Costa Rican Spanish

PHRASEBOOK & DICTIONARY

Acknowledgments
Product Editor Jenna Myers
Production Support Chris Love
Cover Researcher Naomi Parker

Thanks
James Hardy, Kate Mathews, Wayne Murphy, Leif Arne Storset, Angela Tinson, Branislava Vladisavljevic, Tony Wheeler

Published by Lonely Planet Global Limited
CRN 554153

5th edition – Apr 2017
ISBN 978 1 78657 417 6
Text © Lonely Planet 2017

Cover Image Man and woman on a Costa Rican beach
Steve Smith / Getty ©

Printed in China 10 9 8 7 6 5 4

Contact lonelyplanet.com/contact

make the most of this phrasebook ...

Anyone can speak another language! It's all about confidence. Don't worry if you can't remember your school language lessons or if you've never learnt a language before. Even if you learn the very basics (on the inside covers of this book), your travel experience will be the better for it. You have nothing to lose and everything to gain when the locals hear you making an effort.

finding things in this book

For easy navigation, this book is in sections. The Basics chapters are the ones you'll thumb through time and again. The Practical section covers basic travel situations like catching transport and finding a bed. The Social section gives you conversational phrases, pick-up lines, the ability to express opinions – so you can get to know people. Food has a section all of its own: gourmets and vegetarians are covered and local dishes feature. Safe Travel equips you with health and police phrases, just in case. Remember the colours of each section and you'll find everything easily; or use the comprehensive Index. Otherwise, check the two-way traveller's Dictionary for the word you need.

being understood

Throughout this book you'll see coloured phrases on each page. They're phonetic guides to help you pronounce the language. You don't even need to look at the language itself, but you'll get used to the way we've represented particular sounds. The pronunciation chapter in Basics will explain more, but you can feel confident that if you read the coloured phrase slowly, you'll be understood.

communication tips

Body language, ways of doing things, sense of humour – all have a role to play in every culture. 'Local talk' boxes show you common ways of saying things, or everyday language to drop into conversation. 'Listen for ...' boxes supply the phrases you may hear. They start with the language (so local people can point out what they want to say to you) and then lead in to the pronunciation guide and the English translation.

social 97

costa rican spanish

official language

For more details, see the **introduction**.

INTRODUCTION
introducción

Costa Rican Spanish lounges under the beach umbrella of Latin American Spanish – the term given to the many varieties of Spanish that have evolved in the Americas after the Spanish conquests in the 16th century. The language that originally emerged as one of the branches of vulgar Latin successfully took root and spread in the New World and now has official status in 20 countries of Latin America.

Not only did the Spanish language successfully transplant itself, it also hybridised with the indigenous languages and became a colourful array of different varieties of Spanish. Among them, Costa Rican stands out as a unique linguistic entity with its own intriguing quirks of both grammar and vocabulary.

The main grammatical peculiarity is *voseo* vo·se·o – the use of *vos* (meaning 'you') as the second-person singular pronoun, which is considered an archaism in Spain. This is a feature that Costa Rican shares with varieties of Spanish found in other Latin American countries, particularly Argentina, Uruguay, Paraguay, Guatemala, Honduras, Nicaragua and El Salvador. In vocabulary, the abundance of diminutives formed by adding *-tico* ·tee·ko and *-tica* ·tee·ka to the ends of masculine and feminine words respectively – a cutesy way of saying 'small' or expressing affection – has earned Costa Ricans the nickname *Ticos*.

Perhaps what gives Costa Rican Spanish its most distinctive flavour is the rich store of slang expressions commonly known as *tiquismos* tee·kees·mos.

at a glance ...

language name:
Costa Rican Spanish

name in language:
español (costarricense) es·pa·nyol (kos·ta·ree·sen·se), *castellano* kas·te·ya·no

language family: Romance

approximate number of speakers: over 3 million

close relatives:
Castilian Spanish, Latin American Spanish, Italian, French, Portuguese

This phrasebook contains many of these unique turns of phrase to get you talking like a Tico or a Tica and blending in with the crowd. Take it with you and you'll learn exactly why the expression *pura vida* poo·ra vee·da embodies the friendly, unhurried approach to life in Costa Rica. You'll also learn a lot about other key elements of Costa Rican culture expressed in the language.

Though it's a distinct variety of Spanish, Costa Rican does share many similarities with its Latin American siblings which set it apart from the mother language, Castilian Spanish. Costa Rican was influenced by the southern Spanish dialect of Andalucia, from where the first Spanish conquistadors sailed to the New World. The most noticeable trait that sets Costa Rican pronunciation apart from Castilian Spanish is common for the entire continent – *seseo* se·se·o, or the absence of the lisping consonants *c* and *z*, as in *cerveza* ser·ve·sa (beer).

By learning some Costa Rican Spanish, you're opening the door to a world of over 350 million speakers – and be reassured, while it's a distinct variety with its own beautiful individualities, Costa Rican Spanish will be understood by speakers all over Latin America – and even in Spain.

This book gives you the practical phrases you need to get by, as well as the fun, social phrases that lead to a better understanding of Costa Rica and its people. It will also ensure that you can pronounce them like a true *Tico* or *Tica*. To help you get the most out of your travels in beautiful Costa Rica with its many natural wonders, this phrasebook also provides you with an ecotourism section listing the names of flora, fauna and natural features in both Spanish and English.

The contacts you make through speaking Costa Rican Spanish will make your travel experience unique. Local knowledge, new relationships and a sense of satisfaction are on the tip of your tongue – so don't just stand there, say something!

abbreviations used in this book

a	adjective	n	noun
adv	adverb	pl	plural
f	feminine	pol	polite
inf	informal	sg	singular
m	masculine	v	verb

Costa Rican Spanish pronunciation isn't hard, as most of the sounds are also found in English. The best way to learn the correct pronunciation is to listen to the people around you.

Costa Rican Spanish pronunciation differs from the Castilian Spanish spoken in Spain. The most obvious difference is the lack of the lisping 'th' sound. With a little practice you'll soon get the basics and even if you can't roll your *r*'s or hiss out your *j*'s like a Tico or a Tica, your efforts are certain to be rewarded.

vowel sounds

Vowels are generally short and clear. In a number of cases, however, two vowels can be very closely combined (so-called 'diphthongs').

symbol	english equivalent	spanish example	transliteration
a	run	*agua*	***a***·gwa
ai	aisle	*baile*	***bai***·le
ay	say	*seis*	says
e	bed	*edad*	e·***dad***
ee	bee	*idioma, y*	ee·***dyo***·ma, ee
o	not	*ojo*	***o***·kho
oo	good	*uva*	***oo***·va
ow	cow	*autobús*	ow·to·***boos***
oy	boy	*hoy*	oy
ya	yard	*viaje*	***vya***·khe
ye	yes	*tiempo*	***tyem***·po

consonant sounds

symbol	english equivalent	spanish example	transliteration
b	big	*barco*	*bar*·ko
ch	chat	*chico*	*chee*·ko
d	dog	*dedo*	*de*·do
f	friend	*falso*	*fal*·so
g	get	*gato*	*ga*·to
k	kick	*cabeza*, *quitar*	ka·*be*·sa, kee·*tar*
kh	as in the Scottish 'loch' (a harsh, breathy sound from the back of your throat)	*gente*, *jamón*	*khen*·te, kha·*mon*
l	let	*lado*	*la*·do
m	man	*manto*	*man*·to
n	not	*nada*	*na*·da
ny	canyon	*riñón*	ree·*nyon*
p	pig	*padre*	*pa*·dre
r	right (lightly rolled, but at the start of a word and in words with *rr* strongly rolled)	*pero*, *roto*, *carro*	*pe*·ro, *ro*·to, *ka*·ro
s	so	*celos*, *sábado*, *zeta*	*se*·los, *sa*·ba·do, *se*·ta
t	top	*tiempo*	*tyem*·po
v	a soft 'b', half way between a 'v' and a 'b'	*vago*	*va*·go
w	wet	*puedo*	*pwe*·do
y	yes	*ya*, *llamada*	ya, ya·*ma*·da

word stress

Words in Spanish have stress, which means that you emphasise one syllable over another. Rule of thumb: when a word ends in *-n*, *-s* or a vowel, the stress falls on the second-last syllable. Otherwise, the last syllable is stressed. If you see an accent mark over a syllable, it cancels out these rules and you just stress that syllable instead. Don't worry if you can't remember these rules – in our coloured pronounciation guides, the stressed syllable is always in italics.

reading & writing

The Spanish alphabet is presented in the following table. For spelling purposes (eg when you need to spell your name to book into a hotel), the pronunciation of each letter is provided. The order shown below is used in the **menu decoder** and the **costa rican spanish–english dictionary**.

spanish alphabet				
A, a a	*B, b* be *lar*·ga	*C, c* se	*Ch, ch** che	*D, d* de
E, e e	*F, f* *e*·fe	*G, g* khe	*H, h* *a*·che	*I, i* ee
J, j *kho*·ta	*K, k* ka	*L, l* *e*·le	*Ll, ll** *do*·ble *e*·le	*M, m* *e*·me
N, n *e*·ne	*Ñ, ñ* *e*·nye	*O, o* o	*P, p* pe	*Q, q* koo
R, r er	*Rr, rr** *e*·re	*S, s* *e*·se	*T, t* te	*U, u* oo
V, v be *kor*·ta	*W, w* *do*·ble be	*X, x* *e*·kees	*Y, y* ee *grye*·ga	*Z, z* *se*·ta

* The letters *ch*, *ll* and *rr* are no longer officially considered separate letters, but they're still sounds in their own right.

The relationship between Spanish sounds and their spelling is quite straightforward and consistent. The rules given in the table below will help you read any written Costa Rican Spanish that you may come across outside this phrasebook.

letter	pronunciation	example	transliteration
c	before *e* or *i* pronounced as an 's'	*cerveza, cinco*	ser·*ve*·sa, *seen*·ko
	before *a*, *o* and *u* pronounced as a 'k'	*carro, corto, cubo*	*ka*·ro, *kor*·to, *koo*·bo
g	before *e* or *i* pronounced as the 'ch' in 'loch'	*gente, gigante*	*khen*·te, khee·*gan*·te
	before *a*, *o* and *u* pronounced as the 'g' in 'go'	*gato, gordo, guante*	*ga*·to, *gor*·do, *gwan*·te
gu	pronounced as the 'g' in 'go' (the *u* is not pronounced unless there are two dots over the *u*)	*guerra, güiski*	*ge*·ra, *gwees*·kee
h	never pronounced (silent)	*haber, huevo*	a·*ber*, *we*·vo
j	as the 'ch' in 'loch'	*jardín*	khar·*deen*
ll	pronounced as the 'y' in 'yes'	*llave*	*ya*·ve
ñ	pronounced as the 'ny' in 'canyon'	*niño*	*nee*·nyo
qu	pronounced as a 'k' (the *u* is not pronounced)	*quince*	*keen*·se
z	pronounced as an 's'	*zorro*	*so*·ro

contents

The index below shows which grammatical structures you can use to say what you want. Look under each function – listed in alphabetical order – for information on how to build your own sentences. For example, to tell the taxi driver where your hotel is, look for **giving instructions** and you'll be directed to information on **demonstratives** and **prepositions**. A **glossary** of grammatical terms is included at the end of this chapter to help you.

adjectives & adverbs

describing people/things • doing things

When using an adjective to describe a noun, you need to use the appropriate ending depending on whether the noun is masculine or feminine, and singular or plural (see **gender** and **plurals**). Most adjectives have four forms and the endings are easy to remember:

masculine	sg	*un sombrero blanc**o*** oon som·*bre*·ro *blan*·ko	**a white hat**
	pl	*unos sombreros blanc**os*** *oo*·nos som·*bre*·ros *blan*·kos	**some white hats**
feminine	sg	*una camisa blanc**a*** *oo*·na ka·*mee*·sa *blan*·ka	**a white shirt**
	pl	*unas camisas blanc**as*** *oo*·nas ka·*mee*·sas *blan*·kas	**some white shirts**

As you can see above, unlike English adjectives, Spanish adjectives almost always come after the noun. However, 'adjectives' of quantity (such as 'much', 'a lot', 'a little/a few', 'too much'), numbers, and words expressing possession ('my' and 'your') always precede the noun.

many cars	*muchos carros* **m pl** (lit: many cars)	*moo*·chos *ka*·ros
first class	*primera clase* **f sg** (lit: first class)	pree·*me*·ra *kla*·se
my passport	*mi pasaporte* **m sg** (lit: my passport)	mee pa·sa·*por*·te

Adverbs are formed by adding the ending *-mente* to the singular form of an adjective (in the feminine form if there is one). If the adjective has an accent marked in writing, the stress remains on that syllable with the additional stress in pronunciation on *-mente*. Adverbs generally follow the verb they modify.

She has a fantastic voice.
Ella tiene una voz fantástica. e·ya *tye*·ne *oo*·na vos fan·*tas*·tee·ka
(lit: she has a voice fantastic)

She sings fantastically.
Ella canta fantásticamente. e·ya *kan*·ta fan·*tas*·tee·ka·*men*·te
(lit: she sings fantastically)

articles

describing people/things • naming people/things • pointing things out

The articles *el* and *la* both mean 'the'. Whether you use *el* or *la* depends on the gender of the noun talked about, which in Spanish will always be either masculine or feminine. *El* is used with masculine nouns while *la* is used with feminine nouns. When talking about plural nouns you use *los* instead of *el* and *las* instead of *la*. See also **gender** and **plurals**.

	singular		plural	
masculine	***el*** *carro* el *ka*·ro	the car	***los*** *carros* los *ka*·ros	the cars
feminine	***la*** *tienda* la *tyen*·da	the shop	***las*** *tiendas* las *tyen*·das	the shops

Spanish also has masculine and feminine articles meaning 'a/an': *un* and *una*. Again, the gender of the noun determines which one you use. *Un* and *una* also have plural forms: *unos* and *unas*, meaning 'some'.

	singular		plural	
masculine	***un*** *huevo* oon *we*·vo	an egg	***unos*** *huevos* *oo*·nos *we*·vos	some eggs
feminine	***una*** *tortuga* *oo*·na tor·*too*·ga	a turtle	***unas*** *tortugas* *oo*·nas tor·*too*·gas	some turtles

be

doing things • making statements • negating

Spanish has two words for the verb 'be' – *ser* and *estar*. These two verbs have slightly different functions which are outlined below:

use *ser* to express	examples	
permanent characteristics of people/things	*Ángel es muy amable.* an·khel es mooy a·*ma*·ble	**Ángel is very nice.**
occupations or nationalities	*Pablo es de Costa Rica.* *pa*·blo es de *kos*·ta *ree*·ka	**Pablo is from Costa Rica.**
the time & location of events	*Son las tres.* son las tres	**It's 3 o'clock.**
possession	*¿De quién es esta mochila?* de kyen es *es*·ta mo·*chee*·la	**Whose backpack is this?**

use *estar* to express	examples	
temporary characteristics of people/things	*La comida está fría.* la ko·*mee*·da es·*ta* *free*·a	**The meal is cold.**
the time & location of people/things	*Estamos en San José.* es·*ta*·mos en san kho·*se*	**We're in San José.**
the mood of a person	*Estoy contento/a.* **m/f** es·*toy* kon·*ten*·to/a	**I'm happy.**

The forms of both verbs are given on the next page.

forms of *ser*					
I	am	*yo*	yo	*soy*	soy
you sg inf	are	*tú/vos* *	too/vos	*eres/sos* *	e·res/sos
you sg pol	are	*usted*	oos·*ted*	*es*	es
he/she	is	*él/ella*	el/*e*·ya	*es*	es
we	are	*nosotros/as* m/f	no·so·tros/as	*somos*	*so*·mos
you pl	are	*ustedes*	oos·*te*·des	*son*	son
they	are	*ellos/as* m/f	*e*·yos/as	*son*	son

forms of *estar*					
I	am	*yo*	yo	*estoy*	es·*toy*
you sg inf	are	*tú/vos* *	too/vos	*estás*	es·*tas*
you sg pol	are	*usted*	oos·*ted*	*está*	es·*ta*
he/she	is	*él/ella*	el/*e*·ya	*está*	es·*ta*
we	are	*nosotros/as* m/f	no·so·tros/as	*estamos*	es·*ta*·mos
you pl	are	*ustedes*	oos·*te*·des	*estan*	es·*tan*
they	are	*ellos/as* m/f	*e*·yos/as	*estan*	es·*tan*

* For an explanation on the alternate forms, see **personal pronouns.**

demonstratives

giving instructions • indicating location • naming people/things • pointing things out

To refer to or point at a person or thing, use one of the words from the table below, depending on whether someone or something is close (this/these), away from you (that/those) or even further away in time or distance (that/those over there).

Demonstratives can be used on their own or with a noun. They go before the noun they accompany and agree in gender and number with it (see **gender** and **plurals**). They're written without an accent mark when used with a noun. If they're used on their own, an accent mark is added in writing.

masculine	singular		plural	
close (this/these)	*éste*	es·te	*éstos*	es·tos
away (that/those)	*ése*	e·se	*ésos*	e·sos
further away (that/those over there)	*aquél*	a·*kel*	*aquéllos*	a·*ke*·yos
feminine	**singular**		**plural**	
close (this/these)	*ésta*	es·ta	*éstas*	es·tas
away (that/those)	*ésa*	e·sa	*ésas*	e·sas
further away (that/those over there)	*aquélla*	a·*ke*·ya	*aquéllas*	a·*ke*·yas

this plant	*esta mata* **f sg** (lit: this plant)	es·ta *ma*·ta
those animals	*esos animales* **m pl** (lit: those animals)	e·sos a·nee·*ma*·les

gender

describing people/things • naming people/things

In Spanish, all nouns are either masculine or feminine. The gender of a noun is not really concerned with the sex of something – the word for turtle, *tortuga* tor·*too*·ga, is a feminine noun, even if the animal is male! There's no rule as to why, say, the sun (*el sol* el sol) is masculine but a cloud (*la nube* la *noo*·be) is feminine. The gender is often arbitrary, but here are some handy tips to help you determine gender:

- gender is masculine when talking about a man and feminine when talking about a woman
- words ending in *-o* are usually masculine
- words ending in *-a* are usually feminine
- words ending in *-d*, *-z* or *-ión* are usually feminine

All nouns in the **dictionaries**, the **menu decoder** and the word lists in this phrasebook have their gender marked with the abbreviations m and f for masculine and feminine respectively. For more information, see the box **masculine or feminine?** in **feelings & opinions**, page 115.

Remember that the gender of nouns also determines the endings on any articles, adjectives and demonstratives you use to describe them. See also **articles**, **adjectives & adverbs**, **demonstratives**, **plurals** and **possessives**.

have

possessing

The easiest way of expressing possession in Spanish is by using the verb *tener* (have). The present tense forms of this verb are shown in the table on the following page.

I have two brothers.

Tengo dos hermanos. — *ten*·go dos er·*ma*·nos
(lit: I-have two brothers)

forms of *tener*					
I	have	*yo*	yo	*tengo*	*ten*·go
you sg inf	have	*tú/vos* *	too/vos	*tienes/ tenés* *	*tye*·nes/ te·*nes*
you sg pol	have	*usted*	oos·*ted*	*tiene*	*tye*·ne
he/she	has	*él/ella*	el/*e*·ya	*tiene*	*tye*·ne
we	have	*nosotros/ as* m/f	no·*so*·tros/ as	*tenemos*	te·*ne*·mos
you pl	have	*ustedes*	oos·*te*·des	*tienen*	*tye*·nen
they	have	*ellos/as* m/f	*e*·yos/as	*tienen*	*tye*·nen

* For an explanation on the alternate forms, see **personal pronouns.**

Ownership can also be expressed with possessive pronouns – for more information, see **possessives.**

negatives

negating

To make a sentence negative, just add the word *no* (no) before the main verb:

I (don't) live with my family.
(No) Vivo con mi familia. (no) *vee*·vo kon mee fa·*mee*·ya
(lit: (no) I-live with my family)

personal pronouns

making statements • naming people/things

Costa Rican Spanish has three forms for the singular 'you'. The polite form of 'you' singular (*usted*) is used when you're meeting someone for the first time, talking to someone older than you or when you're in a formal situation (eg talking to the police, customs officers etc). When talking to someone familiar to you or younger than you, use the informal forms *tú* or *vos*, rather than the polite form *usted*. *Tú* and *vos* are used more or less interchangeably though *vos* is more common.

All phrases in this book use the form of 'you' that's appropriate for the situation. Where you see the symbols pol (polite) and inf (informal) you're given a choice as either form might be appropriate depending upon the situation. For 'you' plural there's no informal/formal distinction – you just use *ustedes*.

I	*yo*	yo
you sg inf	*tú/vos*	too/vos
you sg pol	*usted*	oos·*ted*
he	*él*	el
she	*ella*	*e*·ya
it	*ello*	*e*·yo
we	*nosotros/as* m/f	no·*so*·tros/as
you pl	*ustedes*	oos·*te*·des
they	*ellos/as* m/f	*e*·yos/as

Personal pronouns are often left out in Spanish because the endings on verbs tell you who is the doer of the action (subject) – you only need to use them if you want to emphasise who or what is doing the action. You may also notice that *tú* verb forms differ slightly from *vos* verb forms – eg *tienes* ('you have' – *tú* form) versus *tenés* ('you have' – *vos* form).

You don't need to worry about this feature of Costa Rican Spanish because all phrases in this book use the appropriate verb forms. If you do want to try your hand at concocting your own phrases, Costa Ricans will understand if you just stick to *tú* rather than trying your hand at the relatively idiosyncratic *vos*. This feature is called *voseo* vo·*se*·o and is limited to only a few varieties of Central American Spanish and the Spanish spoken in Argentina, Paraguay and Uruguay.

See also **be**, **have**, **verbs** and **word order**.

plurals

describing people/things • naming people/things

In general, if the noun ends in a vowel, you add *-s* for plural. If the noun ends in a consonant, you add *-es*:

singular			plural		
bed	*cama*	*ka*·ma	beds	*camas*	*ka*·mas
woman	*mujer*	moo·*kher*	women	*mujeres*	moo·*khe*·res

See also **articles**, **adjectives & adverbs**, **demonstratives**, **gender** and **possessives**.

possessives

naming people/things • possessing

There are a number of words for 'my', 'your' etc in Spanish. Choose the correct form according to the gender and number of the noun – ie the thing owned, not the owner.

	with singular noun		with plural noun	
my	*mi*	mee	*mis*	mees
your sg inf	*tu*	too	*tus*	toos
your sg pol	*su*	soo	*sus*	soos
his/her/its	*su*	soo	*sus*	soos
our	*nuestro/a* **m/f**	*nwes*·tro/a	*nuestros/as* **m/f**	*nwes*·tros/as
your pl	*su*	soo	*sus*	soos
their	*su*	soo	*sus*	soos

Ownership can also be expressed with the word *de* (of) or by using the verb *tener* (have).

This is my friend's tent.

Esta es la carpa de mi amiga. — es·ta es la *kar*·pa de mee a·*mee*·ga

(lit: this is the tent of my friend)

We have two dogs.

Tenemos dos perros. — te·*ne*·mos dos *pe*·ros

(lit: we-have two dogs)

See also **gender, have** and **plurals**.

prepositions

giving instructions • indicating location

Prepositions are used to show the relationship between words in a sentence, just like in English. They're placed before the word they accompany. These are the most useful ones:

at (place)	*en*	en	on (place)	*en*	en
at (time)	*a*	a	on (time)	*a*	a
for (purpose)	*para*	*pa*·ra	outside	*fuera de*	*fwe*·ra de
for (time)	*durante*	doo·*ran*·te	since	*desde*	*des*·de
from (time)	*desde*	*des*·de	to (place)	*a*	a
in (place)	*en*	en	until	*hasta*	*as*·ta
in (time)	*en*	en	with	*con*	kon
inside	*dentro de*	*den*·tro de	without	*sin*	seen

Let's meet at eight o'clock at the entrance.

Veámonos a las ocho en la entrada. — ve·*a*·mo·nos a las *o*·cho en la en·*tra*·da

(lit: let-see-us at the eight at the entrance)

questions

asking questions

To ask a question, simply make a statement, but raise your intonation towards the end of the sentence, as you would in English. The inverted question mark written at the start of a sentence prompts you to do this.

Do you have a car?
¿Tienes un carro? — *tye*·nes oon *ka*·ro
(lit: you-have a car)

You can also place the following question words at the beginning of a phrase:

How?	*¿Cómo?*	*ko*·mo
How many?	*¿Cuántos/as?* **m/f pl**	*kwan*·tos/as
How much?	*¿Cuánto?*	*kwan*·to
What?	*¿Qué?*	ke
When?	*¿Cuándo?*	*kwan*·do
Where?	*¿Dónde?*	*don*·de
Which?	*¿Cuál/Cuáles?* **sg/pl**	kwal/*kwa*·les
Who?	*¿Quién/Quiénes?* **sg/pl**	kyen/*kye*·nes
Why?	*¿Por qué?*	por ke

When does the bus arrive?
¿Cuándo llega el autobús? — *kwan*·do *ye*·ga el ow·to·*boos*
(lit: when arrives the bus)

Where can I buy tickets?
¿Dónde puedo comprar tiquetes? — *don*·de *pwe*·do kom·*prar* tee·*ke*·tes
(lit: where I-can buy tickets)

It's not impolite to answer questions with a simple *sí* (yes) or *no* (no) in Spanish. Unlike in English, there's no direct way in Spanish to say 'Yes, it is/does', or 'No, it isn't/doesn't'.

requests

making requests

A polite and easy way to make a request is by starting with the word *¿Podría …?* (equivalent to 'Could you …?') followed by the infinitive (dictionary form) of the main verb:

Please help me.
¿Podría ayudarme? — po·*dree*·a a·yoo·*dar*·me
(lit: could-you help-me)

See also **questions** and **verbs**.

there is/are

indicating location • pointing things out

To say 'there is/are' in Spanish, use the word *hay* (lit: it-has). Add *no* before it to say 'there isn't/aren't'.

Do you have any rooms?
¿Hay habitaciones? — ai a·bee·ta·*syo*·nes
(lit: it-has rooms)

There aren't any.
No hay. — no ai
(lit: no it-has)

See also **negatives**.

verbs

doing things • making statements

There are three groups of verbs in Spanish – those ending in *-ar* (eg *hablar* 'speak'), *-er* (eg *comer* 'eat') and *-ir* (eg *vivir* 'live'). Tenses are formed by adding different endings for each person to the verb stem (part of the verb that remains after you take off *-ar*, *-er* and *-ir*). These endings vary according to which one of the three groups the verb belongs to. The present tense endings for each person are given in the table below.

present tense						
	hablar		*comer*		*vivir*	
I	*-o*	-o	*-o*	-o	*-o*	-o
you sg inf (*tú*)	*-as*	-as	*-es*	-es	*-es*	-es
you sg inf (*vos*)	*-ás*	*-as*	*-és*	*-es*	*-ís*	*-ees*
you sg pol	*-a*	-a	*-e*	-e	*-e*	-e
he/she	*-a*	-a	*-e*	-e	*-e*	-e
we	*-amos*	*-a*·mos	*-emos*	*-e*·mos	*-imos*	*-ee*·mos
you pl	*-an*	-an	*-en*	-en	*-en*	-en
they	*-an*	-an	*-en*	-en	*-en*	-en

As in any language, some verbs are irregular. The most important ones are *ser* (be), *estar* (be) and *tener* (have). For more details, see **be** and **have**.

word order

asking questions • making statements • negating

Sentences in Spanish have a basic word order of subject–verb–object, just as English does.

I study business.
Yo estudio comercio. yo es·*too*·dyo ko·*mer*·syo
(lit: I study-I business)

However, the subject pronoun is often omitted – '*Estudio comercio*' is enough. Generally, you only use a subject pronoun if you wish to emphasise who is the 'doer' of an action. See also **negatives** and **questions**.

glossary

adjective	word that describes something – '**active** volcanoes are widespread'
adverb	word that explains how an action is done – 'jaguars are **rarely** seen'
article	the words 'a', 'an' and 'the'
demonstrative	word that means 'this' or 'that'
direct object	thing or person in the sentence that has the action directed to it – 'national parks protect the **wildlife**'
gender	grouping of *nouns* into classes (like masculine and feminine), requiring other words (eg *adjectives*) to belong to the same class
indirect object	person or thing in the sentence that is the recipient of the action – 'birds are the main attraction for **nature lovers**'
infinitive	dictionary form of a *verb* – 'monkeys are the easiest to **observe** in the wild'
noun	thing, person or idea – 'the **environment**'
number	whether a word is singular or plural – 'there are deadly poisonous **snakes**'
personal pronoun	word that means 'I', 'you', etc
possessive pronoun	word that means 'mine', 'yours', etc
preposition	word like 'for' or 'before' in English
subject	person or thing in the sentence that does the action – '**sea turtles** are dying out'
tense	form of a *verb* that tells you whether the action is in the present, past or future – eg 'eat' (present), 'ate' (past), 'will eat' (future)
verb	word that tells you what action happened – 'ecotourism **is growing**'
verb ending	ending added to the *verb stem* to indicate the *tense* and/or the *subject* in the sentence
verb stem	part of a *verb* which does not change – 'surf' in '**surf**ing' and '**surf**ed'

language difficulties

dificultades con el lenguaje

Do you speak (English)?
¿Habla (inglés)? — a·bla (een·gles)

Does anyone speak (English)?
¿Alguien habla (inglés)? — al·gyen a·bla (een·gles)

Do you understand (me)?
¿(Me) Entiende? — (me) en·tyen·de

Yes, I understand.
Sí, entiendo. — see en·tyen·do

No, I don't understand.
No, no entiendo. — no no en·tyen·do

talking like a *tico*

If you know any Spanish at all, you're bound to expand your repertoire of slang expressions no end while in Costa Rica. The following colourful turns of phrase are typical Costa Rican slang and colloquialisms (known as *tiquismos* tee·kees·mos).

agüevado/a m/f	a·gwe·va·do/a	bored/boring
buena nota f	bwe·na no·ta	all right
chapulín m	cha·poo·leen	young thief
chunche m	choon·che	thingumajig
guavero/a m/f	gwa·ve·ro/a	lucky
macho/a m/f	ma·cho/a	blonde person
sabanero m	sa·ba·ne·ro	cowboy
salado m	sa·la·do	bad luck

For other *tiquismos*, see the box **talking *tiquismos***, page 134.

I speak (English).
Hablo (inglés). — *a*·blo (een·*gles*)

I don't speak (Spanish).
No hablo (español). — no *a*·blo (es·pa·*nyol*)

I speak a little.
Hablo un poquito. — *a*·blo oon po·*kee*·to

I'd like to practise (Spanish).
Quisiera practicar (español). — kee·*sye*·ra prak·tee·*kar* (es·pa·*nyol*)

Let's speak (Spanish).
Hablemos (español). — a·*ble*·mos (es·pa·*nyol*)

Pardon?
¿Perdón? — per·*don*

What does (*pura vida*) mean?
¿Que significa (pura vida)? — ke seeg·nee·*fee*·ka (*poo*·ra *vee*·da)

How do you ...?	*¿Cómo ...?*	*ko*·mo ...
pronounce this	*se pronuncia esto*	se pro·*noon*·sya *es*·to
write (*pura vida*)	*se escribe (pura vida)*	se es·*kree*·be (*poo*·ra *vee*·da)

Could you please ...?	*¿Podría ...?*	po·*dree*·a ...
repeat that	*repetir eso*	re·pe·*teer* *e*·so
speak more slowly	*hablar más despacio*	a·*blar* mas des·*pa*·syo
write it down	*escribirlo*	es·kree·*beer*·lo

rev it up

When you see the letter *r* at the beginning of a Spanish word, or when you see a double *rr*, remember to trill the 'r' sound. It's a case of blowing air past your tongue so that it produces a sound like a cat purring. It may help to visualise yourself sitting astride a powerful motorbike revving on the throttle as you do so. Try practising on the word *Costarricense(s)* **sg/pl** kos·ta·ree·*sen*·se(s), the official name for the Costa Rican people.

numbers & amounts

los números y las cantidades

cardinal numbers

números cardinales

0	*cero*	*se*·ro	6	*seis*	says
1	*uno*	*oo*·no	7	*siete*	*sye*·te
2	*dos*	dos	8	*ocho*	*o*·cho
3	*tres*	tres	9	*nueve*	*nwe*·ve
4	*cuatro*	*kwa*·tro	10	*diez*	dyes
5	*cinco*	*seen*·ko			

11	*once*	*on*·se
12	*doce*	*do*·se
13	*trece*	*tre*·se
14	*catorce*	ka·*tor*·se
15	*quince*	*keen*·se
16	*dieciséis*	dye·see·*says*
17	*diecisiete*	dye·see·*sye*·te
18	*dieciocho*	dye·see·*o*·cho
19	*diecinueve*	dye·see·*nwe*·ve
20	*veinte*	*vayn*·te
21	*veintiuno*	vayn·tee·*oo*·no
22	*veintidós*	vayn·tee·*dos*
30	*treinta*	*trayn*·ta
40	*cuarenta*	kwa·*ren*·ta
50	*cincuenta*	seen·*kwen*·ta
60	*sesenta*	se·*sen*·ta
70	*setenta*	se·*ten*·ta
80	*ochenta*	o·*chen*·ta
90	*noventa*	no·*ven*·ta
100	*cien*	syen
200	*doscientos*	do·*syen*·tos
1000	*mil*	meel
2000	*dos mil*	dos meel
1,000,000	*un millón*	oon mee·*yon*

numbers & amounts

ordinal numbers

números ordinales

Ordinal numbers are written with a degree sign – 1st is written '1º', 2nd is '2º', and so on.

1st	*primero/a* **m/f**	pree·*me*·ro/a
2nd	*segundo/a* **m/f**	se·*goon*·do/a
3rd	*tercero/a* **m/f**	ter·*se*·ro/a
4th	*cuarto/a* **m/f**	*kwar*·to/a
5th	*quinto/a* **m/f**	*keen*·to/a

fractions

fracciones

a quarter	*un cuarto*	oon *kwar*·to
a third	*un tercio*	oon *ter*·syo
a half	*un medio*	oon *me*·dyo
three-quarters	*tres cuartos*	tres *kwar*·tos
all	*todos/as* **m/f pl**	*to*·dos/as
none	*ninguno/a* **m/f**	neen·*goo*·no/a

useful amounts

cantidades útiles

How much?	*¿Cuánto/a?* **m/f**	*kwan*·to/a
How many?	*¿Cuántos/as?* **m/f pl**	*kwan*·tos/as
Please give me ...	*Por favor deme ...*	por fa·*vor de*·me ...
(just) a little	*un poquitito*	oon po·kee·*tee*·to
a lot	*mucho/a* **m/f**	*moo*·cho/a
many	*muchos/as* **m/f pl**	*moo*·chos/as
some	*unos/as* **m/f pl**	*oo*·nos/as

For more amounts, see **self-catering**, page 165.

telling the time

diciendo la hora

Time is expressed by the phrase *Son las …* (It is …) followed by a number. Times past the hour are expressed using *y* (and) while times before the hour take *para* (to). The words *medianoche* me·dya·*no*·che (midnight) and *mediodía* me·dyo·*dee*·a (midday) are used instead of 12am and 12pm.

Costa Ricans refer to a 12-hour clock. The terms 'am' and 'pm', however, are used only in writing. When speaking, time is designated by the part of the day. The day is roughly broken up into four time periods. To specify whether a time is am or pm, just state the hour and link it to the time of the day using the phrase *de la* (lit: of the).

What time is it?	*¿Qué hora es?*	ke *o*·ra es
It's one o'clock.	*Es la una.*	es la *oo*·na
It's (ten) o'clock.	*Son las (diez).*	son las (dyes)
Five past (ten).	*(Diez) y cinco.*	(dyes) ee *seen*·ko
Quarter past (ten).	*(Diez) y cuarto.*	(dyes) ee *kwar*·to
Half past (ten).	*(Diez) y media.*	(dyes) ee *me*·dya
Quarter to (eleven).	*Cuarto para las (once).*	*kwar*·to *pa*·ra las (*on*·se)
am (dawn)	*de la madrugada*	de la ma·droo·*ga*·da
am (morning)	*de la mañana*	de la ma·*nya*·na
pm (afternoon)	*de la tarde*	de la *tar*·de
pm (evening)	*de la noche*	de la *no*·che
At what time …?	*¿A qué hora …?*	a ke *o*·ra …
At (five).	*A las (cinco).*	a las (*seen*·ko)
At (7.57pm).	*A las (siete y cincuenta y siete de la noche).*	a las (*sye*·te ee seen·*kwen*·ta ee *sye*·te de la *no*·che)

the calendar

el calendario

days

Monday	*lunes*	*loo*·nes
Tuesday	*martes*	*mar*·tes
Wednesday	*miércoles*	*myer*·ko·les
Thursday	*jueves*	*hwe*·ves
Friday	*viernes*	*vyer*·nes
Saturday	*sábado*	*sa*·ba·do
Sunday	*domingo*	do·*meen*·go

months

January	*enero*	e·*ne*·ro
February	*febrero*	fe·*bre*·ro
March	*marzo*	*mar*·so
April	*abril*	a·*breel*
May	*mayo*	*ma*·yo
June	*junio*	*khoo*·nyo
July	*julio*	*khoo*·lyo
August	*agosto*	a·*gos*·to
September	*septiembre*	se·*tyem*·bre
October	*octubre*	ok·*too*·bre
November	*noviembre*	no·*vyem*·bre
December	*diciembre*	dee·*syem*·bre

dates

Dates are expressed using cardinal numbers. The exception to this rule is the first day of the month which uses the ordinal number – eg *el primero de octubre* el pree·*me*·ro de ok·*too*·bre (lit: the first of October).

What date is it today?
¿Qué fecha es hoy? ke *fe*·cha es oy

It's (18 October).
Es (el dieciocho de octubre). es (el dye·see·*o*·cho de ok·*too*·bre)

seasons

dry season	*estación seca* **f**	es·ta·*syon* *se*·ka
wet season	*estación lluviosa* **f**	es·ta·*syon* yoo·*vyo*·sa
spring	*primavera* **f**	pree·ma·*ve*·ra
summer	*verano* **m**	ve·*ra*·no
autumn	*otoño* **m**	o·*to*·nyo
winter	*invierno* **m**	een·*vyer*·no

present

el presente

now	*ahora*	a·*o*·ra
today	*hoy*	oy
tonight	*hoy en la noche*	oy en la *no*·che
this morning	*hoy en la mañana*	oy en la ma·*nya*·na
this afternoon	*hoy en la tarde*	oy en la *tar*·de
this week	*esta semana*	*es*·ta se·*ma*·na
this month	*este mes*	*es*·te mes
this year	*este año*	*es*·te *a*·nyo

past

el pasado

yesterday	*ayer*	a·*yer*
day before yesterday	*anteayer*	an·te·a·*yer*
(three days) ago	*hace (tres días)*	*a*·se (tres *dee*·as)
since (May)	*desde (mayo)*	*des*·de (*ma*·yo)
last night	*anoche*	a·*no*·che
last week	*la semana pasada*	la se·*ma*·na pa·*sa*·da
last month	*el mes pasado*	el mes pa·*sa*·do
last year	*el año pasado*	el *a*·nyo pa·*sa*·do

yesterday …	*ayer …*	a·*yer* …
morning	*en la mañana*	en la ma·*nya*·na
afternoon	*en la tarde*	en la *tar*·de
evening	*en la noche*	en la *no*·che

future

el futuro

tomorrow	*mañana*	ma·*nya*·na
day after tomorrow	*pasado mañana*	pa·*sa*·do ma·*nya*·na
in (two days)	*dentro de (dos días)*	*den*·tro de (dos *dee*·as)
until (June)	*hasta (junio)*	*as*·ta (*khoo*·nyo)
next …	*… entrante*	… en·*tran*·te
week	*la semana*	la se·*ma*·na
month	*el mes*	el mes
year	*el año*	el *a*·nyo
tomorrow …	*mañana …*	ma·*nya*·na …
morning	*en la mañana*	en la ma·*nya*·na
afternoon	*en la tarde*	en la *tar*·de
evening	*en la noche*	en la *no*·che

during the day

durante el día

afternoon	*tarde* **f**	*tar*·de
dawn	*madrugada* **f**	ma·droo·*ga*·da
day	*día* **m**	*dee*·a
evening	*noche* **f**	*no*·che
midday	*mediodía* **m**	*me*·dyo·*dee*·a
midnight	*medianoche* **f**	*me*·dya·*no*·che
morning	*mañana* **f**	ma·*nya*·na
night	*noche* **f**	*no*·che
sunrise	*amanecer* **m**	a·ma·ne·*ser*
sunset	*atardecer* **m**	a·tar·de·*ser*

money
dinero

How much is it?		
	¿Cuánto es?	*kwan*·to es
Can you write down the price?		
	¿Podría escribir el precio?	po·*dree*·a es·kree·*beer* el *pre*·syo
What's the exchange rate?		
	¿A cómo está el tipo de cambio?	a *ko*·mo es·*ta* el *tee*·po de *kam*·byo
What's the charge?		
	¿Cuánto me cobrás?	*kwan*·to me ko·*bras*

I'd like to …	*Quiero …*	*kye*·ro …
cash a cheque	*cambiar un cheque*	kam·*byar* oon *che*·ke
change a travellers cheque	*cambiar un cheque de viajero*	kam·*byar* oon *che*·ke de vya·*khe*·ro
change money into *colones*	*cambiar dinero a colones*	kam·*byar* dee·*ne*·ro a ko·*lo*·nes
change money/ dollars	*cambiar plata/ dólares*	kam·*byar* *pla*·ta/ *do*·la·res
get a cash advance	*que me den un adelanto en efectivo*	ke me den oon a·de·*lan*·to en e·fek·*tee*·vo
withdraw money	*sacar plata*	sa·*kar* *pla*·ta

Do you accept …?	*¿Acepta …?*	a·*sep*·ta …
credit cards	*tarjetas de crédito*	tar·*khe*·tas de *kre*·dee·to
debit cards	*tarjetas de débito*	tar·*khe*·tas de *de*·bee·to
travellers cheques	*cheques de viajero*	*che*·kes de vya·*khe*·ro

I'd like ..., please.	*Quiero ..., por favor.*	kye·ro ... por fa·vor
a receipt	*un recibo*	oon re·see·bo
a refund	*un reintegro*	oon re·een·te·gro
my change	*mi vuelto*	mee vwel·to
to return this	*devolver ésto*	de·vol·ver es·to

Where's a/an ...?	*¿Dónde hay ...?*	don·de ai ...
automated teller machine	*un cajero automático*	oon ka·khe·ro ow·to·ma·tee·ko
foreign exchange office	*una casa de cambio*	oo·na ka·sa de kam·byo

How much is it per ...?	*¿Cuánto es por ...?*	kwan·to es por ...
day	*día*	dee·a
hour	*hora*	o·ra
night	*noche*	no·che
person	*persona*	per·so·na
visit	*visita*	vee·see·ta

the colour of money

The Costa Rican currency is the *colón* ko·lon, named after the explorer Christopher Columbus (whose name in Spanish is *Cristóbal Colón* krees·to·bal ko·lon). One *colón* comprises 100 *centavos* sen·ta·vos (cents). The plural of *colón* is *colones* ko·lo·nes. In practice though, *pesos* pe·sos – the slang term for money – is often used. In addition, you may come across the following colourful terms for individual amounts:

media teja f (lit: half tile)	me·dya te·kha	50 *colón* coin
teja f (lit: tile)	te·kha	100 *colón* coin
rojo m 'red' – refers to the red colour of the bill. Also known as *pargo* par·go 'red snapper' (type of fish).	ro·kho	1000 *colón* bill
tucán m 'toucan' – depicts one of Costa Rica's avian emblems	too·kan	5000 *colón* bill

getting around

para transportarse

Which … goes to (Quepos)?	*¿Cuál … va para (Quepos)?*	kwal … va *pa*·ra (*ke*·pos)
4WD	*cuatro por cuatro*	*kwa*·tro por *kwa*·tro
boat	*barco*	*bar*·ko
bus	*bus*	boos
jeep	*jeep*	yeep
train	*tren*	tren
Is this the … to (Limón)?	*Este es el … que va para (Limón)?*	*es*·te es el … ke va *pa*·ra (lee·*mon*)
boat	*barco*	*bar*·ko
bus	*bus*	boos
train	*tren*	tren
When's the … (bus)?	*¿A qué hora sale el … (bus)?*	a ke *o*·ra *sa*·le el … (boos)
first	*primer*	pree·*mer*
last	*último*	*ool*·tee·mo
next	*próximo*	*prok*·see·mo

What time does it leave?
¿A qué hora sale? — a ke *o*·ra *sa*·le

What time does it get to (San José)?
¿A qué hora llega a (San José)? — a ke *o*·ra *ye*·ga a (san kho·*se*)

How long will it be delayed?
¿Cuánto se va a atrasar? — *kwan*·to se va a a·tra·*sar*

Is this seat taken?
¿Está ocupado? es·*ta* o·koo·*pa*·do

That's my seat.
Este es mi asiento. *es*·te es mee a·*syen*·to

Please tell me when we get to (Alajuela).
Por favor, avíseme cuando lleguemos a (Alajuela). por fa·*vor* a·*vee*·se·me *kwan*·do ye·*ge*·mos a (a·la·*khwe*·la)

Please stop here.
Puede parar aquí, por favor. *pwe*·de pa·*rar* a·*kee* por fa·*vor*

How long do we stop here?
¿Cuánto tiempo vamos a parar aquí? *kwan*·to *tyem*·po *va*·mos a pa·*rar* a·*kee*

tickets

tiquetes

Transportation in Costa Rica is mainly on cheap and cheerful (and often crowded) buses. Seating on buses isn't divided up into separate classes. The only time you may need to specify which class you wish to travel is on international flights in and out of San José.

Where do I buy a ticket?
¿Dónde puedo comprar un pasaje? *don*·de *pwe*·do kom·*prar* oon pa·*sa*·khe

Do I need to book (well in advance)?
¿Necesito reservar el tiquete (muy por adelantado)? ne·se·*see*·to re·ser·*var* el tee·*ke*·te (mooy por a·de·lan·*ta*·do)

A … ticket (to Monteverde).	*Un pasaje … para (Monteverde).*	oon pa·*sa*·khe … *pa*·ra (mon·te·*ver*·de)
child's	*para niño*	*pa*·ra *nee*·nyo
one-way	*solo de ida*	*so*·lo de *ee*·da
return	*de ida y vuelta*	de *ee*·da ee *vwel*·ta
student	*de estudiante*	de es·too·*dyan*·te

PRACTICAL

I'd like a/an ... seat.	*Quiero un asiento en ...*	*kye*·ro oon a·*syen*·to en ...
aisle	*el pasillo*	el pa·*see*·yo
nonsmoking	*el área de no fumado*	el *a*·re·a de no foo·*ma*·do
smoking	*el área de fumado*	el *a*·re·a de foo·*ma*·do
window	*la ventana*	la ven·*ta*·na

Is there a ...?	*¿Tiene ...?*	*tye*·ne ...
blanket	*una cobija*	*oo*·na ko·*bee*·kha
sick bag	*una bolsa para vomitar*	*oo*·na *bol*·sa *pa*·ra vo·mee·*tar*
toilet	*un baño*	oon *ba*·nyo

Is there air conditioning?
¿Tiene aire acondicionado? — *tye*·ne *ai*·re a·kon·dee·syo·*na*·do

How long does the trip take?
¿Cuánto dura el viaje? — *kwan*·to *doo*·ra el *vya*·khe

Is it a direct route?
¿Es un viaje directo? — es oon *vya*·khe dee·*rek*·to

How much is it?
¿Cuánto cuesta? — *kwan*·to *kwes*·ta

Can I get a stand-by ticket?
¿Puedo comprar un tiquete de stand-by? — *pwe*·do kom·*prar* oon tee·*ke*·te de sten·*bai*

What time should I check in?
¿A qué hora debo hacer el chequeo? — a ke *o*·ra *de*·bo a·*ser* el che·*ke*·o

I'd like to ... my ticket, please.	*Quisiera ... mi tiquete, por favor.*	kee·*sye*·ra ... mee tee·*ke*·te por fa·*vor*
cancel	*cancelar*	kan·se·*lar*
change	*cambiar*	kam·*byar*
confirm	*confirmar*	kon·feer·*mar*

listen for ...		
agente de viajes m&f	a·*khen*·te de vee·*a*·khes	**travel agent**
atrasado/a m/f	a·tra·*sa*·do/a	**delayed**
cancelado/a m/f	kan·se·*la*·do/a	**cancelled**
huelga f	*wel*·ga	**strike** n
itinerario m	ee·tee·ne·*ra*·ryo	**timetable**
lleno/a m/f	*ye*·no/a	**full**
plataforma f	pla·ta·*for*·ma	**platform**
ventanilla f	ven·ta·*nee*·ya	**ticket window**

luggage

equipaje

Where's (a/the) ...?	*¿Dónde está el ...?*	*don*·de es·*ta* el ...
baggage claim	*reclamo de equipaje*	re·*kla*·mo de e·kee·*pa*·khe
left-luggage office	*cuarto para guardar equipaje*	*kwar*·to *pa*·ra gwar·*dar* e·kee·*pa*·khe
luggage locker	*lócker para equipaje*	*lo*·ker *pa*·ra e·kee·*pa*·khe
trolley	*carrito para equipaje*	ka·*ree*·to *pa*·ra e·kee·*pa*·khe

Can I have some coins/tokens?
¿Me puede dar monedas/fichas? me *pwe*·de dar mo·*ne*·das/*fee*·chas

My luggage has been damaged.
Me dañaron el equipaje. me da·*nya*·ron el e·kee·*pa*·khe

My luggage has been lost.
Se perdieron mis maletas. se per·*dye*·ron mees ma·*le*·tas

My luggage has been stolen.
Se robaron mis maletas. se ro·*ba*·ron mees ma·*le*·tas

That's (not) mine.
Eso (no) es mío. *e*·so (no) es *mee*·o

plane

avión

Where does flight (CO52) arrive/depart?
¿Dónde llega/sale el vuelo (CO52)? — don·de *ye*·ga/*sa*·le el *vwe*·lo (se o seen·*kwen*·ta dos)

A (1st-class) ticket to (New York).
Un pasaje (en primera clase) para (Nueva York). — oon pa·*sa*·khe (en pree·*me*·ra *kla*·se) *pa*·ra (*nwe*·va york)

Where's (the) ...?	*¿Dónde está ...?*	*don*·de es·*ta* ...
airport shuttle	*la buseta del aeropuerto*	la boo·*se*·ta del a·e·ro·*pwer*·to
arrivals hall	*el área de llegadas*	el *a*·re·a de ye·*ga*·das
departures hall	*el área de salidas*	el *a*·re·a de sa·*lee*·das
duty-free shop	*el duty-free*	el *dyoo*·tee·free
gate (7)	*la puerta (siete)*	la *pwer*·ta (*sye*·te)

listen for ...

cambio m	*kam*·byo	**transfer**
pasaporte m	pa·sa·*por*·te	**passport**
tiquete de abordaje m	tee·*ke*·te de a·bor·*da*·khe	**boarding pass**
tránsito m	*tran*·see·to	**transit**

bus

bus

There are two main types of buses in Costa Rica – *directos* dee·*rek*·tos and *colectivos* ko·lek·*tee*·vos. The term *directos* is a bit of a misnomer because they still stop frequently. Not as frequently, however, as the *colectivos*, which require a Latin American patience to endure. *Buses de turistas* *boo*·ses de too·*rees*·tas are privately owned and used only for tours.

Is this a bus stop?
¿Esta es una parada de bus? es·ta es *oo*·na pa·*ra*·da de boos

How often do buses come?
¿Cada cuánto pasa el bus? *ka*·da *kwan*·to *pa*·sa el boos

Does it stop at (Puerto Viejo)?
¿Hace parada en (Puerto Viejo)? *a*·se pa·*ra*·da en (*pwer*·to *vye*·kho)

What's the next stop?
¿Cuál es la próxima parada? kwal es la *prok*·see·ma pa·*ra*·da

I'd like to get off at (San Pedro).
Quiero bajarme en (San Pedro). *kye*·ro ba·*khar*·me en (san *pe*·dro)

bus station	*estación de buses* f	es·ta·*syon* de *boo*·ses
bus terminal	*terminal de buses* f	ter·mee·*nal* de *boo*·ses
departure bay	*área de salida* m	*a*·re·a de sa·*lee*·da
local bus station	*estación de buses locales* f	es·ta·*syon* de *boo*·ses lo·*ka*·les
minibus	*microbús* m	mee·kro·*boos*
shuttle bus	*buseta* f	boo·*se*·ta
timetable display	*pizarra con itinerario* f	pee·*sa*·ra kon ee·tee·ne·*ra*·ryo

listen for ...

equipaje de mano m	e·ke·*pa*·khe de *ma*·no	**carry-on baggage**
exceso de equipaje m	ek·*se*·so de e·kee·*pa*·khe	**excess baggage**
ficha f	*fee*·cha	**token**

bussing it

Travelling by bus can be a chaotic affair in Costa Rica. In San José there's no central terminal of the kind that you might be used to – just an area called 'the Coca Cola' in honour of a bottling plant that used to occupy the site. Other terminals and offices are scattered all over the city.

Brightly painted timetables on station walls may not have been updated ... ever. Always ask at the ticket office about departure times. If there isn't one, try your luck with the women who clean the restrooms. These phrases might help:

Where's the bus terminal?
¿Dónde está la terminal de buses? — *don*·de es·*ta* la ter·mee·*nal* de *boo*·ses

What time does bus number (five) leave?
¿A qué hora sale el bus número (cinco)? — a ke *o*·ra *sa*·le el boos *noo*·me·ro (*seen*·ko)

boat

barco

What's the lake/sea like today?
¿Cómo está el lago/ mar hoy? — *ko*·mo es·*ta* el *la*·go/ mar oy

What island/beach is this?
¿Cuál isla/playa es esta? — kwa *ees*·la/*pla*·ya es *es*·ta

I feel seasick.
Me siento mareado/a. m/f — me *syen*·to ma·re·*a*·do/a

Are there life jackets?
¿Hay chalecos salvavidas? — ai cha·*le*·kos sal·va·*vee*·das

Can I dine at the captain's table?
¿Podría cenar con el capitán? — po·*dree*·a se·*nar* kon el ka·pee·*tan*

boat (general)	*barco* m	*bar*·ko
boat (small)	*bote* m	*bo*·te
cabin	*cabina* f	ka·*bee*·na
captain	*capitán* m	ka·pee·*tan*
car deck	*plataforma para carros* f	pla·ta·*for*·ma *pa*·ra *ka*·ros
deck	*cubierta* f	koo·*byer*·ta
ferry	*ferry* m	*fe*·ree
hammock	*hamaca* f	a·*ma*·ka
lifeboat	*bote salvavidas* m	*bo*·te sal·va·*vee*·das
life jacket	*chaleco salvavidas* m	cha·*le*·ko sal·va·*vee*·das
yacht	*yate* m	*ya*·te

taxi

taxi

I'd like a (shared) taxi …	*Quiero un taxi (compartido) …*	*kye*·ro oon *tak*·see (kom·par·*tee*·do) …
at (9am)	*para las (nueve de la mañana)*	*pa*·ra las (*nwe*·ve de la ma·*nya*·na)
for a full day	*para un día entero*	*pa*·ra oon *dee*·a en·*te*·ro
for a half day	*para medio día*	*pa*·ra *me*·dyo *dee*·a
for (two) hours	*para (dos) horas*	*pa*·ra (dos) *o*·ras
now	*para ahora*	*pa*·ra a·*o*·ra
tomorrow	*para mañana*	*pa*·ra ma·*nya*·na

Where's the taxi stand?
¿Dónde está la parada de taxis? — *don*·de es·*ta* la pa·*ra*·da de *tak*·sees

Is there a taxi available?
¿Hay un taxi disponible? — ai oon *tak*·see dees·po·*nee*·ble

Please take me to (this address).
Por favor, lléveme a (esta dirección). — por fa·*vor* *ye*·ve·me a (*es*·ta dee·rek·*syon*)

How much is it to (San Isidro)?
¿Cuánto es hasta (San Isidro)? — *kwan*·to es *as*·ta (san ee·*see*·dro)

How much is the (initial) charge?
¿Cuánto es la tarifa (básica)? — *kwan*·to es la ta·*ree*·fa (*ba*·see·ka)

Please put the meter on.
Por favor, ponga la maría. — por fa·*vor* *pon*·ga la ma·*ree*·a

I don't want to pay a flat fare.
No quiero pagar una tarifa fija. — no *kye*·ro pa·*gar* *oo*·na ta·*ree*·fa *fee*·kha

Please …	*Por favor, …*	por fa·*vor* …
come back at (10pm)	*vuelva a las (diez de la noche)*	*vwel*·va a las (dyes de la *no*·che)
slow down	*baje la velocidad*	*ba*·khe la ve·lo·see·*dad*
stop here	*pare aquí*	*pa*·re a·*kee*
wait here	*espéreme aquí*	es·*pe*·re·me a·*kee*

For other useful phrases, see **directions**, page 57, and **money**, page 39.

all the way to Chepe

Both the man's name *José* kho·*se* and the capital city *San José* san kho·*se* carry the nickname *Chepe* *che*·pe. Rumour has it that if you ask a taxi driver to take you from the airport to *Chepe*, rather than to *San José*, you'll get a better deal on the taxi fare.

car & motorbike hire

I'd like to hire a/an ...	*Quiero alquilar ...*	*kye*·ro al·kee·*lar* ...
4WD	*un cuatro por cuatro*	oon *kwa*·tro por *kwa*·tro
automatic	*un carro automático*	oon *ka*·ro ow·to·*ma*·tee·ko
car	*un carro*	oon *ka*·ro
manual	*un carro de marchas*	oon *ka*·ro de *mar*·chas
motorbike	*una motocicleta*	*oo*·na mo·to·see·*kle*·ta
with ...	*con ...*	kon ...
air conditioning	*aire acondicionado*	*ai*·re a·kon·dee·syo·*na*·do
a driver	*un chofer*	oon cho·*fer*

How much for daily/weekly hire?
¿Cuánto cuesta el alquiler por día/semana? — *kwan*·to *kwes*·ta el al·kee·*ler* por *dee*·a/se·*ma*·na

Does that include insurance/mileage?
¿Incluye seguro/ kilometraje? — een·*kloo*·ye se·*goo*·ro/ kee·lo·me·*tra*·khe

Do you have a guide to the road rules (in English)?
¿Tiene un manual de tránsito (en inglés)? — *tye*·ne oon ma·*nwal* de *tran*·see·to (en een·*gles*)

Do you have a road map?
¿Tiene un mapa de carreteras? — *tye*·ne oon *ma*·pa de ka·re·*te*·ras

on the road

What's the speed limit?
¿Cuál es el límite de velocidad? — kwal es el *lee*·mee·te de ve·lo·see·*dad*

Is this the road to (Tamarindo)?
¿Por aquí se va a (Tamarindo)? — por a·*kee* se va a (ta·ma·*reen*·do)

Where's a petrol station?
¿Dónde hay una bomba? — *don*·de ai *oo*·na *bom*·ba

Please fill it up.
Lleno, por favor. — *ye*·no por fa·*vor*

I'd like (25) litres.
Échele (veinticinco) litros, por favor. — e·che·le (*vayn*·tee·*seen*·ko) *lee*·tros por fa·*vor*

diesel	*diesel* m	*dee*·sel
premium	*súper* m	*soo*·per
regular	*regular* m	re·goo·*lar*

Can you check the ...?	*¿Le revisa ..., por favor?*	le ree·*vee*·sa ... por fa·*vor*
oil	*el aceite*	el a·*say*·te
tyre pressure	*las llantas*	las *yan*·tas
water	*el agua*	el *a*·gwa

(How long) Can I park here?
¿(Cuánto tiempo) Puedo parquear aquí? — (*kwan*·to *tyem*·po) *pwe*·do par·ke·*ar* a·*kee*

Do I have to pay?
¿Tengo que pagar? — *ten*·go ke pa·*gar*

signs

Alto	*al*·to	**Stop**
Ceda	*se*·da	**Give Way**
Desvío	des·*vee*·o	**Detour**
Entrada	en·*tra*·da	**Entrance**
No Hay Paso	no ai *pa*·so	**No Entry**
Peaje	pe·*a*·khe	**Toll**
Peligro	pe·*lee*·gro	**Danger**
Salida	sa·*lee*·da	**Exit**
Una Vía	*oo*·na *vee*·a	**One Way**

problems

I need a mechanic.
Necesito un mecánico. — ne·se·*see*·to oon me·*ka*·nee·ko

I've had an accident.
Tuve un accidente. — *too*·ve oon ak·see·*den*·te

The car has broken down (at Golfito).
El carro se varó (en Golfito). — el *ka*·ro se va·*ro* (en gol·*fee*·to)

The motorbike has broken down (at Golfito).
La moto se varó (en Golfito). — la *mo*·to se va·*ro* (en gol·*fee*·to)

The car won't start.
El carro no arranca. — el *ka*·ro no a·*ran*·ka

The motorbike won't start.
La moto no arranca. — la *mo*·to no a·*ran*·ka

I have a flat tyre.
Se me estalló una llanta. — se me es·ta·*yo* *oo*·na *yan*·ta

I've lost my car keys.
Se me perdieron las llaves del carro. — se me per·*dye*·ron las *ya*·ves del *ka*·ro

I've locked the keys inside.
Dejé las llaves adentro. — de·*khe* las *ya*·ves a·*den*·tro

I've run out of petrol.
Me quedé sin gasolina. — me ke·*de* seen ga·so·*lee*·na

Can you fix it (today)?
¿Lo puede arreglar (hoy)? — lo *pwe*·de a·reg·*lar* (oy)

How long will it take?
¿Cuánto va a durar? — *kwan*·to va a doo·*rar*

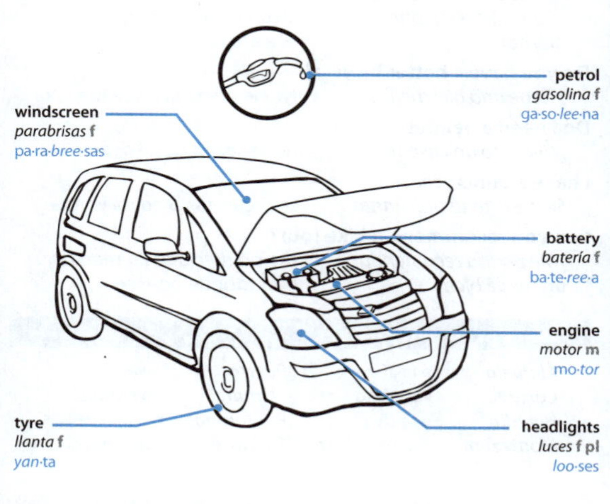

bicycle

bicicleta

I'd like …	*Quiero …*	*kye*·ro …
my bicycle repaired	*que me arreglen la bicicleta*	ke me a·*re*·glen la bee·see·*kle*·ta
to buy a bicycle	*comprar una bicicleta*	kom·*prar* *oo*·na bee·see·*kle*·ta
to hire a bicycle	*alquilar una bicicleta*	al·kee·*lar* *oo*·na bee·see·*kle*·ta

I'd like a … bike.	*Quiero una bicicleta …*	*kye*·ro *oo*·na bee·see·*kle*·ta …
mountain	*montañera*	mon·ta·*nye*·ra
racing	*de carreras*	de ka·*re*·ras
second-hand	*de segunda mano*	de se·*goon*·da *ma*·no

How much is it per day/hour?
¿Cuánto cuesta por día/hora? — *kwan*·to *kwes*·ta por *dee*·a/*o*·ra

Do you have a better bicycle?
¿Tiene una bici mejor? — *tye*·ne *oo*·na *bee*·see me·*khor*

Do I need a helmet?
¿Necesito un casco? — ne·se·*see*·to oon *kas*·ko

I have a puncture.
Se me estalló una llanta. — se me es·ta·*yo* *oo*·na *yan*·ta

Can you recommend a bike tour?
¿Me podría recomendar un tur de bici? — me po·*dree*·a re·ko·men·*dar* oon toor de *bee*·see

costa rican place names

Alajuela	a·la·*khwe*·la	*Puerto Limón*	*pwer*·to lee·*mon*
Cartago	kar·*ta*·go	*Puntarenas*	poon·ta·*re*·nas
Heredia	e·*re*·dya	*San José*	san kho·*se*
Montezuma	mon·te·*soo*·ma		

border crossing

cruzando la frontera

I'm ...	*Estoy ...*	es·*toy* ...
in transit	*de paso*	de *pa*·so
on business	*de negocios*	de ne·*go*·syos
on holiday	*de vacaciones*	de va·ka·*syo*·nes
I'm here for ...	*Voy a estar aquí por ...*	voy a es·*tar* a·*kee* por ...
(10) days	*(diez) días*	(dyes) *dee*·as
(three) weeks	*(tres) semanas*	(tres) se·*ma*·nas
(two) months	*(dos) meses*	(dos) *me*·ses

I'm going to (Jacó).
Voy para (Jacó). — voy *pa*·ra (kha·*ko*)

I'm staying at (the Hotel Tropical).
Estoy hospedado en (el Hotel Tropical). — es·*toy* o·spe·*da*·do en (el o·*tel* tro·pee·*kal*)

listen for ...

familia f	fa·*mee*·lya	**family**
grupo m	*groo*·po	**group**
impuesto de salida m	eem·*pwes*·to de sa·*lee*·da	**departure tax**
pasaporte m	pa·sa·*por*·te	**passport**
solo/a m/f	*so*·lo/a	**alone**
visa f	*vee*·sa	**visa**

at customs

en la aduana

I have nothing to declare.

No tengo nada que declarar.	no *ten*·go *na*·da ke de·kla·*rar*

I have something to declare.

Tengo algo para declarar.	*ten*·go *al*·go *pa*·ra de·kla·*rar*

Do I have to declare this?

¿Tengo que declarar esto?	*ten*·go ke de·kla·*rar es*·to

That's (not) mine.

Eso (no) es mío.	*e*·so (no) es *mee*·o

I didn't know I had to declare it.

Yo no sabía que tenía que declararlo.	yo no sa·*bee*·a ke te·*nee*·a ke de·kla·*rar*·lo

Do you have this form in (English)?

¿Tiene este formulario en (inglés)?	*tye*·ne *es*·te for·moo·*la*·ryo en (een·*gles*)

Could I please have an (English) interpreter?

¿Podría conseguirme un intérprete (en inglés), por favor?	po·*dree*·a kon·se·*geer*·me oon een·*ter*·pre·te (en een·*gles*) por fa·*vor*

For phrases on payments and receipts, see **money**, page 39.

signs

Aduana	a·*dwa*·na	**Customs**
Control de Pasaporte	kon·*trol* de pa·sa·*por*·te	**Passport Control**
Cuarentena	kwa·ren·*te*·na	**Quarantine**
Duty-Free	*dyoo*·tee·free	**Duty-Free**
Migración	mee·gra·*syon*	**Immigration**

directions
direcciones

Where's (the bank)?
¿Dónde está (el banco)? — *don*·de es·*ta* (el *ban*·ko)

What's the address?
¿Cuál es la dirección? — kwal es la dee·rek·*syon*

How do I get there?
¿Cómo llego ahí? — *ko*·mo *ye*·go a·*ee*

How far is it?
¿Qué tan largo está? — ke tan *lar*·go es·*ta*

Can you show me (on the map)?
¿Me puede enseñar (en el mapa)? — me *pwe*·de en·se·*nyar* (en el *ma*·pa)

What … is this?	*¿Cuál … es este/a?* **m/f**	kwal … es *es*·te/a
square	*plaza* **f**	*pla*·sa
street	*calle* **f**	*ka*·ye
village	*pueblo* **m**	*pwe*·blo

It's …	*Está …*	es·*ta* …
behind …	*detrás de …*	de·*tras* de …
close	*cerrado*	se·*ra*·do
here	*aquí*	a·*kee*
in front of …	*en frente de …*	en *fren*·te de …
near …	*cerca de …*	*ser*·ka de…
next to …	*a la par de …*	a la par de …
opposite …	*opuesto a …*	o·*pwes*·to a …
straight ahead	*aquí directo*	a·*kee* dee·*rek*·to
there	*ahí*	a·*ee*

just around the corner

Costa Ricans will often give directions using the phrase *cien metros* syen *me*·tros (100 metres). This is really shorthand for 'one city block', known locally as *una cuadra* oo·na *kwa*·dra.

Turn ...	*Doble ...*	*do*·ble ...
at the corner	*en la esquina*	en la es·*kee*·na
at the traffic lights	*en el semáforo*	en el se·*ma*·fo·ro
left	*a la izquierda*	a la ees·*kyer*·da
right	*a la derecha*	a la de·*re*·cha
north	*norte*	*nor*·te
south	*sur*	soor
east	*este*	*es*·te
west	*oeste*	o·*es*·te
by bus	*por bus*	por boos
by taxi	*por taxi*	por *tak*·see
by train	*por tren*	por tren
on foot	*por a pie*	a pye

For information on Costa Rican addresses, see the box **return to sender**, page 82.

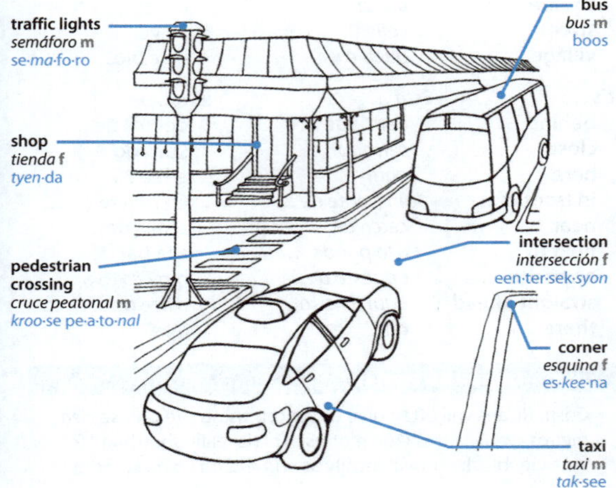

PRACTICAL

finding accommodation

encontrando un lugar para hospedarse

An *apartotel* is basically a hotel room equipped with a kitchen to allow for self-catering. The word *cabina* is loosely used to cover cheap to mid-range accommodation. Both the words *pensión* pen·*syon* and *casa de huéspedes* are used for 'guesthouse'. Bed and breakfasts are an increasingly popular accommodation option and the English term is used.

Where's a/an ...?	*¿Dónde hay ...?*	*don*·de ai ...
apartotel	*un apartotel*	oon a·par·to·*tel*
cabina	*una cabina*	oo·na ka·*bee*·na
camping ground	*una área para acampar*	oo·na *a*·re·a *pa*·ra a·kam·*par*
ecolodge	*un ecolodge*	oon *e*·ko·loj
guesthouse	*una casa de huéspedes*	oo·na *ka*·sa de *wes*·pe·des
hostel	*un hospedaje*	oon os·pe·*da*·khe
hotel	*un hotel*	oon o·*tel*
youth hostel	*un albergue juvenil*	oon al·*ber*·ge khoo·ve·*neel*
Can you recommend somewhere ...?	*¿Me podría recomendar algún lugar ...?*	me po·*dree*·a re·ko·men·*dar* al·*goon* loo·*gar* ...
cheap	*barato*	ba·*ra*·to
good	*bueno*	*bwe*·no
luxurious	*lujoso*	loo·*kho*·so
nearby	*cerca de aquí*	*ser*·ka de a·*kee*
romantic	*romántico*	ro·*man*·tee·ko
safe for women travellers	*que sea seguro para mujeres*	ke *se*·a se·*goo*·ro *pa*·ra moo·*khe*·res

I want something near the ...	*Quiero algo que esté cerca ...*	kye·ro al·go ke es·te ser·ka ...
beach	*de la playa*	de la pla·ya
bus stop	*de la parada de buses*	de la pa·ra·da de boo·ses
city centre	*del centro*	del sen·tro
shops	*de las tiendas*	de las tyen·das
What's the address?	*¿Cuál es la dirección?*	kwal es la dee·rek·syon

For responses, see **directions**, page 57.

local talk

dive n	*chinchorro* m	cheen·cho·ro
roach motel	*cucarachero* m	koo·ka·ra·che·ro
top spot	*lugar pura vida* m	loo·gar poo·ra vee·da

booking ahead & checking in

haciendo una reservación y llegando

I'd like to book a room, please.
Quiero reservar una habitación, por favor. — kye·ro re·ser·var oo·na a·bee·ta·syon por fa·vor

I have a reservation.
Tengo una reservación. — ten·go oo·na re·ser·va·syon

My name's ...
Mi nombre es ... — mee nom·bre es ...

For (three) nights/weeks.
Por (tres) noches/semanas. — por (tres) no·ches/se·ma·nas

From (2 July) to (6 July).
Del (dos de julio) al (seis de julio). — del (dos de khoo·lyo) al (says de khoo·lyo)

Do I need to pay upfront?
¿Necesito pagar por adelantado? — ne·se·see·to pa·gar por a·de·lan·ta·do

listen for ...

¿Cuántas noches?	*kwan*·tas *no*·ches	**How many nights?**
llave **f**	*ya*·ve	**key**
lleno/a **m/f**	*ye*·no/a	**full**
pasaporte **m**	pa·sa·*por*·te	**passport**
recepción **f**	re·sep·*syon*	**reception**

Do you have a ... room?	*¿Tiene una habitación ...?*	*tye*·ne *oo*·na a·bee·ta·*syon* ...
single	*sencilla*	sen·*see*·ya
double	*doble*	*do*·ble
twin	*con dos camas sencillas*	kon dos *ka*·mas sen·*see*·yas
How much is it per ...?	*¿Cuánto es por ...?*	*kwan*·to es por ...
night	*noche*	*no*·che
person	*persona*	per·*so*·na
week	*semana*	se·*ma*·na
Can I pay by ...?	*¿Puedo pagar con ...?*	*pwe*·do pa·*gar* kon ...
credit card	*tarjeta de crédito*	tar·*khe*·ta de *kre*·dee·to
debit card	*tarjeta de débito*	tar·*khe*·ta de *de*·bee·to
travellers cheque	*cheque de viajero*	*che*·ke de vya·*khe*·ro
Can I see it?	*¿Puedo verla?*	*pwe*·do *ver*·la
I'll take it.	*Sí, la quiero.*	see la *kye*·ro

signs

Baño	*ba*·nyo	**Bathroom**
Espacio Disponible	es·*pa*·syo dees·po·*nee*·ble	**Vacancy**
Lavandería	la·van·de·*ree*·a	**Laundry**
No Hay Espacio	no ai es·*pa*·syo	**No Vacancy**

requests & queries

preguntas y peticiones

Is breakfast included?
¿Incluye el desayuno? — een·*kloo*·ye el de·sa·*yoo*·no

When/Where is breakfast served?
¿Cuándo/Dónde sirven el desayuno? — *kwan*·do/*don*·de *seer*·ven el de·sa·*yoo*·no

Is there hot water all day?
¿Hay agua caliente todo el día? — ai *a*·gwa ka·*lyen*·te *to*·do el *dee*·a

Please wake me at (seven).
Por favor, despiérteme a las (siete). — por fa·*vor* des·*pyer*·te·me a las (*sye*·te)

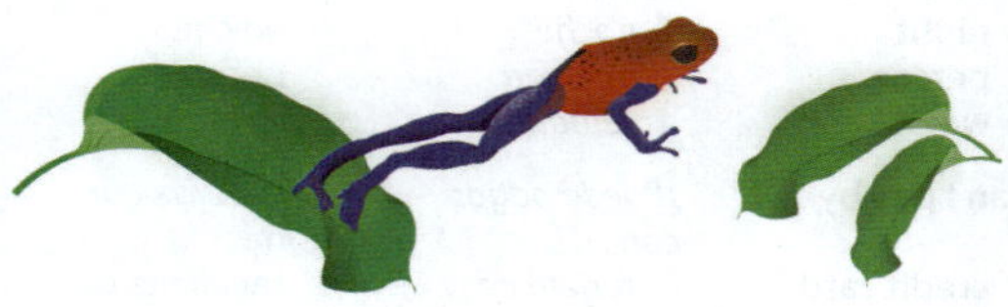

Do you have a/an ...?	*¿Tienen ...?*	*tye*·nen ...
elevator	*ascensor*	a·sen·*sor*
laundry service	*servicio de lavandería*	ser·*vee*·syos de la·van·de·*ree*·a
message board	*pizarra de mensajes*	pee·*sa*·ra de men·*sa*·khes
safe	*caja fuerte*	*ka*·kha *fwer*·te
swimming pool	*piscina*	pee·*see*·na

Can I use the ...?	*¿Podría usar ...?*	po·*dree*·a oo·*sar* ...
kitchen	*la cocina*	la ko·*see*·na
laundry	*la lavandería*	la la·van·de·*ree*·a
telephone	*el teléfono*	el te·*le*·fo·no

a knock at the door …

Who is it?	*¿Quién es?*	kyen es
Just a moment.	*Un momento.*	oon mo·*men*·to
Come in.	*Pase.*	*pa*·se
Come back later, please.	*Vuelva más tarde, por favor.*	*vwel*·va mas *tar*·de por fa·*vor*

Could I have (a) …, please?	*¿Me podría dar …, por favor?*	me po·*dree*·a dar … por fa·*vor*
mosquito net	*un mosquitero*	oon mos·kee·*te*·ro
my key	*la llave*	la *ya*·ve
receipt	*una factura*	*oo*·na fak·*too*·ra

Do you … here?	*¿Aquí …?*	a·*kee* …
arrange tours	*organizan tours*	or·ga·*nee*·san toors
change money	*cambian dinero*	*kam*·byan dee·*ne*·ro

Is there a message for me?
¿Tengo algún mensaje? — *ten*·go al·*goon* men·*sa*·khe

Can I leave a message for someone?
¿Le puedo dejar un mensaje a alguien? — le *pwe*·do de·*khar* oon men·*sa*·khe a *al*·gyen

I'm locked out of my room.
No puedo entrar al cuarto. — no *pwe*·do en·*trar* al *kwar*·to

complaints

quejas

It's too …	*Está demasiado …*	es·*ta* de·ma·*sya*·do …
bright	*claro*	*kla*·ro
cold	*frío*	*free*·o
dark	*oscuro*	os·*koo*·ro
expensive	*caro*	*ka*·ro
hot	*caliente*	ka·*lyen*·te
noisy	*ruidoso*	rwee·*do*·so
small	*pequeño*	pe·*ke*·nyo

The … doesn't work.	*El … no sirve.*	el … no *seer*·ve
air conditioner	*aire acondicionado*	*ai*·re a·kon·dee·syo·*na*·do
fan	*ventilador*	ven·tee·la·*dor*
toilet	*baño*	*ba*·nyo

Can I get (another blanket)?
¿Me podría dar (otra cobija)? — me po·*dree*·a dar (*o*·tra ko·*bee*·kha)

This … isn't clean.
Este/a … está sucio/a. m/f — *es*·te/a … es·*ta soo*·syo/a

There's no hot water.
No hay agua caliente. — no ai *a*·gwa ka·*lyen*·te

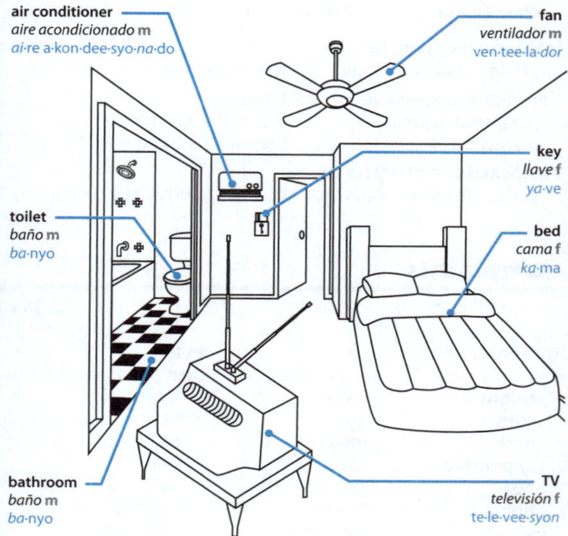

checking out

salida

What time is checkout?
¿A qué hora es la salida? — a ke *o*·ra es la sa·*lee*·da

Can I have a late checkout?
¿Puedo salir más tarde? — *pwe*·do sa·*leer* mas *tar*·de

Can you call a taxi for me (for 11 o'clock)?
¿Usted me podría llamar un taxi (para las once)? — oos·*ted* me po·*dree*·a ya·*mar* oon *tak*·see (*pa*·ra las *on*·se)

I'm leaving now.
Ya me voy. — ya me voy

Can I leave my bags here?
¿Puedo dejar mis maletas aquí? — *pwe*·do de·*khar* mees ma·*le*·tas a·*kee*

There's a mistake in the bill.
Hay un error en la cuenta. — ai oon e·*ror* en la *kwen*·ta

I had a great stay, thanks.
La pasé muy bien, muchas gracias. — la pa·*se* mooy byen *moo*·chas *gra*·syas

I'll recommend it to my friends.
Voy a recomendar a mis amigos. — voy a re·ko·men·*dar* a mees a·*mee*·gos

Could I have my ..., please?	*¿Me puede dar ..., por favor?*	me *pwe*·de dar ... por fa·*vor*
deposit	*mi depósito*	mee de·*po*·see·to
passport	*mi pasaporte*	mee pa·sa·*por*·te
valuables	*mis valores*	mees va·*lo*·res

I'll be back ...	*Voy a volver ...*	voy a vol·*ver* ...
in (three) days	*en (tres) días*	en (tres) *dee*·as
on (Tuesday)	*el (martes)*	el (*mar*·tes)

camping

acampar

Can I …?	*¿Puedo …?*	pwe·do …
camp here	*acampar aquí*	a·kam·*par* a·*kee*
park next to my tent	*parquearme a la par de la tienda*	par·ke·*ar*·me a la par de la *tyen*·da
How much is it per …?	*¿Cuánto cuesta por …?*	*kwan*·to *kwes*·ta por …
person	*persona*	per·*so*·na
tent	*tienda de campaña*	*tyen*·da de kam·*pa*·nya
vehicle	*carro*	*ka*·ro
Do you have (a) …?	*¿Tiene …?*	*tye*·ne …
electricity	*electricidad*	e·lek·tree·see·*dad*
laundry service	*servicio de lavandería*	ser·*vee*·syos de la·van·de·*ree*·a
shower facilities	*duchas*	*doo*·chas
site	*un espacio*	oon es·*pa*·syo
tents for hire	*tiendas de campaña para alquilar*	*tyen*·das de kam·*pa*·nya *pa*·ra al·kee·*lar*
toilets	*baños*	*ba*·nyos

Who do I ask to stay here?
¿A quién le pregunto para quedarme aquí? — a kyen le pre·*goon*·to *pa*·ra ke·*dar*·me a·*kee*

Is it coin-operated?
¿Es de monedas? — es de mo·*ne*·das

Is the water drinkable?
¿Se puede beber el agua? — se *pwe*·de be·*ber* el *a*·gwa

Could I borrow …?
¿Podría prestarme …? — po·*dree*·a pres·*tar*·me …

For cooking utensils, see **self-catering,** page 167.

renting

alquilando

I'm here about the … for rent.	*Vengo por el/la … que está alquilando.* m/f	ven·go por el/la … ke es·*ta* al·kee·*lan*·do
Do you have a/an … for rent?	*¿Tiene un/una … para alquilar?* m/f	*tye*·ne oon/*oo*·na … *pa*·ra al·kee·*lar*
apartment	*apartamento* m	a·par·ta·*men*·to
cabina	*cabina* f	ka·*bee*·na
house	*casa* f	*ka*·sa
room	*cuarto* m	*kwar*·to
villa	*villa* f	*vee*·ya
(partly) furnished	*(parcialmente) amueblado*	(par·syal·*men*·te) a·mwe·*bla*·do
unfurnished	*sin amueblar*	seen a·mwe·*blar*

Is there a deposit?
¿Hay que dejar depósito? — ai ke de·*khar* de·*po*·see·to

Are utilities included?
¿Incluye los servicios de luz y agua? — een·*kloo*·ye los ser·*vee*·syos de loos ee *a*·gwa

staying with locals

hospedárse con la gente de la zona

If you're invited to stay with a local family, make sure you not only bring a small gift (such as food or a souvenir), but also offer to help with the housework. You may need to insist on helping out, as your offer will usually be declined on first attempt.

Can I stay at your place?
¿Puedo quedarme en su casa? — *pwe*·do ke·*dar*·me en soo *ka*·sa

I have my own ...	*Yo tengo mi propio/a ...* **m/f**	yo *ten*·go mee *pro*·pyo/a ...
sleeping bag	*saco de dormir* **m**	*sa*·ko de dor·*meer*
sleeping mat	*colchoneta* **f**	kol·cho·*ne*·ta

Is there anything I can do to help?
¿En que le puedo ayudar? — en ke le *pwe*·do a·yoo·*dar*

Can I bring anything for the meal?
¿Le traigo algo para la comida? — le *trai*·go *al*·go *pa*·ra la ko·*mee*·da

Can I set/clear the table?
¿Pongo/Quito la mesa? — *pon*·go/*kee*·to la *me*·sa

Can I take out the rubbish?
¿Saco la basura? — *sa*·ko la ba·*soo*·ra

Thanks for your hospitality.
Muchas gracias por hospedarme. — *moo*·chas *gra*·syas por os·pe·*dar*·me

the host with the most

If you're invited to share a meal in a Costa Rican home, your solicitous hosts will ply you with food and drink. Remember that politeness is highly valued in their culture, so be sure to extoll the virtues of your hosts' cooking. This phrase should do the trick:

La comida está muy rica!
la ko·*mee*·da es·*ta* mooy *ree*·ka — **The food is very good!**

For more dining-related phrases, see **eating out**, page 153.

PRACTICAL

looking for ...

buscando ...

Are shops open (on Independence Day)?
¿El comercio abre (el día de la independencia)? el ko·*mer*·syo *a*·bre (el *dee*·a de la een·de·pen·*den*·sya)

What hours are shops open?
¿Cuál es el horario de las tiendas? kwal es el o·*ra*·ryo de las *tyen*·das

Where can I buy (a padlock)?
¿Dónde puedo comprar (un candado)? *don*·de *pwe*·do kom·*prar* (oon kan·*da*·do)

Where's (a/the) ...?	*¿Dónde hay ...?*	*don*·de ai ...
department store	*una tienda*	*oo*·na *tyen*·da
kiosk	*un quiosco*	oon *kyos*·ko
mall	*un mall*	oon mol
neighbourhood store	*una pulpería*	*oo*·na pool·pe·*ree*·a
market	*un mercado*	oon mer·*ka*·do

For more items and shopping locations, see the **dictionary**.

making a purchase

al comprar

I'm just looking.
Sólo estoy viendo. *so*·lo es·*toy* *vyen*·do

I'd like to buy (an adaptor plug).
Quiero (un adaptador). *kye*·ro (oon a·dap·ta·*dor*)

How much is it?

¿Cuánto cuesta?	*kwan*·to *kwes*·ta

Can you write down the price?

¿Podría escribir el precio?	po·*dree*·a es·kree·*beer* el *pre*·syo

Can I look at it?

¿Lo/la puedo ver? m/f	lo/la *pwe*·do ver

Do you have any others?

¿Tiene más?	*tye*·ne mas

Is this (240) volts?

¿Éste es de (doscientos cuarenta) voltios?	*es*·te es de (do·*syen*·tos kwa·*ren*·ta) *vol*·tee·os

Do you accept ...?	*¿Acepta ...?*	a·*sep*·ta ...
credit cards	*tarjetas de crédito*	tar·*khe*·tas de *kre*·dee·to
debit cards	*tarjetas de débito*	tar·*khe*·tas de *de*·bee·to
travellers cheques	*cheque de viajero*	*che*·ke de vya·*khe*·ro

Could I have a ..., please?	*¿Me da ..., por favor?*	me da ... por fa·*vor*
bag	*una bolsa*	*oo*·na *bol*·sa
receipt	*un recibo*	oon re·*see*·bo

I don't need a bag, thanks.

No necesito bolsa, gracias.	no ne·se·*see*·to *bol*·sa *gra*·syas

Could I have it wrapped?

¿Me lo puede envolver, por favor?	me lo *pwe*·de en·vol·*ver* por fa·*vor*

Does it have a guarantee?

¿Tiene garantía?	*tye*·ne ga·ran·*tee*·a

Can I have it sent abroad?

¿Lo puedo mandar al extranjero?	lo *pwe*·do man·*dar* al eks·tran·*khe*·ro

Can you order it for me?

¿Usted me lo podría pedir?	oos·*ted* me lo po·*dree*·a pe·*deer*

Can I pick it up later?
¿Puedo pasar a recogerlo después? — *pwe*·do pa·*sar* a re·ko·*kher*·lo des·*pwes*

The quality isn't good.
No es de buena calidad. — no es de *bwe*·na ka·lee·*dad*

It doesn't work.
No funciona. — no foon·see·*o*·na

It's broken/damaged.
Está roto/dañado. — es·*ta ro*·to/da·*nya*·do

It's dirty/stained.
Está sucio/manchado. — es·*ta soo*·syo/man·*cha*·do

I'd like to return this.
Quiero devolver ésto. — *kye*·ro de·vol·*ver es*·to

I'd like (a) ..., please.	*Me da ..., por favor.*	me da ... por fa·*vor*
my change	*el vuelto*	el *vwel*·to
receipt	*un recibo*	oon re·*see*·bo
refund	*un reintegro*	oon re·een·*te*·gro

local talk

bargain n	*ganga* **f**	*gan*·ga
rip-off	*robo* **m**	*ro*·bo
sale	*promoción* **f**	pro·mo·*syon*

bargaining

el regateo

That's too expensive.
Está muy caro. — es·*ta* mooy *ka*·ro

Can you lower the price?
¿Podría bajarle el precio? — po·*dree*·a ba·*khar*·le el *pre*·syo

Do you have something cheaper?
¿Tiene algo más barato? — *tye*·ne *al*·go mas ba·*ra*·to

What's your final price?
¿Entonces, cuál es el precio final? — en·*ton*·ses kwal es el *pre*·syo fee·*nal*

I'll give you (1000 *colones*).
Le doy (mil colones). — le doy (meel ko·*lo*·nes)

listen for ...

¿Algo más?	*al*·go mas	**Anything else?**
¿Le puedo ayudar en algo?	le *pwe*·do a·yoo·*dar* en *al*·go	**Can I help you?**
No tenemos.	no te·*ne*·mos	**We don't have any.**

books & reading

libros y lectura

Can you recommend a book to me?
¿Me podría recomendar un libro? — me po·*dree*·a re·ko·men·*dar* oon *lee*·bro

Do you have ...?	*¿Tiene ...?*	*tye*·ne ...
a book by (Carmen Lyra)	*un libro de (Carmen Lyra)*	oon *lee*·bro de (*kar*·men *lee*·ra)
an entertainment guide	*una guía de entretenimientos*	*oo*·na *gee*·a de en·tre·te·nee·*myen*·tos
Is there an English-language ...?	*¿Hay alguna ... de (inglés)?*	ai al·*goo*·na ... de (een·*gles*)
bookshop	*librería*	lee·bre·*ree*·a
section	*sección*	sek·*syon*
I'd like a ...	*Quiero ...*	*kye*·ro ...
dictionary	*un diccionario*	oon deek·syo·*na*·ryo
newspaper (in English)	*un periódico (en inglés)*	oon pe·*ryo*·dee·ko (en een·*gles*)
Do you have ...?	*¿Tiene ...?*	*tye*·ne ...
guidebooks	*guías*	*gee*·as
phrasebooks	*libros de frases*	*lee*·bros de *fra*·ses

PRACTICAL

clothes

ropa

My size is …	*Mi talla es …*	mee *ta*·ya es …
small	*pequeño*	pe·*ke*·nyo
medium	*mediano*	me·*dya*·no
large	*grande*	*gran*·de

Can I try it on?
¿Me lo puedo probar? — me lo *pwe*·do pro·*bar*

It doesn't fit.
No me queda. — no me *ke*·da

hairdressing

peluquería

I'd like (a) …	*Quiero …*	*kye*·ro …
colour	*un tinte*	oon *teen*·te
my beard trimmed	*que me recorten la barba*	ke me re·*kor*·ten la *bar*·ba
my hair washed/dried	*que me laven/ sequen el pelo*	ke me *la*·ven/ *se*·ken el *pe*·lo
shave	*que me afeiten*	ke me a·*fay*·ten
streaks	*hacerme unos rayitos*	a·*ser*·me *oo*·nos ra·*yee*·tos
trim	*que me recorten el pelo*	ke me re·*kor*·ten el *pe*·lo

Don't cut it too short.
No me lo corte demasiado corto. — no me lo *kor*·te de·ma·*sya*·do *kor*·to

Please use a new blade.
Por favor, use una navajilla nueva. — por fa·*vor* *oo*·se *oo*·na na·va·*khee*·ya *nwe*·va

Shave it all off!
Córtemelo todo. — *kor*·te·me·lo *to*·do

music

música

I'd like a ...	*Quiero un ...*	*kye*·ro oon ...
blank tape	*cassette en blanco*	ka·*se*·te en *blan*·ko
CD/DVD	*CD/DVD*	se de/de ve de
video	*vídeo*	*vee*·de·o

I'm looking for something by (Editus).
Estoy buscando algo de (Editus). — es·*toy* boos·*kan*·do *al*·go de (e·*dee*·toos)

Can I listen to this?
¿Lo puedo escuchar? — lo *pwe*·do es·koo·*char*

Will this work on any DVD player?
¿Este servirá en cualquier DVD? — es·te ser·vee·*ra* en kwal·*kyer* de ve de

Is this for a (PAL/NTSC) system?
¿Es para un sistema (PAL/NTSC)? — es *pa*·ra oon sees·*te*·ma (pe a *e*·le/*e*·ne te *e*·se se)

photography

fotografía

Can you ...?	*¿Puede ...?*	*pwe*·de ...
develop digital photos	*revelar fotos digitales*	re·ve·*lar* *fo*·tos dee·khee·*ta*·les
develop this film	*revelar este rollo*	re·ve·*lar* *es*·te *ro*·yo
load my film	*ponerme este rollo en la cámara*	po·*ner*·me *es*·te *ro*·yo en la *ka*·ma·ra
recharge the battery for my digital camera	*recargar la batería de mi cámara digital*	re·kar·*gar* la ba·te·*ree*·a de mee *ka*·ma·ra dee·khee·*tal*
transfer photos from my camera to CD	*pasar las fotos de mi cámara digital a un CD*	pa·*sar* las *fo*·tos de mee *ka*·ma·ra dee·khee·*tal* a oon se de

I need a/an … film for this camera.	*Necesito un rollo … para esta cámara.*	ne·se·*see*·to oon *ro*·yo … *pa*·ra *es*·ta *ka*·ma·ra
APS	*APS*	a pe *e*·se
B&W	*blanco y negro*	*blan*·ko ee *ne*·gro
colour	*a color*	a ko·*lor*
slide	*para diapositivas*	*pa*·ra dee·a·po·see·*tee*·vas
(200) speed	*asa (doscientos)*	*a*·sa (do·*syen*·tos)

Do you have a … for this camera?	*¿Tiene un … para esta cámara?*	*tye*·ne oon … *pa*·ra *es*·ta *ka*·ma·ra
flash	*flash*	flash
light meter	*medidor de luz*	me·dee·*dor* de loos
telephoto lens	*teleobjetivo*	te·le·ob·*khe*·tee·vo
zoom lens	*zoom*	soom

Do you have … for this camera?	*¿Tiene … para esta cámara?*	*tye*·ne … *pa*·ra *es*·ta *ka*·ma·ra
batteries	*baterías*	ba·te·*ree*·as
memory cards	*memorias*	me·*mo*·ree·as

… camera	*… cámara*	… *ka*·ma·ra
digital	*digital*	dee·khee·*tal*
disposable	*desechable*	de·se·*cha*·ble
underwater	*sumergible*	soo·mer·*khee*·ble
video	*de vídeo*	de *vee*·de·o

I need a cable to connect my camera to a computer.

Necesito un cable para conectar mi cámara a la computadora.	ne·se·*see*·to oon *ka*·ble *pa*·ra ko·nek·*tar* mee *ka*·ma·ra a la kom·poo·ta·*do*·ra

I need a cable to recharge this battery.

Necesito un cable para recargar esta batería.	ne·se·*see*·to oon *ka*·ble *pa*·ra re·kar·*gar* *es*·ta ba·te·*ree*·a

I need a video cassette for this camera.

Necesito un cassette para esta cámara de vídeo.	ne·se·*see*·to oon ka·*se*·te *pa*·ra *es*·ta *ka*·ma·ra de *vee*·de·o

I need a passport photo taken.

Necesito tomarme una foto tamaño pasaporte.	ne·se·*see*·to to·*mar*·me *oo*·na *fo*·to ta·*ma*·nyo pa·sa·*por*·te

I'm not happy with these photos.

No me gusta la calidad de estas fotos.	no me *goos*·ta la ka·lee·*dad* de *es*·tas *fo*·tos

I don't want to pay the full price.

No quiero pagarle el precio completo.	no *kye*·ro pa·*gar*·le el *pre*·syo kom·*ple*·to

repairs

reparaciones

Can I have my ... repaired here?	*¿Me pueden arreglar ... aquí?*	me *pwe*·den a·reg·*lar* ... a·*kee*
backpack	*mi mochila*	mee mo·*chee*·la
bag	*mi bolso*	mee *bol*·so
(video) camera	*mi cámara (de vídeo)*	mee *ka*·ma·ra (de *vee*·de·o)
(sun)glasses	*mis anteojos (oscuros)*	mees an·te·*o*·khos (os·*koo*·ros)
shoes	*mis zapatos*	mees sa·*pa*·tos

When will it be ready?

¿Cuándo va a estar listo?	*kwan*·do va a es·*tar lees*·to

souvenirs		
ceramics	*cerámica* **f**	se·*ra*·mee·ka
hammock	*hamaca* **f**	a·*ma* ka
handicraft	*artesanías* **f pl**	ar·te·sa·*nee*·as
jewellery	*joyas* **f pl**	*kho*·yas
painted miniature ox carts	*carretas* **f pl**	ka·*re*·tas

the internet

internet

Where's the local Internet café?
¿Dónde hay un café internet? — *don*·de ai oon ka·*fe* een·ter·*net*

I'd like to ...	*Quiero ...*	*kye*·ro ...
burn a CD	*quemar un disco*	ke·*mar* oon *dees*·ko
check my email	*revisar mi correo*	re·vee·*sar* mee ko·*re*·o
download my photos	*bajar mis fotos*	ba·*khar* mees *fo*·tos
get Internet access	*tener acceso al internet*	te·*ner* ak·*se*·so al een·ter·*net*
use a printer	*usar una impresora*	oo·*sar oo*·na eem·pre·*so*·ra
use a scanner	*usar un escáner*	oo·*sar* oon es·*ka*·ner

Do you have ...?	*¿Tiene ...?*	*tye*·ne ...
PCs	*PCs*	pe ses
Macs	*Macs*	maks
a Zip drive	*unidad de Zip*	oo·nee·*dad* de seep

Can I connect my ... to this computer?	*¿Puedo conectar mi ... a esta computadora?*	*pwe*·do ko·nek·*tar* mee ... a *es*·ta kom·poo·ta·*do*·ra
camera	*cámara*	*ka*·ma·ra
media player	*reproductor media*	re·pro·dook·*tor me*·dya
portable hard drive	*disco duro portátil*	*dees*·ko *doo*·ro por·*ta*·teel

How much per …?	*¿Cuánto es por …?*	*kwan*·to es por …
hour	*hora*	*o*·ra
(five) minutes	*(cinco) minutos*	(*seen*·ko) mee·*noo*·tos
page	*página*	*pa*·khee·na
How do I log on?	*¿Cómo entro?*	*ko*·mo *en*·tro
It's crashed.	*Está caída.*	es·*ta* ka·*ee*·da
I've finished.	*Ya terminé.*	ya ter·mee·*ne*

where the @!*# is it?

Spanish-language and English-language keyboard layouts differ because the two alphabets aren't quite the same. This shouldn't generally be a problem, but for one pesky – all too useful in the age of email – key.

The @ ('at') symbol – in Spanish this symbol is called *la arroa* la a·*ro*·a – isn't necessarily labeled on keyboards or may not be accessed by simply pressing the keys you're used to. Try the F2 key, use an ALT code – or ask for help:

Where's the @ key?
¿Dónde está la arroa? — *don*·de es·*ta* la a·*ro*·a

mobile/cell phone

teléfono celular

I'd like a …	*Necesito …*	ne·se·*see*·to …
charger for my phone	*un cargador para mi celular*	oon kar·ga·*dor* *pa*·ra mee se·loo·*lar*
mobile/cell phone for hire	*alquilar un teléfono celular*	al·kee·*lar* oon te·*le*·fo·no se·loo·*lar*
prepaid mobile/cell phone	*un celular prepagado*	oon se·loo·*lar* pre·pa·*ga*·do
SIM card for your network	*una tarjeta SIM para su red*	*oo*·na tar·*khe*·ta seem *pa*·ra soo red

PRACTICAL

What are the call rates?

¿Cuánto es la tarifa?	*kwan*·to es la ta·*ree*·fa

(30) *colones* per (30) minutes.

(Treinta) colones por (treinta) minutos.	(*trayn*·ta) ko·*lo*·nes por (*trayn*·ta) mee·*noo*·tos

phone

el teléfono

What's your phone number?

¿Cuál es tu número de teléfono?	kwal es too *noo*·me·ro de te·*le*·fo·no

Where's the nearest public phone?

¿Dónde está el teléfono público más cercano?	*don*·de es·*ta* el te·*le*·fo·no *poo*·blee·ko mas ser·*ka*·no

Can I look at a phone book?

¿Puedo ver la guía telefónica?	*pwe*·do ver la *gee*·a te·le·*fo*·nee·ka

What's the area/country code for (Panama)?

¿Cuál es el código de área/país para (Panamá)?	kwal es el *ko*·dee·go de *a*·re·a/pa·*ees pa*·ra (pa·na·*ma*)

The number is ...

El número es ...	el *noo*·me·ro es ...

I want to ...	*Quiero ...*	*kye*·ro ...
buy a phonecard	*comprar una tarjeta telefónica*	kom·*prar oo*·na tar·*khe*·ta te·le·*fo*·nee·ka
call (Canada)	*llamar a (Canadá)*	ya·*mar* a (ka·na·*da*)
make a (local) call	*hacer una llamada (local)*	a·*ser oo*·na ya·*ma*·da (lo·*kal*)
reverse the charges	*llamar de cobro revertido*	ya·*mar* de *ko*·bro re·ver·*tee*·do
speak for (three) minutes	*hablar (tres) minutos*	a·*blar* (tres) mee·*noo*·tos

communications

How much does … cost?	*¿Cuánto cuesta …?*	kwan·to kwes·ta …
a (three)-minute call	*una llamada de (tres) minutos*	oo·na ya·ma·da de (tres) mee·noo·tos
each extra minute	*cada minuto extra*	ka·da mee·noo·to eks·tra
It's engaged.	*Está ocupado.*	es·ta o·koo·pa·do
I've been cut off.	*Se cortó.*	se kor·to
The connection's bad.	*La conexión está muy mala.*	la ko·nek·syon es·ta mooy ma·la
Hello.	*Aló.*	a·lo
It's …	*Es …*	es …

listen for …

¿Con quién quiere hablar?	kon kyen kye·re a·blar	**Who do you want to speak to?**
No está.	no es·ta	**He/She isn't here.**
Número equivocado.	noo·me·ro e·kee·vo·ka·do	**Wrong number.**
¿Quién llama?	kyen ya·ma	**Who's calling?**
Un momento.	oon mo·men·to	**One moment.**

Please tell him/her I called.
¿Le podría decir que yo llamé, por favor? — le po·dree·a de·seer ke yo ya·me por fa·vor

Can I leave a message?
¿Le puedo dejar un mensaje? — le pwe·do de·khar oon men·sa·khe

I don't have a contact number.
No tengo un número dónde me pueda llamar. — no ten·go oon noo·me·ro don·de me pwe·da ya·mar

I'll call back later.
Yo llamo después. — yo ya·mo des·pwes

What time should I call?
¿A qué hora debo llamar? — a ke o·ra de·bo ya·mar

post office

correo

I want to send a …	*Quiero mandar …*	kye·ro man·dar …
fax	*un fax*	oon faks
letter	*una carta*	oo·na kar·ta
parcel	*un paquete*	oon pa·ke·te
postcard	*una postal*	oo·na pos·tal
I want to buy a/an …	*Quiero comprar…*	kye·ro kom·prar…
(padded) envelope	*un sobre (acolchonado)*	oon so·bre (a·kol·cho·na·do)
stamp	*una estampilla*	oo·na es·tam·pee·ya

Please send it by air/surface mail to (Australia).
Por favor, envíelo por avión/tierra a (Australia). por fa·vor en·vee·e·lo por a·vyon/tye·ra a (ow·stra·lya)

It contains (souvenirs).
Contiene (recuerdos). kon·tye·ne (re·kwer·dos)

Is there any mail for me?
¿Me llegó algo? me ye·go al·go

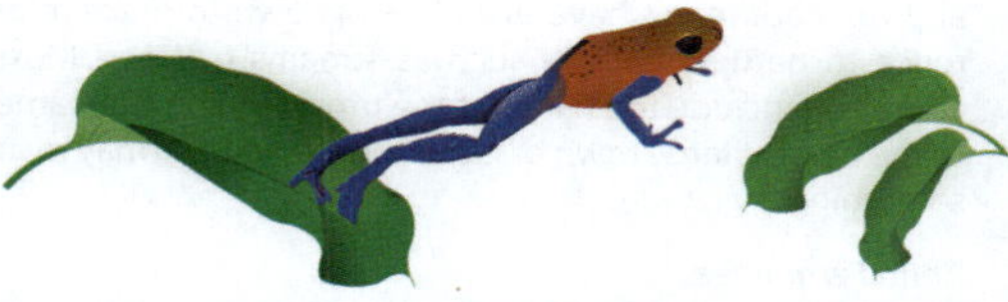

snail mail

… mail	*correo …*	ko·re·o …
air	*aéreo*	a·e·re·o
express	*express*	eks·pres
registered	*certificado*	ser·tee·fee·ka·do
sea	*marítimo*	ma·ree·tee·mo
surface	*por tierra*	por tye·ra

customs declaration	*declaración de aduana* **f**	de·kla·ra·*syon* de a·*dwa*·na
domestic	*local* **m&f**	lo·*kal*
fragile	*frágil* **m&f**	*fra*·kheel
international	*internacional* **m&f**	een·ter·na·syo·*nal*
mail n	*correo* **m**	ko·*re*·o
mailbox	*buzón* **m**	boo·*son*
PO box	*apartado* **m**	a·par·*ta*·do
postcode	*código postal* **m**	*ko*·dee·go pos·*tal*

return to sender

Addresses in Costa Rica sometimes take a surprising form. For one thing, outside San José and other larger cities, numbered addresses and street names don't really exist. Instead, Costa Ricans use descriptive addresses.

People can get quite creative in their choice of landmarks, and rural addresses have even been known to make reference to natural features such as streams or trees! Most addresses include the name of the province and the name of the nearest large town or city. A house address may read something like:

Anna Fernández
2km después de la fábrica hacia el Aguila
(2km after the factory on the way to Aguila)
Pejibaye de Perez Zeledón
San Isidro el General (closest major town)
Costa Rica
Centroamérica

What times/days is the bank open?
¿A qué horas/días está abierto el banco? — a ke o·ras/*dee*·as es·*ta* a·*byer*·to el *ban*·ko

Where can I ...?	*¿Dónde puedo ...?*	*don*·de *pwe*·do ...
I'd like to ...	*Quisiera ...*	kee·*sye*·ra ...
cash a cheque	*cambiar un cheque*	kam·*byar* oon *che*·ke
change a travellers cheque	*cambiar un cheque de viajero*	kam·*byar* oon *che*·ke de vya·*khe*·ro
change money into ***colones***	*cambiar dinero a colones*	kam·*byar* dee·*ne*·ro a ko·*lo*·nes
change money/ dollars	*cambiar plata/ dólares*	kam·*byar pla*·ta/ *do*·la·res
get a cash advance	*obtener un adelanto en efectivo*	ob·te·*ner* oon a·de·*lan*·to en e·fek·*tee*·vo
get change for this note	*cambiar este pagaré*	kam·*byar es*·te pa·ga·*re*
withdraw money	*sacar dinero*	sa·*kar* dee·*ne*·ro

Where's a/an ...?	*¿Dónde hay ...?*	*don*·de ai ...
automated teller machine	*un cajero automático*	oon ka·*khe*·ro ow·to·*ma*·tee·ko
foreign exchange office	*una casa de cambio*	*oo*·na *ka*·sa de *kam*·byo

For more information on the Costa Rican currency, the *colón*, see the box **the colour of money**, page 40.

What's the exchange rate?

¿A cómo está el tipo de cambio?	a *ko*·mo es·*ta* el *tee*·po de *kam*·byo

What's the charge for that?

¿Cuánto cobran por eso?	*kwan*·to *ko*·bran por *e*·so

The automated teller machine took my card.

El cajero automático se dejó mi tarjeta.	el ka·*khe*·ro ow·to·*ma*·tee·ko se de·*kho* mee tar·*khe*·ta

I've forgotten my PIN.

Se me olvidó mi PIN.	se me ol·vee·*do* mee peen

Can I use my credit card to withdraw money?

¿Puedo usar mi tarjeta de crédito para sacar plata?	*pwe*·do oo·*sar* mee tar·*khe*·ta de *kre*·dee·to *pa*·ra sa·*kar pla*·ta

Has my money arrived yet?

¿Ya llegó mi plata?	ya ye·*go* mee *pla*·ta

How long will it take to arrive?

¿Cuánto va a durar en llegar?	*kwan*·to va a doo·*rar* en ye·*gar*

For other useful phrases, see **money**, page 39.

listen for ...

Firme aquí. *feer*·me a·*kee*	**Sign here.**
Hay un problema. ai oon pro·*ble*·ma	**There's a problem.**
No podemos hacer eso. no po·*de*·mos a·*ser e*·so	**We can't do that.**
Usted no tiene fondos. oos·*ted* no *tye*·ne *fon*·dos	**You have no funds left.**

identificación **f**	ee·den·tee·fee·ka·*syon*	**identification**
pasaporte **m**	pa·sa·*por*·te	**passport**

sightseeing
turismo

I'd like a ...	*Quisiera ...*	kee·*sye*·ra ...
brochure	*un panfleto*	oon pan·*fle*·to
catalogue	*un catálogo*	oon ka·*ta*·lo·go
guide	*un guía*	oon *gee*·a
guidebook (in English)	*una guía turística (en inglés)*	*oo*·na *gee*·a too·*rees*·tee·ka (en een·*gles*)
(local) map	*un mapa (local)*	oon *ma*·pa (lo·*kal*)

Do you have information on ... sights?	*¿Tiene información sobre atracciones ...?*	*tye*·ne een·for·ma·*syon* *so*·bre a·trak·*syo*·nes ...
cultural	*culturales*	kool·too·*ra*·les
historical	*históricas*	ees·*to*·ree·kas
religious	*religiosas*	re·lee·*khyo*·sas

I'd like to see ...
Me gustaría ver ... — me goos·ta·*ree*·a ver ...

What's that?
¿Qué es eso? — ke es *e*·so

Who built/made it?
¿Quién lo construyó/hizo? — kyen lo kons·troo·*yo*/*ee*·so

How old is it?
¿Qué tan viejo es? — ke tan *vye*·kho es

Could you take a photo of me?
¿Podría/Podrías tomarme una foto? **pol/inf** — po·*dree*·a/po·*dree*·as to·*mar*·me *oo*·na *fo*·to

Can I take a photo (of you)?
¿(Le/Te) Puedo sacar una foto? **pol/inf** — (le/te) *pwe*·do sa·*kar* *oo*·na *fo*·to

I'll send you the photo.
Yo le/te mando la foto. **pol/inf** — yo le/te *man*·do la *fo*·to

getting in

para entrar

What time does it open/close?
¿A qué hora abren/cierran? — a ke *o*·ra *a*·bren/*sye*·ran

What's the admission charge?
¿Cuánto cuesta la entrada? — *kwan*·to *kwes*·ta la en·*tra*·da

Is there a discount for …?	*¿Hay algún descuento para …?*	ai al·*goon* des·*kwen*·to *pa*·ra …
children	*niños*	*nee*·nyos
families	*familias*	fa·*mee*·lyas
groups	*grupos*	*groo*·pos
older people	*personas mayores*	per·*so*·nas ma·*yo*·res
pensioners	*pensionados*	pen·syo·*na*·dos
students	*estudiantes*	es·too·*dyan*·tes

tours

Can you recommend a/an ...?	*¿Me podría recomendar un/una ...?* **m/f**	me po·*dree*·a re·ko·men·*dar* oon/*oo*·na ...
When's the next ...?	*¿Cuándo es el/la próximo/a ...?* **m/f**	*kwan*·do es el/la *prok*·see·mo/a ...
boat trip	*excursión en lancha* **f**	eks·koor·*syon* en *lan*·cha
day trip	*tour de un día* **m**	toor de oon *dee*·a
ecotour	*ecotour* **m**	e·ko·*toor*
natural history tour	*tour de historia natural* **m**	toor de ees·*to*·rya na·too·*ral*
tour	*tour* **m**	toor

I'd like to go ...	*Me gustaría ...*	me goos·ta·*ree*·a ...
bird watching	*ver pájaros*	ver *pa*·kha·ros
canoeing	*hacer canoa*	a·*ser* ka·*no*·a
horse riding	*hacer una cabalgata*	a·*ser oo*·na ka·bal·*ga*·ta
on a guided trek	*hacer trekking con guía*	a·*ser tre*·keen kon *gee*·a
river rafting	*ir rafting*	eer *raf*·teen
walking on the beach	*caminar en la playa*	ka·mee·*nar* en la *pla*·ya
wildlife spotting	*ver fauna*	ver *fow*·na

Is ... included?	*¿Incluye ...?*	een·*kloo*·ye ...
accommodation	*la dormida*	la dor·*mee*·da
food	*la comida*	la ko·*mee*·da
transport	*el transporte*	el trans·*por*·te

I want to hire a guide.
Quiero contratar un guía. *kye*·ro kon·tra·*tar* oon *gee*·a

How much for one day?
¿Cuánto cuesta por un día? *kwan*·to *kwes*·ta por oon *dee*·a

How long is the tour?
¿Cuánto dura el tour? — kwan·to doo·ra el toor

What time should we be back?
¿A qué hora volvemos? — a ke o·ra vol·ve·mos

Where will we meet?
¿Dónde nos encontramos? — don·de nos en·kon·tra·mos

I'm with them.
Yo vengo con ellos. — yo ven·go kon e·yos

I've lost my group.
Perdí mi grupo. — per·dee mee groo·po

biological reserve	*reserva biológica* **f**	re·ser·va byo·lo·khee·ka
botanical garden	*jardín botánico* **m**	khar·deen bo·ta·nee·ko
habitat	*hábitat* **m**	a·bee·tat
indigenous reserve	*reserva indígena* **f**	re·ser·va een·dee·khe·na
national park	*parque nacional* **m**	par·ke na·syo·nal
wildlife refuge	*refugio de fauna silvestre* **m**	re·foo·khyo de fow·na seel·ves·tre

For more on habitats and wildlife, see **ecotourism**, page 149.

costa rican national parks

Parque Nacional Chirripó	par·ke na·syo·nal chee·ree·po	Chirripó National Park
Parque Nacional Corcovado	par·ke na·syo·nal kor·ko·va·do	Corcovado National Park
Parque Nacional Santa Rosa	par·ke na·syo·nal san·ta ro·sa	Santa Rosa National Park
Parque Nacional Tortuguero	par·ke na·syo·nal tor·too·ge·ro	Tortuguero National Park
Reserva Monteverde	re·ser·va mon·te·ver·de	Monteverde Nature Reserve

I'm attending a …	*Estoy aquí para …*	es·*toy* a·*kee* *pa*·ra …
conference	*una conferencia*	*oo*·na kon·fe·*ren*·sya
course	*un curso*	oon *koor*·so
meeting	*una reunión*	*oo*·na re·oo·*nyon*
trade fair	*una feria de comercio*	*oo*·na *fe*·rya de ko·*mer*·syo

I'm here with …	*Estoy aquí con …*	es·*toy* a·*kee* kon …
my colleague(s)	*mi(s) colega(s)*	mee(s) ko·*le*·ga(s)
(two) others	*(dos) personas más*	(dos) per·*so*·nas mas

I'm alone.
Estoy aquí solo/a. m/f — es·*toy* a·*kee* *so*·lo/a

I have an appointment with …
Tengo una cita con … — *ten*·go *oo*·na *see*·ta kon …

I'm staying at (the Hotel Brisamar), room (200).
Me estoy quedando en (el Hotel Brisamar), habitación (doscientos). — me es·*toy* ke·*dan*·do en (el o·*tel* bree·sa·*mar*) a·bee·ta·*syon* (do·*syen*·tos)

I'm here for (two) days/weeks.
Voy a estar aquí (dos) días/semanas. — voy a es·*tar* a·*kee* (dos) *dee*·as/se·*ma*·nas

Can I have your business card?
¿Me podría dar su tarjeta de presentación? — me po·*dree*·a dar soo tar·*khe*·ta de pre·sen·ta·*syon*

Here's my ...	*Este es mi ...*	es·te es mee ...
What's your ...?	*¿Cuál es su ...?*	kwal es soo ...
address	*dirección*	dee·rek·*syon*
email address	*correo electrónico*	ko·*re*·o e·lek·*tro*·nee·ko
fax number	*número de fax*	*noo*·me·ro de faks
mobile/cell phone number	*número de celular*	*noo*·me·ro de se·loo·*lar*
pager number	*número de beeper*	*noo*·me·ro de *bee*·per
work number	*número de teléfono del trabajo*	*noo*·me·ro de te·*le*·fo·no del tra·*ba*·kho

Where's the ...?	*¿Dónde es la ...?*	*don*·de es la ...
business centre	*sala ejecutiva*	*sa*·la e·khe·koo·*tee*·va
conference	*conferencia*	kon·fe·*ren*·sya
meeting	*reunión*	re·oo·*nyon*

I need (a/an) ...	*Necesito ...*	ne·se·*see*·to ...
computer	*una computadora*	*oo*·na kom·poo·ta·*do*·ra
Internet connection	*una conexión de internet*	*oo*·na ko·nek·*syon* de een·ter·*net*
interpreter who speaks (English)	*un traductor que hable (inglés)*	oon tra·dook·*tor* ke *a*·ble (een·*gles*)
to send a fax	*mandar un fax*	man·*dar* oon faks

Thank you for your attention.
Gracias por su atención. — *gra*·syas por soo a·ten·*syon*

That went very well.
Estuvo muy bien. — es·*too*·vo mooy byen

Shall we go for a drink/meal?
¿Vamos a comer/tomar algo? — *va*·mos a ko·*mer*/to·*mar* *al*·go

It's on me.
Yo invito. — yo een·*vee*·to

senior & disabled travellers
viajeros discapacitados o de edad avanzada

Costa Rica is making strides to implement facilities for the elderly and people with disabilities. There are already special seats, parking spots and, in government offices, express queues reserved for people with disabilities (*filas para discapacitados* fee·las pa·ra dees·ka·pa·see·ta·dos). Wheelchair ramps are increasingly common in San José, and the country has recently established its first disabled taxi service (*taxi para discapacitados* tak·see pa·ra dees·ka·pa·see·ta·dos).

I have a disability.
Tengo una discapacidad. — ten·go oo·na dees·ka·pa·see·dad

I need assistance.
Necesito asistencia. — ne·se·see·to a·sees·ten·sya

I'm deaf.
Soy sordo/a. m/f — soy sor·do/a

I have a hearing aid.
Tengo un audífono. — ten·go oon ow·dee·fo·no

My (companion) is blind.
Mi (compañero/a) es ciego/a. m/f — mee (kom·pa·nyer·o/a) es sye·go/a

What services do you have for people with a disability?
¿Qué servicios tiene para personas con discapacidad? — ke ser·vee·syos tye·ne pa·ra per·so·nas kon dees·ka·pa·see·dad

Are guide dogs permitted?
¿Se permiten perros guías? — se per·mee·ten pe·ros gee·as

Are there disabled parking spaces?
¿Hay parqueo para discapacitados? — ai par·ke·o para dees·ka·pa·see·ta·dos

Is there wheelchair access?
¿Hay acceso para silla de ruedas? — ai ak·se·so pa·ra see·ya de rwe·das

How wide is the entrance?

¿Qué tan ancha es la entrada? — ke tan *an*·cha es la en·*tra*·da

How many steps are there?

¿Cuántas gradas hay? — *kwan*·tas *gra*·das ai

Is there an elevator?

¿Hay ascensor? — ai a·sen·*sor*

Are there disabled toilets?

¿Hay baños para discapacitados? — ai *ba*·nyos *pa*·ra dees·ka·pa·see·*ta*·dos

Are there rails in the bathroom?

¿Hay barras para sostenerse en el baño? — ai *ba*·ras *pa*·ra sos·te·*ner*·se en el *ba*·nyo

Could you call me a disabled taxi?

¿Me podría llamar un taxi para discapacitados? — me po·*dree*·a ya·*mar* oon *tak*·see *pa*·ra dees·ka·pa·see·*ta*·dos

Could you help me cross the street safely?

¿Me podría ayudar a cruzar la calle? — me po·*dree*·a a·yoo·*dar* a kroo·*sar* la *ka*·ye

Is there somewhere I can sit down?

¿Hay algún lugar donde me pueda sentar? — ai al·*goon* loo·*gar* *don*·de me *pwe*·da sen·*tar*

guide dog	*perro guía* **m**	*pe*·ro *gee*·a
older person	*persona mayor* **f**	per·*so*·na ma·*yor*
person with a disability	*discapacitado/a* **m/f**	dees·ka·pa·see·*ta*·do/a
ramp	*rampa* **f**	*ram*·pa
walking frame	*baranda* **f**	ba·*ran*·da
walking stick	*bastón* **m**	bas·*ton*
wheelchair	*silla de ruedas* **f**	*see*·ya de *rwe*·das

golden age

Costa Rican senior citizens are designated *ciudadanos de oro* syoo·da·*da*·nos de *o*·ro (lit: golden citizens) and have ID cards which entitle them to special privileges.

travelling with children

viajando con niños

Is there a ...?	*¿Tienen ...?*	*tye*·nen ...
baby change room	*un lugar para cambiar bebés*	oon loo·*gar pa*·ra kam·*byar* be·*bes*
child discount	*un descuento para niños*	oon des·*kwen*·to *pa*·ra *nee*·nyos
child-minding service	*una guardería*	*oo*·na gwar·de·*ree*·a
children's menu	*un menú para niños*	oon me·*noo pa*·ra *nee*·nyos
child's portion	*una porción para niños*	*oo*·na por·*syon pa*·ra *nee*·nyos
family ticket	*un tiquete familiar*	oon tee·*ke*·te fa·mee·*lyar*

I need a/an ...	*Necesito ...*	ne·se·*see*·to ...
baby seat	*una silla para bebé*	*oo*·na *see*·ya *pa*·ra be·*be*
(English-speaking) babysitter	*una niñera (que hable inglés)*	*oo*·na nee·*nye*·ra (ke *a*·ble een·*gles*)
booster seat	*una silla de carro para niños*	*oo*·na *see*·ya de *ka*·ro *pa*·ra *nee*·nyos
cot	*un catre*	oon *ka*·tre
highchair	*una silla para comer*	*oo*·na *see*·ya *pa*·ra ko·*mer*
plastic bag	*una bolsa plástica*	*oo*·na *bol*·sa *plas*·tee·ka
potty	*una vacenilla*	*oo*·na va·se·*nee*·ya
pram	*un coche*	oon *ko*·che
stroller	*un coche sombrilla*	oon *ko*·che som·*bree*·ya

Where's the nearest ...?	*¿Dónde está el/la ... más cercano/a?* **m/f**	*don*·de es·*ta* el/la ... mas ser·*ka*·no/a
drinking fountain	*fuente de agua* **m**	*fwen*·te de *a*·gwa
park	*parque* **m**	*par*·ke
playground	*play* **m**	plai
swimming pool	*piscina* **f**	pee·*see*·na
tap	*tubo* **m**	*too*·bo
toyshop	*juguetería* **f**	khoo·ge·te·*ree*·a

Do you sell ...?	*¿Venden ...?*	*ven*·den ...
baby wipes	*pañitos desechables para bebé*	pa·*nyee*·tos de·se·*cha*·bles *pa*·ra be·*be*
disposable nappies/diapers	*pañales desechables*	pa·*nya*·les de·se·*cha*·bles
painkillers for infants	*pastillas pediátricas para el dolor*	pas·*tee*·yas pe·dee·*a*·tree·kas *pa*·ra el do·*lor*
tissues	*klíneks*	*klee*·neks

Are there any good places to take children around here?
¿Hay algún lugar bonito para llevar niños por aquí? — ai al·*goon* loo·*gar* bo·*nee*·to *pa*·ra ye·*var* *nee*·nyos por a·*kee*

Are children allowed?
¿Se permiten niños? — se per·*mee*·ten *nee*·nyos

Where can I change a nappy/diaper?
¿Dónde puedo cambiar un pañal? — *don*·de *pwe*·do kam·*byar* oon pa·*nyal*

Do you mind if I breast-feed here?
¿Le molestaría si doy de mamar aquí? — le mo·les·ta·*re*·a see doy de ma·*mar* a·*kee*

Could I have some paper and pencils, please?
¿Me podría dar un papel y lápices, por favor? — me po·*dree*·a dar oon pa·*pel* ee *la*·pee·ses por fa·*vor*

Is this suitable for (five)-year-old children?
¿Ésto está bien para niños de (cinco) años? — *es*·to es·*ta* byen *pa*·ra *nee*·nyos de (*seen*·ko) *a*·nyos

Do you know a dentist/doctor who is good with children?
¿Usted conoce algún dentista/doctor que sea bueno con los niños? — oos·*ted* ko·*no*·se al·*goon* den·*tees*·ta/dok·*tor* ke *se*·a *bwe*·no kon los *nee*·nyos

If your child is sick, see **health**, page 183.

talking with children

hablando con niños

What's your name?
¿Cómo te llamás? — *ko*·mo te ya·*mas*

How old are you?
¿Cuántos años tenés? — *kwan*·tos *a*·nyos te·*nes*

When's your birthday?
¿Cuándo cumplís años? — *kwan*·do koom·*plees a*·nyos

Do you go to kindergarten?
¿Vas al kínder? — vas al *keen*·der

Do you go to school?
¿Vas a la escuela? — vas a la es·*kwe*·la

What grade are you in?
¿En qué grado estás? — en ke *gra*·do es·*tas*

Do you like (school)?
¿Te gusta (la escuela)? — te *goos*·ta (la es·*kwe*·la)

Do you learn (English)?
¿Aprendés (ingles)? — a·pren·*des* (een·*gles*)

What do you do after school?
¿Qué hacés después de la escuela? — ke a·*ses* des·*pwes* de la es·*kwe*·la

talking about children

hablando sobre niños

When's the baby due?
¿Para cuándo está el bebé? — pa·ra *kwan*·do es·*ta* el be·*be*

What are you going to call the baby?
¿Cómo le va/vas a poner? **pol/inf** — *ko*·mo le va/vas a po·*ner*

Is this your first child?
¿Es su primer hijo/a? **pol m/f** — es soo pree·*mer ee*·kho/a
¿Es tu primer hijo/a? **inf m/f** — es too pree·*mer ee*·kho/a

How many children do you have?
¿Cuántos hijos tiene/tenés? **pol/inf** — *kwan*·tos *ee*·khos *tye*·ne/te·*nes*

What a beautiful child!
¡Qué chiquito/a más lindo/a! **m/f** — ke chee·*kee*·to/a mas *leen*·do/a

Is it a boy or a girl?
¿Es chiquito o chiquita? — es chee·*kee*·to o chee·*kee*·ta

How many months is he/she?
¿Cuántos meses tiene? — *kwan*·tos *me*·ses *tye*·ne

How old is he/she?
¿Cuántos años tiene? — *kwan*·tos *a*·nyos *tye*·ne

What's his/her name?
¿Cómo se llama? — *ko*·mo se *ya*·ma

who's who in the zoo?

Ever wondered how a rooster says 'cock-a-doodle-do' in Costa Rica? To break the ice with the local domestic fauna, try addressing them in their native tongue:

cat	*miau*	myow
chicken	*pío pío*	*pee*·o *pee*·o
cow	*muu*	moo
dog	*guau guau*	wow wow
rooster	*ki ki ri ki*	kee kee ree kee

basics

lo básico

Yes.	*Sí.*	see
No.	*No.*	no
Please.	*Por favor.*	por fa·*vor*
Thank you (very much).	*(Muchas) Gracias.*	(*moo*·chas) *gra*·syas
You're welcome.	*Con mucho gusto.*	kon *moo*·cho *goos*·to
Excuse me. (to get attention/ to get past)	*Con permiso.*	kon per·*mee*·so
Excuse me. (apology)	*Discúlpeme.*	dees·*kool*·pe·me
Sorry. (apology)	*Perdón.*	per·*don*
Sorry. (condolence)	*Lo siento.*	lo *syen*·to

greetings & goodbyes

saludos y despedidas

Costa Ricans are very conscious of civilities in their public behaviour. Never address a stranger without first extending a greeting such as *buenos días* (good morning), *buenas tardes* (good afternoon) or *buenas noches* (good evening). These may be abbreviated to simply *buenos* (for *buenos días*) and *buenas* (for *buenas tardes* and *buenas noches*).

Good …		
day	*Buen día.*	bwen *dee*·a
morning	*Buenos (días).*	*bwe*·nos (*dee*·as)
afternoon	*Buenas (tardes).*	*bwe*·nas (*tar*·des)
evening	*Buenas (noches).*	*bwe*·nas (*no*·ches)

In addition to the formal greetings on the preceding page, you can use the expressions below to greet a friend or someone you're familiar with. The expressions *pura vida* (lit: pure life) and *tuanis* (lit: too nice – from the English) are quintessential *tiquismos* tee·*kees*·mos (Costa Rican slang). If you bandy them about you might soon be taken for a *Tico* *tee*·ko or *Tica* *tee*·ka (Costa Rican man or woman) yourself. See the box **talking *tiquismos***, page 134, for more on these expressions.

Hello/Hi.	*Hola.*	o·la
Hello. How's it going?	*Hola. ¿Pura vida?*	o·la *poo*·ra *vee*·da
Hello. How are things?	*Hola. ¿Todo bien?*	o·la *to*·do byen
Great, thanks.	*Tuanis.*	too·*a*·nees

How are you?

¿Cómo va/vas? **sg pol/inf**	*ko*·mo va/vas
¿Cómo van? **pl**	*ko*·mo van

Fine. And you?

Bien. ¿Y usted/vos? **sg pol/inf**	byen ee oos·*ted*/vos
Bien. ¿Y ustedes? **pl**	byen ee oos·*te*·des

What's your name?

¿Cómo se llama? **pol**	*ko*·mo se *ya*·ma
¿Cómo te llamás? **inf**	*ko*·mo te ya·*mas*

My name is ...

Me llamo ...	me *ya*·mo ...

I'd like to introduce you to (Daniel).

Quiero presentarle/ presentarte a (Daniel). **pol/inf**	*kye*·ro pre·sen·*tar*·le/ pre·sen·*tar*·te a (da·*nyel*)

I'm pleased to meet you.

Mucho gusto.	*moo*·cho *goos*·to

knock knock ...

If you're paying a visit to someone's house and can't find a doorbell, call out the following greeting to announce your presence:

¡Upe!	*oo*·pe	**Anyone home?**

SOCIAL

This is my ...	*Él/Ella es mi ...* **m/f**	el/*e*·ya es mee ...
boyfriend	*novio*	*no*·vyo
child	*hijo/a* **m/f**	*ee*·kho/a
colleague	*colega* **m&f**	ko·*le*·ga
friend	*amigo/a* **m/f**	a·*mee*·go/a
girlfriend	*novia*	*no*·vya
husband	*esposo*	es·*po*·so
partner	*compañero/a* **m/f**	kom·pa·*nye*·ro/a
wife	*esposa*	es·*po*·sa

See you later.	*Nos vemos.*	nos *ve*·mos
Bye.	*Chao.*	chao
Goodbye.	*Adiós.*	a·*dyos*
Good night.	*Buenas (noches).*	*bwe*·nas (*no*·ches)
Bon voyage!	*¡Buen viaje!*	bwen *vya*·khe

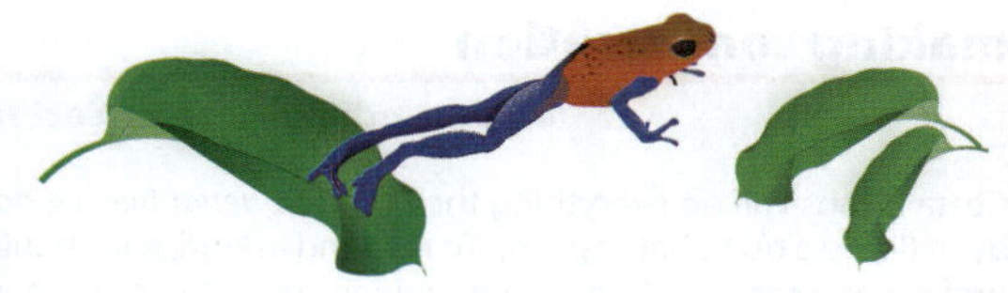

addressing people

modos de saludar

The usual nonverbal greetings are either shaking hands or kissing once on the cheek. In a formal situation or when you're meeting someone for the first time, it's probably best to shake hands. For a more informal everyday encounter, one kiss on the cheek is the usual protocol – unless it's between men, who usually just shake hands. The following titles are used in formal situations, and they're frequently abbreviated in writing:

Mr/Sir	*Señor (Sr)*	se·*nyor*
Mrs/Madam	*Señora (Sra)*	se·*nyo*·ra
Miss	*Señorita (Srta)*	se·nyo·*ree*·ta

hey mate!

The most common word for friend is *amigo/a* a·*mee*·go/a **m/f**, but Costa Rican Spanish has a number of colourful alternatives. You might hear young people call each other *mae* mai (or less commonly *maje* *ma*·khe), or refer to each other using this term. It roughly translates as 'dude' or 'mate'. It's also used for women but relatively rarely, in which case it equates to 'chick' or 'sheila' (to use an Australian expression).

Yet another term for 'mate/buddy' is *compa* *kom*·pa, an abbreviated form of *compañero* kom·pa·*nye*·ro (companion). In addition, there are quite a few rather vulgar terms used between men, but we'll spare you those …

making conversation

empezando una conversación

Costa Ricans will do everything they can to *quedar bien* ke·*dar* byen (leave a good impression). To respond in kind, you should preface any conversation with enquiries about the other person's wellbeing and engage in a little small talk too.

Everything fine?
¿Pura vida? — *poo*·ra *vee*·da

What's going down?
¿Qué hay de nuevo? — ke ai de *nwe*·vo

Everything cool?
¿Qué, todo bien? — ke *to*·do byen

What's the news?
¿Qué me cuenta? — ke me *kwen*·ta

What a beautiful day!
¡Qué día más bonito! — ke *dee*·a mas bo·*nee*·to

Nice/Awful weather, isn't it?
Qué tiempo más bonito/feo, ¿verdad? — ke *tyem*·po mas bo·*nee*·to/*fe*·o ver·*dad*

SOCIAL

Do you live here?	
¿Vive/Vivís por aquí? **pol/inf**	*vee*·ve/vee·*vees* por a·*kee*
Where are you going?	
¿Dónde va/vas? **pol/inf**	*don*·de va/vas
What are you doing?	
¿Qué está/estás haciendo? **pol/inf**	ke es·*ta*/es·*tas* a·*syen*·do
Do you like it here?	
¿Le/Te gusta aquí? **pol/inf**	le/te *goos*·ta a·*kee*
I love it here.	
Me encanta aquí.	me en·*kan*·ta a·*kee*
Can I take a photo of you?	
¿Puedo tomarle/tomarte una foto? **pol/inf**	*pwe*·do to·*mar*·le/to·*mar*·te *oo*·na *fo*·to

I'll send you the photo.
Yo le/te mando la foto. pol/inf — yo le/te la *man*·do la *fo*·to

That's (beautiful), isn't it?
Qué (bonito), ¿verdad? — ke (bo·*nee*·to) ver·*dad*

How long are you here for?
¿Cuánto tiempo va/vas a estar aquí? pol/inf — *kwan*·to *tyem*·po va/vas a es·*tar* a·*kee*

I'm here for (four) weeks/days.
Voy a estar aquí (cuatro) semanas/días. — voy a es·*tar* a·*kee* (*kwa*·tro) se·*ma*·nas/*dee*·as

Are you here on holiday?
¿Está/Estás aquí de vacaciones? pol/inf — es·*ta*/es·*tas* a·*kee* de va·ka·*syo*·nes

I'm here ...	*Estoy aquí ...*	es·*toy* a·*kee* ...
for a holiday	*de vacaciones*	de va·ka·*syo*·nes
on business	*de negocios*	de ne·*go*·syos
to study	*estudiando*	es·too·*dyan*·do

local talk

Hey!	*¡Hey!*	khe
Great!	*¡Tuanis!*	too·*a*·nees
Just a minute.	*Dame un toque.*	da·me oon *to*·ke
Just joking.	*Estoy vacilando.*	es·*toy* va·see·*lan*·do
Maybe.	*Tal vez.*	tal ves
No problem.	*No te preocupés.*	no te pre·o·koo·*pes*
No way!	*¡Qué va!*	ke va
Sure.	*Claro.*	*kla*·ro

nationalities

nacionalidades

Where are you from?
¿De dónde es/sos? **sg pol/inf** — de *don*·de es/sos

I'm from ...	*Soy de ...*	soy de ...
Australia	*Australia*	ow·*stra*·lya
Canada	*Canadá*	ka·na·*da*
the USA	*los Estados Unidos*	los es·*ta*·dos oo·*nee*·dos

ticomania

Costa Ricans are nicknamed *Ticos* *tee*·kos and *Ticas* *tee*·kas due to their affinity for adding endings such as *-tico/a* ·*tee*·ko/a, *-ito/a* ·*ee*·to/a or *-(c)illo/a* ·(s)*ee*·yo/a **m/f**, to the ends of words. These endings are known as diminutives. Diminutives can indicate the smallness of something – eg *gato* *ga*·to (cat) becomes *gatico* ga·*tee*·ko 'kitten' – but they also express how a speaker feels about something. Not surprisingly, many terms of endearment are in the form of diminutives – eg *palomita* pa·lo·*mee*·ta (darling) is a diminutive of *paloma* pa·*lo*·ma (dove). Diminutives can also give a friendly tone to a conversation. For instance, *un momentito* oon mo·men·*tee*·to (just a moment) sounds more lighthearted than *un momento* oon mo·*men*·to (one moment).

age

edad

How old ...?	*¿Cuantos años ...?*	*kwan*·tos *a*·nyos ...
are you	*tiene/tenés* **pol/inf**	*tye*·ne/te·*nes*
is your daughter	*tiene su hija* **pol**	*tye*·ne soo *ee*·kha
	tiene tu hija **inf**	*tye*·ne too *ee*·kha
is your son	*tiene su hijo* **pol**	*tye*·ne soo *ee*·kho
	tiene tu hijo **inf**	*tye*·ne too *ee*·kho

I'm … years old.
Tengo … años. — *ten*·go … *a*·nyos

He/She is … years old.
Él/Ella tiene … años. — el/*e*·ya *tye*·ne … *a*·nyos

Too old!
¡Demasiado viejo/a! m/f — de·ma·*sya*·do *vye*·kho/a

I'm younger than I look.
Soy menor de lo que parezco. — soy me·*nor* de lo ke pa·*res*·ko

For your age, see **numbers & amounts**, page 33.

occupations & studies

trabajo y estudio

What's your occupation?
¿Qué hace usted? pol — ke *a*·se oos·*ted*
¿Vos qué hacés? inf — vos ke a·*ses*

I'm self-employed.
Tengo mi propio negocio. — *ten*·go mee *pro*·pyo ne·*go*·syo

I'm a …	*Soy …*	soy …
chef	*chef* m&f	shef
engineer	*ingeniero/a* m/f	een·khe·*nye*·ro/a
journalist	*periodista* m&f	pe·ryo·*dees*·ta
student	*estudiante* m&f	es·too·*dyan*·te
teacher	*profesor/ profesora* m/f	pro·fe·*sor* pro·fe·*so*·ra

I work in …	*Yo trabajo en …*	yo tra·*ba*·kho en …
administration	*administración*	ad·mee·nees·tra·*syon*
health	*salud*	sa·*lood*
sales & marketing	*ventas y mercadeo*	*ven*·tas ee mer·ka·*de*·o

I'm …	*Soy …*	soy …
retired	*pensionado/a* m/f	pen·syo·*na*·do/a
unemployed	*desempleado/a* m/f	de·sem·ple·*a*·do/a

What are you studying?
¿Qué estás estudiando? — ke es·*tas* es·too·*dyan*·do

I'm studying …	*Estudio …*	es·*too*·dyo …
humanities	*humanidades*	oo·ma·nee·*da*·des
science	*ciencias*	*syen*·syas
Spanish	*español*	es·pa·*nyol*

family

familia

Family is one of the sacred pillars of Costa Rican society, so this vocabulary could well come in handy.

Do you have (a) …?	*¿Tiene …?* **pol**	*tye*·ne …
	¿Tenés…? **inf**	te·*nes* …
I (don't) have (a) …	*(No) Tengo…*	(no) *ten*·go …
boyfriend	*novio*	*no*·vyo
brother	*un hermano*	oon er·*ma*·no
children	*hijos*	*ee*·khos
daughter	*una hija*	*oo*·na *ee*·kha
girlfriend	*novia*	*no*·vya
husband	*esposo*	es·*po*·so
partner	*una pareja* **m&f**	*oo*·na pa·*re*·kha
sister	*una hermana*	*oo*·na er·*ma*·na
son	*un hijo*	oon *ee*·kho
wife	*esposa*	es·*po*·sa

Are you married?
¿Está casado/a? **pol m/f** — es·*ta* ka·*sa*·do/a
¿Estás casado/a? **inf m/f** — es·*tas* ka·*sa*·do/a

I live with someone.
Vivo con alguien. — *vee*·vo kon *al*·gyen

I'm …	*Soy …*	soy …
married	*casado/a* **m/f**	ka·*sa*·do/a
separated	*separado/a* **m/f**	se·pa·*ra*·do/a
single	*soltero/a* **m/f**	sol·*te*·ro/a

farewells

despedidas

Tomorrow is my last day here.

Mañana es mi último día acá.	ma·*nya*·na es mee *ool*·tee·mo *dee*·a a·*ka*

If you come to (the States) you can stay with me.

Si usted venga a (los Estados Unidos) se puede quedar conmigo. **pol**	see oos·*ted ven*·ga a (los es·*ta*·dos oo·*nee*·dos) se *pwe*·de ke·*dar* kon·*mee*·go
Si venís a (los Estados Unidos) te podés quedar conmigo. **inf**	see ve·*nees* a (los es·*ta*·dos oo·*nee*·dos) te po·*des* ke·*dar* kon·*mee*·go

It's been great meeting you.

Fue un placer conocerle/ conocerte. **pol/inf**	fwe oon pla·*ser* ko·no·*ser*·le/ ko·no·*ser*·te

Here's my …	*Este es mi …*	es·*te* es mee …
What's your …?	*¿Cuál es su/tu …?* **pol/inf**	kwal es soo/too …
address	*dirección*	dee·rek·*syon*
email address	*correo electrónico*	ko·*re*·o e·lek·*tro*·nee·ko
phone number	*teléfono*	te·*le*·fo·no

well-wishing

All the best!	*¡Qué te vaya bien!*	ke te *va*·ya byen
Congratulations!	*¡Felicidades!*	fe·lee·see·*da*·des
Good luck!	*¡Buena suerte!*	*bwe*·na *swer*·te
Happy Birthday!	*¡Feliz cumpleaños!*	fe·*lees* koom·ple·*a*·nyos
May God be with you!	*¡Qué Dios te acompañe!*	ke dee·*os* te a·kom·*pa*·nye
God bless you!	*¡Qué Dios te bendiga!*	ke dee·*os* te ben·*dee*·ga
Merry Christmas!	*¡Feliz Navidad!*	fe·*lees* na·vee·*dad*
Take care!	*¡Cuidate!*	*kwee*·da·te

interests
intereses

In this chapter, phrases are given in the informal *tú* and *vos* forms. For more details on polite and informal forms, see the **phrasebuilder**, page 23.

common interests

intereses comunes

What do you do in your spare time?

	¿Qué te gusta hacer en el tiempo libre?	ke te *goos*·ta a·*ser* en el *tyem*·po *lee*·bre
Do you like ...?	*¿Te gusta ...?*	te *goos*·ta ...
I (don't) like ...	*(No) Me gusta ...*	(no) me *goos*·ta ...
art	*el arte*	el *ar*·te
cooking	*cocinar*	ko·see·*nar*
dancing	*bailar*	bai·*lar*
drawing	*dibujar*	dee·boo·*khar*
gardening	*hacer el jardín*	a·*ser* el khar·*deen*
hiking	*ir a caminar*	eer a ka·mee·*nar*
listening to music	*escuchar música*	es·koo·*char moo*·see·ka
painting	*pintar*	peen·*tar*
reading	*leer*	le·*er*
shopping	*ir de compras*	eer de *kom*·pras
socialising	*socializar*	so·sya·lee·*sar*
sport	*hacer deporte*	a·*ser* de·*por*·te
surfing the Internet	*navegar el internet*	na·ve·*gar* el een·ter·*net*
travelling	*viajar*	vya·*khar*
watching films	*ver películas*	ver pe·*lee*·koo·las
watching TV	*ver tele*	ver *te*·le

For types of sports, see **sport**, page 135, and the **dictionary.**

music

música

Do you dance/sing?
¿Bailás/Cantás? — bai·*las*/kan·*tas*

Do you go to concerts?
¿Vas a conciertos? — vas a kon·*syer*·tos

Do you listen to music?
¿Escuchás música? — es·koo·*chas* *moo*·see·ka

Do you play an instrument?
¿Tocás algún instrumento? — to·*kas* al·*goon* eens·troo·*men*·to

What music do you like?
¿Qué música te gusta? — ke *moo*·see·ka te *goos*·ta

Which bands/singers do you like?
¿Qué grupos/cantantes te gustan? — ke *groo*·pos/kan·*tan*·tes te *goos*·tan

blues	*blues*	bloos
classical music	*música clásica*	*moo*·see·ka *kla*·see·ka
electronic music	*música electrónica*	*moo*·see·ka e·lek·*tro*·nee·ka
folk music	*música folklórica*	*moo*·see·ka fol·*klo*·ree·ka
jazz	*jazz*	shass
pop	*pop*	pop
rock	*rock*	rok
traditional music	*música tradicional*	*moo*·see·ka tra·dee·syo·*nal*
world music	*música internacional*	*moo*·see·ka een·ter·na·syo·*nal*

SOCIAL

costa rican grooves

In Costa Rica you'll hear music from all over the world, but your ears will also become attuned to Latin American rhythms. Guanacaste province, in particular, is known for its traditional music, often based around the marimba. Here are some of the musical styles that may get you jumping:

cumbia — *koom*·bya
Rhythmic dance music incorporating guitars, accordions, brass, drums and percussion. It encompasses indigenous, Spanish and African influences and was originally a courtship dance among slave populations.

merengue — me·*ren*·ge
Lively dance music originating in the Dominican Republic, combining African and Spanish influences. Signature instruments include the tambora drum, saxophone and accordion.

reggaetón — re·ge·*ton*
Reggae music reborn for a new generation. It's sung in Spanish and is a hip hop and dancehall hybrid originating in Puerto Rico and New York City. Eminently danceable and wildly popular with Costa Rican youth.

salsa — *sal*·sa
Popular dance music originating in New York, which spread like wildfire throughout the Caribbean in the 1960s .

Planning to go to a concert? See **tickets**, page 42, and **going out**, page 119.

cinema & theatre

cine y teatro

I feel like going to a ...	*Tengo ganas de ir a ...*	*ten*·go *ga*·nas de eer a ...
concert	*un concierto*	oon kon·*syer*·to
film	*una película*	*oo*·na pe·*lee*·ko·la
play	*una obra de teatro*	*oo*·na *o*·bra de te·*a*·tro

Did you like (the concert)?
¿Te gustó (el concierto)? te goos·*to* (el kon·*syer*·to)

What's showing at the cinema/theatre tonight?
¿Qué están dando en el cine/teatro hoy en la noche? ke es·*tan* *dan*·do en el *see*·ne/te·*a*·tro hoy en la *no*·che

Is it in (English)?
¿Es en (inglés)? es en (een·*gles*)

Does it have (English) subtitles?
¿Tiene subtítulos en (inglés)? *tye*·ne soob·*tee*·too·los en (een·*gles*)

Do you have tickets for ...?
¿Tenés entradas para ...? te·*nes* en·*tra*·das *pa*·ra ...

Are there any extra tickets for ...?
¿Hay más entradas para ...? ai mas en·*tra*·das *pa*·ra ...

Have you seen ...?
¿Has visto ...? as *vees*·to ...

Who's in it?
¿Quién tiene? kyen *tye*·ne

It stars ...
Protagoniza ... pro·ta·go·*nee*·sa ...

Is this seat taken?
¿Está ocupado? es·*ta* o·ko·*pa*·do

Is there a/an ...?	*¿Hay un ...?*	ai oon ...
intermission	*intermedio*	een·ter·*me*·dyo
programme	*programa*	pro·*gra*·ma

I thought it was ...	*Me pareció ...*	me pa·re·*syo* ...
excellent	*excelente*	ek·se·*len*·te
long	*larga*	*lar*·ga
OK	*bien*	byen

getting friendly

There are three ways of saying 'you' (singular) in Costa Rica. In formal situations or when you don't know someone well, it's best to use the polite (**pol**) form *usted* oos·*ted*. When the situation is informal or you're well acquainted with someone, the informal (**inf**) form *vos* vos is used. *Tú* too may also be used for informal situations, although it's less common than *vos*. In plural, however, there's only one 'you' form for both polite and informal situations – *ustedes* oos·*te*·des.

The words *usted*, *tú* and *vos* take different verb forms. Throughout this book the correct verb forms are given according to the real-life context of the phrases. Note that the pronouns are often left out in Spanish, as the verb endings tell you who's doing the action. For more information, see the **phrasebuilder**, page 23.

I (don't) like …	*(No) Me gusta/ gustan …* **sg/pl**	(no) me *goos*·ta/ *goos*·tan …
action movies	*las películas de acción* **pl**	las pe·*lee*·koo·las de ak·*syon*
animated films	*las películas animadas* **pl**	las pe·*lee*·koo·las a·nee·*ma*·das
(Costa Rican) cinema	*el cine (costarricense)* **sg**	el *see*·ne (kos·ta·ree·*sen*·se)
comedies	*las comedias* **pl**	las ko·*me*·dyas
documentaries	*los documentales* **pl**	los do·koo·men·*ta*·les
drama	*el drama* **sg**	el *dra*·ma
horror movies	*las películas de miedo* **pl**	las pe·*lee*·koo·las de *mye*·do
sci-fi	*la ciencia ficción* **sg**	la *syen*·sya feek·*syon*
short films	*los cortos* **pl**	los *kor*·tos
thrillers	*las películas de terror* **pl**	las pe·*lee*·koo·las de te·*ror*
war movies	*las películas de guerras* **pl**	las pe·*lee*·koo·las de *ge*·ras

limón creole

If you're visiting popular destinations along the Caribbean coast, in the province of Limón, you'll notice striking differences in the language spoken by its Afro-Costa Rican community. This idiom, often referred to as *criollo limones* kree·o·yo lee·*mo*·nes (Limón Creole) is a mix of various languages and cultures in the region.

Limón Creole isn't a standardised language like English or Spanish – it changes from generation to generation and even from speaker to speaker. The idiom is a colourful hybrid of Jamaican Creole (a variation of English) and Spanish, which gradually developed among the descendents of the black 19th-century Jamaican immigrants.

An example that shows the great degree of Spanish influence in Limón Creole, particularly among younger people, is the y sound – just like the Costa Rican pronunciation of the Spanish letter *ll* – so that, for instance, the 'zh' sound in the word *gendarme* is actually pronounced as the 'y' in 'yes'.

Words in Limón Creole which are derived from English vocabulary don't necessarily have the same meaning. 'All right' often means 'hello' and 'OK' can mean 'thank you' or 'goodbye'. The Spanish phrase *es que* es ke (lit: it's that) is a common way to begin a sentence.

Looking at the same sentence in standard English, Spanish, Jamaican Creole and Limón Creole can give a good indication of the interaction between the languages and the way sentences are formed. Note that the sentences in both Jamaican and Limón Creole are spelled only phonetically to give a better idea of how they actually sound (and because the languages exist primarily in spoken form):

English	In three years, he will be ten.
Spanish	*Le faltan tres años para cumplir diez.* le *fal*·tan tres *a*·nyos *pa*·ra koom·*pleer* dyes (lit: him need three years to turn ten)
Jamaican Creole	heem *a*·ve tree *yee*·as lef fe toon ten
Limón Creole	*fal*·ta tree *yee*·as eem get ten

feelings & opinions

sentimientos y opiniones

In this chapter, phrases are given in the informal *tú* and *vos* forms. For more details on polite and informal forms, see the **phrasebuilder**, page 23.

feelings

sentimientos

Feelings are described with either nouns or adjectives. The nouns use forms of the verb *tener* (have) in Spanish (eg 'I have hunger'), while the adjectives use forms of *estar* (be).

I'm (not) …	*(No) Tengo …*	(no) *ten*·go …
Are you …?	*¿Tenés …?*	te·*nes* …
cold	*frío*	*free*·o
hot	*calor*	ka·*lor*
hungry	*hambre*	*am*·bre
thirsty	*sed*	sed

I'm (not) …	*(No) Estoy …*	(no) es·*toy* …
Are you …?	*¿Estás …?*	es·*tas* …
happy	*contento/a* m/f	kon·*ten*·to/a
OK	*bien* m&f	byen
sad	*triste* m&f	*trees*·te
tired	*cansado/a* m/f	kan·*sa*·do/a

pregnant pause

If you want to say in Spanish that you're embarrassed, beware the following pitfall or you could end up with red faces all round. The word *embarazada* em·ba·ra·*sa*·da might look like the translation equivalent of 'embarrassed', but in actual fact means 'pregnant', as in the phrase *Estoy embarazada* es·*toy* em·ba·ra·*sa*·da (I'm pregnant). The correct word for embarrassed is *avergonzado/a* a·ver·gon·*sa*·do/a m/f.

mixed emotions		
not at all	*para nada*	*pa*·ra *na*·da
I don't care at all.	*No me importa para nada.*	no me eem·*por*·ta *pa*·ra *na*·da
a little	*un poco*	oon *po*·ko
I'm a little sad.	*Estoy un poco triste.*	es·*toy* oon *po*·ko *trees*·te
very	*muy*	mooy
I feel very tired.	*Estoy muy cansado/a.* **m/f**	es·*toy* mooy kan·*sa*·do/a
extremely	*muchísimo*	moo·*chee*·see·mo
I'm extremely sorry.	*Lo siento muchísimo.*	lo *syen*·to moo·*chee*·see·mo

If you're not feeling well, see **health**, page 183.

opinions

opiniones

Did you like it?
¿Te gustó? te goos·*to*

What do you think of it?
¿Qué opinás? ke o·pee·*nas*

I thought it was …	*Pienso que estuvo …*	*pyen*·so ke es·*too*·vo …
It's …	*Es …*	es …
awful	*pésimo/a* **m/f**	*pe*·see·mo/a
bad	*malo/a* **m/f**	*ma*·lo/a
beautiful	*muy bonito/a* **m/f**	mooy bo·*nee*·to/a
boring	*aburrido/a* **m/f**	a·boo·*ree*·do/a
(too) expensive	*(demasiado) caro/a* **m/f**	(de·ma·*sya*·do) *ka*·ro/a
great	*excelente* **m&f**	ek·se·*len*·te
interesting	*interesante* **m&f**	een·te·re·*san*·te
strange	*raro/a* **m/f**	*ra*·ro/a

politics & social issues

la política y asuntos sociales

Costa Rica is a progressive country and has by far the most stable government and economy in Central America. The country hasn't had a military for over 50 years. Immigration, drugs, the ongoing battle against deforestation, political corruption and how to properly manage and develop the tourism boom are issues of social and political interest and debate. A growing problem in Costa Rica is also the high number of young thieves (*chapulines* cha·poo·*lee*·nes).

Who do you vote for?
¿Por quién votaste? — por kyen vo·*tas*·te

I support the ... party.	*Yo soy ...*	yo soy ...
I'm a member of the ... party.	*Yo soy ...*	yo soy ...
communist	*comunista* m&f	ko·moo·*nees*·ta
conservative	*conservador/ conservadora* m/f	kon·ser·va·*dor*/ kon·ser·va·*do*·ra
democratic	*demócrata* m&f	de·*mo*·kra·ta
green	*verde* m&f	*ver*·de
liberal	*liberal* m&f	lee·be·*ral*
social democratic	*social demócrata* m&f	so·*syal* de·*mo*·kra·ta
socialist	*socialista* m&f	so·sya·*lees*·ta

masculine or feminine?

In this phrasebook, masculine forms of nouns, pronouns and adjectives appear before the feminine forms. If you see a word ending in *-o/a*, it means the masculine form ends in *-o*, and the feminine form ends in *-a* (that is, you replace the *-o* ending with the *-a* ending to make it feminine). The same goes for the plural endings *-os/as*. In other cases we spell out the whole word.

party on

The major political parties in Costa Rica are:

Partido Acción Ciudadana (PAC)	
par·*tee*·do ak·*syon* syoo·da·*da*·na	Citizens' Action Party
Partido Liberación Nacional (PLN)	
par·*tee*·do lee·be·ra·*syon* na·syo·*nal*	National Liberation Party
Partido Unidad Social Cristiana (PUSC)	
par·*tee*·do oo·nee·*dad* so·*syal* krees·*tya*·na	United Christian Social Party

Is there help for (the) ...?	*¿Hay ayuda para los ...?*	ai a·*yoo*·da *pa*·ra los ...
aged	*ancianos*	an·*sya*·nos
beggars	*mendigos*	men·*dee*·gos
disabled	*discapacitados*	dees·ka·pa·see·*ta*·dos
homeless	*indigentes*	een·dee·*khen*·tes
street kids	*niños de la calle*	*nee*·nyos de la *ka*·ye

Did you hear about ...?
¿Escuchaste que ...? — es·koo·*chas*·te ke ...

Do you agree with ...?
¿Estás de acuerdo con ...? — es·*tas* de a·*kwer*·do kon ...

I don't agree with ...
No estoy de acuerdo con ... — no es·*toy* de a·*kwer*·do kon ...

How do people feel about ...?
¿Qué piensa la gente sobre ...? — ke *pyen*·sa la *khen*·te *so*·bre ...

How can we protest against ...?
¿Cómo podemos protestar contra ...? — *ko*·mo po·*de*·mos pro·tes·*tar kon*·tra ...

How can we support ...?
¿Cómo podemos apoyar ...? — *ko*·mo po·*de*·mos a·po·*yar* ...

abortion	*aborto* m	a·*bor*·to
animal rights	*derechos de los animales* m pl	de·*re*·chos de los a·nee·*ma*·les
corruption	*corrupción* f	ko·roop·*syon*
crime	*crimen* m	*kree*·men
discrimination	*discriminación* f	dees·kree·mee·na·*syon*
drugs	*drogas* f pl	*dro*·gas
the economy	*economía* f	e·ko·no·*mee*·a
education	*educación* f	e·doo·ka·*syon*
the environment	*medio ambiente* m	*me*·dyo am·*byen*·te
equal opportunity	*igualdad de oportunidades* f	ee·gwal·*dad* de o·por·too·nee·*da*·des
euthanasia	*eutanasia* f	e·oo·ta·*na*·sya
globalisation	*globalización* f	glo·ba·lee·sa·*syon*
human rights	*derechos humanos* m pl	de·*re*·chos oo·*ma*·nos
immigration	*inmigración* f	een·me·gra·*syon*
indigenous issues	*Indígenas* m pl	een·*dee*·khe·nas
inequality	*desigualdad* f	des·ee·gwal·*dad*
party politics	*partidos políticos* m pl	par·*tee*·dos po·*lee*·tee·kos
poverty	*pobreza* f	po·*bre*·sa
privatisation	*privatización* f	pree·va·tee·sa·*syon*
racism	*racismo* m	ra·*sees*·mo
sexism	*sexismo* m	sek·*sees*·mo
social welfare	*bienestar social* m	byen·es·*tar* so·*syal*
terrorism	*terrorismo* m	te·ro·*rees*·mo
the war in (Iraq)	*la guerra en (Irak)* f	la *ge*·ra en (ee·*rak*)
unemployment	*desempleo* m	des·em·*ple*·o

tongue torture

Tongue twisters are known as *trabalenguas* tra·ba·*len*·gwas. Try rolling this tricky number off the tip of your tongue:

Tres tristes tigres trigo comieron.

tres *trees*·tes *tee*·gres *tree*·go ko·*mye*·ron	Three sad tigers ate wheat.

the environment

el medio ambiente

Is there a … problem here?
¿Hay un problema de … aquí? — ai oon pro·*ble*·ma de … a·*kee*

What should be done about …?
¿Qué se debería hacer con respecto a …? — ke se de·be·*ree*·a a·*ser* kon re·*spek*·to a …

conservation	*protección del medio ambiente* **f**	pro·tek·*syon* del *me*·dyo am·*byen*·te
deforestation	*deforestación* **f**	de·fo·res·ta·*syon*
drought	*sequías* **f pl**	se·*kee*·as
ecosystem	*ecosistema* **m**	e·ko·sees·*te*·ma
endangered species	*especies en peligro de extinción* **f pl**	es·*pe*·syas en pe·*lee*·gro de eks·teen·*syon*
genetically modified food	*alimentos transgénicos* **m pl**	a·lee·*men*·tos trans·*khe*·nee·kos
hunting	*caza* **f**	*ka*·sa
hydroelectricity	*proyectos hidroeléctricos* **m pl**	pro·*yek*·tos ee·dro·e·*lek*·tree·kos
irrigation	*irrigación* **f**	ee·ree·ga·*syon*
nuclear energy	*energía nuclear* **f**	e·ner·*khee*·a noo·kle·*ar*
nuclear testing	*pruebas nucleares* **f pl**	*prwe*·bas noo·kle·*a*·res
ozone layer	*capa de ozono* **f**	*ka*·pa de o·*so*·no
pesticides	*pesticidas* **m pl**	pes·tee·*see*·das
pollution	*contaminación* **f**	kon·ta·mee·na·*syon*
recycling programme	*programas de reciclaje* **m pl**	pro·*gra*·mas de re·see·*kla*·khe
toxic waste	*desechos tóxicos* **m pl**	de·*se*·chos *tok*·see·kos
water supply	*suministro de agua* **m**	soo·mee·*nees*·tro de *a*·gwa
wildlife poaching	*caza ilegal* **f**	*ka*·sa ee·le·*gal*

going out
al salir

In this chapter, phrases are given in the informal *tú* and *vos* forms. For more details on polite and informal forms, see the **phrasebuilder**, page 23.

where to go

a dónde ir

What's there to do in the evenings?
¿Qué se puede hacer en la noche? — ke se *pwe*·de a·*ser* en la *no*·che

What's on ...?	*¿Qué actividades hay ...?*	ke ak·tee·vee·*da*·des ai ...
locally	*por aquí*	por a·*kee*
this weekend	*este fin de semana*	*es*·te feen de se·*ma*·na
today	*hoy*	oy
tonight	*hoy en la noche*	oy en la *no*·che

out of the closet

Homosexuality is generally kept hidden in the closet in Costa Rica – as is the case throughout Central America. While most locals will be familiar with the terms *gay* gay and *lesbiana* les·*bya*·na, gay travellers should also be on the lookout for the term *playo* *pla*·yo. This is an offensive term for a gay man and might signal a potentially threatening situation.

On the bright side, Costa Rica does have some gay-friendly beaches and international resorts. Check ahead of your departure for information about these facilities.

Where are the ...?	*¿Dónde hay ...?*	*don*·de ai ...
bars	*bares*	*ba*·res
clubs	*discotecas*	dees·ko·*te*·kas
gay/lesbian venues	*lugares gay/ lesbianas*	loo·*ga*·res gay/ les·*bya*·nas
places to eat	*lugares para comer*	loo·*ga*·res *pa*·ra ko·*mer*
pubs	*bares*	*ba*·res
Is there a local ... guide?	*¿Existe una guía local ...?*	ek·*sees*·te *oo*·na *gee*·a lo·*kal* ...
entertainment	*de entretenimiento*	de en·tre·te·nee·*myen*·to
film	*de películas*	de pe·*lee*·koo·las
gay/lesbian	*para personas gay/lesbianas*	*pa*·ra per·*so*·nas gay/les·*bya*·nas
music	*de música*	de *moo*·see·ka
I feel like going to a ...	*Tengo ganas de ir a ...*	*ten*·go *ga*·nas de eer a ...
bar	*un bar*	oon bar
café	*un café*	oon ka·*fe*
concert	*un concierto*	oon kon·*syer*·to
film	*ver una película*	ver *oo*·na pe·*lee*·koo·la
(football) game	*un partido de (fútbol)*	oon par·*tee*·do de (*foot*·bol)
karaoke bar	*un karaoke*	oon ka·ra·*o*·ke
nightclub	*un club*	oon kloob
party	*una fiesta*	*oo*·na *fyes*·ta
performance	*una presentación*	*oo*·na pre·sen·ta·*syon*
play	*una obra de teatro*	*oo*·na *o*·bra de te·*a*·tro
pub	*un bar*	oon bar
restaurant	*un restaurante*	oon res·tow·*ran*·te

For more on bars, drinks and partying, see **romance**, page 125, and **eating out**, page 153.

invitations

invitaciones

What are you doing …?	*¿Qué vas a hacer …?*	ke vas a a·*ser* …
now	*ahora*	a·*o*·ra
this weekend	*el fin de semana*	el feen de se·*ma*·na
tonight	*hoy en la noche*	oy en la *no*·che
I feel like going (for a) …	*Tengo ganas de ir a …*	*ten*·go *ga*·nas de eer a …
Would you like to go (for a) …?	*¿Querés ir a …?*	ke·*res* eer a …
coffee	*tomar un café*	to·*mar* oon ka·*fe*
dancing	*bailar*	bai·*lar*
drink	*tomar algo*	to·*mar al*·go
meal	*comer algo*	ko·*mer al*·go
out somewhere	*algún lado*	al·*goon la*·do
walk	*caminar*	ka·mee·*nar*

My round.
Me toca. me *to*·ka

Do you know a good restaurant?
¿Conocés un buen restaurante? ko·no·*ses* oon bwen res·tow·*ran*·te

Do you want to come to the concert with me?
¿Querés acompañarme al concierto? ke·*res* a·kom·pa·*nyar*·me al kon·*syer*·to

We're having a party.
Tenemos una fiesta. te·*ne*·mos *oo*·na *fyes*·ta

You should come.
Vení. ve·*nee*

responding to invitations

respondiendo a invitaciones

Sure! *¡Claro!*	*kla*·ro
Yes, I'd love to. *Si, me encantaría.*	see me en·kan·ta·*ree*·a
That's very kind of you. *Qué amable.*	ke a·*ma*·ble
Where shall we go? *¿Dónde vamos?*	*don*·de *va*·mos
No, I'm afraid I can't. *No, no puedo.*	no no *pwe*·do
What about tomorrow? *¿Y mañana?*	ee ma·*nya*·na
Sorry, I can't sing/dance. *Perdoná, no sé cantar/bailar.*	per·do·*na* no se kan·*tar*/bai·*lar*

arranging to meet

para encontrarse

What time will we meet? *¿A qué hora nos vemos?*		a ke *o*·ra nos *ve*·mos
Where will we meet? *¿Dónde nos vemos?*		*don*·de nos *ve*·mos
Let's meet at …	*Veámonos …*	ve·*a*·mo·nos …
(eight) o'clock	*a las (ocho)*	a las (*o*·cho)
the entrance	*en la entrada*	en la en·*tra*·da

I'll pick you up.
Yo paso por vos. yo *pa*·so por vos

Are you ready?
¿Estás listo/a? m/f es·*tas lees*·to/a

I'm ready.
Yo estoy listo/a. m/f yo es·*toy lees*·to/a

I'll be coming later.
Voy a llegar más tarde. voy a ye·*gar* mas *tar*·de

Where will you be?
¿Dónde vas a estar? *don*·de vas a es·*tar*

If I'm not there by (nine), don't wait for me.
Si no he llegado a (las nueve) no me esperés. see no e ye·*ga*·do a (las *nwe*·ve) no me es·pe·*res*

I'll see you then.
Nos vemos. nos *ve*·mos

See you later.
Nos vemos más tarde. nos *ve*·mos mas *tar*·de

See you tomorrow.
Nos vemos mañana. nos *ve*·mos ma·*nya*·na

Sorry I'm late.
Perdoná que llegara tarde. per·*do*·na ke ye·*ga*·ra *tar*·de

Never mind.
No importa. no eem·*por*·ta

don't worry, don't hurry

The ideas about punctuality are more relaxed in Costa Rica than in English-speaking countries. You can expect *Ticos* to be at least half an hour late for most social occasions. Costa Ricans do differentiate, however, between formal and social situations and are usually more punctual for the former.

Where punctuality is important, you could try adding the expression *en punto* en *poon*·to – meaning 'exactly' – after arranging to meet. If it's a rendez-vous for a football match you're trying to arrange, you can count on your Costa Rican friends being on time!

drugs

drogas

I don't take drugs.
Yo no uso drogas. yo no *oo*·so *dro*·gas

Do you want to have a smoke?
¿Querés fumarte un puro? ke·*res* foo·*mar*·te oon *poo*·ro

Do you have a light?
¿Tenés fuego? te·*nes* *fwe*·go

If the police are talking to you about drugs, see **police**, page 180, for useful phrases.

fiesta fiends

Various local festivals, known as *fiestas* *fyes*·tas, add plenty of colour to life in Costa Rica. These are a few festivals of national significance:

Día de los Muertos *dee*·a de los *mwer*·tos
All Souls' Day (November 2nd) – families visit graveyards to make flower offerings to their loved ones. Religious parades are also held in honour of the deceased.

Semana Santa se·*ma*·na *san*·ta
Holy Week – the week leading up to Easter, celebrated with colourful religious processions and masses.

Virgen de los Ángeles *veer*·khen de los *an*·khe·les
Costa Rica's patron saint is celebrated on 2 August with a particularly important procession from San José to Cartago.

romance

In this chapter, phrases are given in the informal *tú* and *vos* forms. For more details on polite and informal forms, see the **phrasebuilder**, page 23.

asking someone out

invitando a alguien a salir

Where would you like to go (tonight)?
¿Dónde te gustaría ir (hoy en la noche)? — *don*·de te goos·ta·*ree*·a eer (oy en la *no*·che)

Would you like to do something (tomorrow)?
¿Querés hacer algo (mañana)? — ke·*res* a·*ser al*·go (ma·*nya*·na)

Yes, I'd love to.
Sí, me encantaría. — see me en·kan·ta·*ree*·a

Sorry, I can't.
Perdoná, no puedo. — per·do·*na* no *pwe*·do

local talk

How …!	*¡Qué …!*	ke …
cool	*buena nota*	*bwe*·na *no*·ta
sexy	*sexy*	*sek*·see
He/She …	*Él/Ella es …*	el/*e*·ya es …
is hot	*rico/a* m/f	*ree*·ko/a
He/She is a babe.	*Él/Ella está guapo/a.* m/f	el/*e*·ya es·*ta gwa*·po/a

pick-up lines

frases para ligar

Would you like a drink?	
¿Querés tomar algo?	ke·*res* to·*mar* *al*·go
You look like someone I know.	
Me parecés conocido/a. m/f	me pa·re·*ses* ko·no·*see*·do/a
You're a fantastic dancer.	
Sos un/una excelente bailarín/bailarina. m/f	sos oon/*oo*·na ek·se·*len*·te bai·la·*reen*/bai·la·*ree*·na

Can I ...?	*¿Puedo ...?*	*pwe*·do ...
dance with you	*bailar contigo*	bai·*lar* kon·*tee*·go
sit here	*sentarme acá*	sen·*tar*·me a·*ka*
take you home	*llevarte a la casa*	ye·*var*·te a la *ka*·sa

macho a go go

When it comes to mating, *machismo* ma·*chees*·mo is Costa Rica's law of the jungle – men initiate most flirting. Typically a man will ask a woman to dance and will also buy drinks. Even merely striking up a conversation is usually left to the initiative of men. Feminists need not despair though, as in San José and other more cosmopolitan areas, women will sometimes make the first move and have even been known to whistle at passing men.

rejections

rechazamientos

You're cool, but no thanks.	
Me caes muy bien, pero no gracias.	me *ka*·es mooy byen *pe*·ro no *gra*·syas
I love you like a friend.	
Te quiero como amigo/a. m/f	te *kye*·ro *ko*·mo a·*mee*·go/a

I'm here with my girlfriend/boyfriend.

Estoy aquí con mi novio/novia.	es·*toy* a·*kee* kon mee *no*·vyo/*no*·vya

I'd rather not.

Mejor no.	me·*khor* no

No, thank you.

No, gracias.	no *gra*·syas

Excuse me, I have to go now.

Con permiso, ya me tengo que ir.	kon per·*mee*·so ya me *ten*·go ke eer

giving someone the flick

Get out of here!

¡Andáte ya!	an·*da*·te ya

Leave me in peace!

¡Dejáme en paz!	de·*kha*·me en pas

Piss off!

¡Largáte!	lar·*ga*·te

getting closer

acercando

I really like you.

Me gustás mucho.	me goos·*tas moo*·cho

You're great.

Sos muy tuanis.	sos mooy too·*a*·nees

Can I kiss you?

¿Te puedo dar un beso?	te *pwe*·do dar oon *be*·so

Do you want to come inside for a while?

¿Querés entrar un rato?	ke·*res* en·*trar* oon *ra*·to

Do you want a massage?

¿Querés que te dé un masaje?	ke·*res* ke te de oon ma·*sa*·khe

Would you like to stay over?
¿Te querés quedar? te ke·*res* ke·*dar*

Can I stay over?
¿Me puedo quedar? me *pwe*·do ke·*dar*

sex

sexo

Kiss me.
Dáme un beso. *da*·me oon *be*·so

I want you.
Te deseo. te de·*se*·o

Let's go to bed.
Vamos a la cama. *va*·mos a la *ka*·ma

Touch me here.
Tocáme aquí. to·*ka*·me a·*kee*

Do you like this?
¿Ésto te gusta? *es*·to te *goos*·ta

I (don't) like that.
Éso (no) me gusta. *e*·so (no) me *goos*·ta

I think we should stop now.
Mejor paremos ya. me·*khor* pa·*re*·mos ya

Do you have a (condom)?
¿Tenés (preservativo)? te·*nes* (pre·ser·va·*tee*·vo)

Let's use a (condom).
Usémos (preservativo). oo·*se*·mos (pre·ser·va·*tee*·vo)

I won't do it without protection.
No lo voy a hacer sin protección. no lo voy a a·*ser* seen pro·tek·*syon*

It's my first time.
Es mi primera vez. es mee pree·*me*·ra ves

Oh my God!
¡Dios mío! dee·os *mee*·o

That's great.
¡Qué bueno! ke *bwe*·no

Easy tiger!
¡Suave tigre! *swa*·ve *tee*·gre

That was ...	*Eso estuvo ...*	e·so es·*too*·vo ...
amazing	*increíble*	een·kre·*ee*·ble
romantic	*romántico*	ro·*man*·tee·ko
wild	*salvaje*	sal·*va*·khe

love

amor

I think we're good together.
Hacemos buena pareja. a·*se*·mos *bwe*·na pa·*re*·kha

I love you.
Te amo. te *a*·mo

Will you go out with me?
¿Saldrías conmigo? sal·*dree*·as kon·*mee*·go

Will you marry me?
¿Te casarías conmigo? te ka·sa·*ree*·as kon·*mee*·go

Will you meet my parents?
¿Conocerías a mis papás? ko·no·se·*ree*·as a mees pa·*pas*

pillow talk

It's a peculiarity of Costa Rican Spanish that seemingly unflattering turns of phrase are, in fact, terms of endearment:

My ...	*Mi ...*	mee ...
baby	*bebé* m&f	be·*be*
chicken	*pollo/a* m/f	*po*·yo/a
fatty	*gordo/a* m/f	*gor*·do/a
love	*amor* m&f	a·*mor*

problems

problemas

Are you seeing someone else?
¿Me estás dando vuelta? — me es·*tas* *dan*·do *vwel*·ta

He's just a friend.
Él es sólo un amigo. — el/*e*·ya es *so*·lo oon a·*mee*·go

She's just a friend.
Ella es sólo una amiga. — el/*e*·ya es *so*·lo *oo*·na a·*mee*·ga

You're just using me for sex.
Sólo estás jugando conmigo. — *so*·lo es·*tas* khoo·*gan*·do kon·*mee*·go

I never want to see you again.
No te quiero ver nunca más. — no te *kye*·ro ver *noon*·ka mas

I don't think it's working out.
Creo que no está funcionando. — *kre*·o ke no es·*ta* foon·see·o·*nan*·do

We'll work it out.
Vamos a resolverlo. — *va*·mos a re·sol·*ver*·lo

leaving

despidiendo

I have to leave (tomorrow).
(Mañana) Me tengo que ir. — (ma·*nya*·na) me *ten*·go ke eer

I'll call you.
Yo te llamo. — yo te *ya*·mo

I'll write to you.
Yo te escribo. — yo te es·*kree*·bo

I'll miss you.
Me vas a hacer falta. — me vas a a·*ser* *fal*·ta

For more phrases, see **farewells**, page 106.

beliefs & cultural differences

creencias y diferencias culturales

religion

religión

What's your religion?

¿De qué religión es/sos? pol/inf		de ke re·lee·*khyon* es/sos

I'm not religious.

No soy religioso/a. m/f		no soy re·lee·*khyo*·so/a

I'm (a/an) …	*Soy …*	soy …
agnostic	*agnóstico/a* m/f	ag·*nos*·tee·ko/a
Buddhist	*budista* m&f	boo·*dees*·ta
Catholic	*católico/a* m/f	ka·*to*·lee·ko/a
Christian	*cristiano/a* m/f	krees·*tya*·no/a
Hindu	*hindú* m&f	een·*doo*
Jewish	*judío/a* m/f	khoo·*dee*·o/a
Muslim	*musulmán/ musulmána* m/f	moo·sool·*man*/ moo·sool·*ma*·na
Rastafarian	*rastafarián/ rastafariana* m/f	ras·ta·fa·*ryan*/ ras·ta·fa·*rya*·na

I (don't) believe in …	*Yo (no) creo en …*	yo (no) *kre*·o en …
astrology	*la astrología*	la as·tro·lo·*khee*·a
fate	*el destino*	el des·*tee*·no
God	*Dios*	dee·*os*

Can I … here?	*¿Puedo … aquí?*	*pwe*·do … a·*kee*
Where can I …?	*¿Dónde puedo …?*	*don*·de *pwe*·do …
attend a service	*participar en un servicio*	par·tee·see·*par* en oon ser·*vee*·syo
attend mass	*ir a misa*	eer a *mee*·sa
pray	*rezar*	re·*sar*

cultural differences

diferencias culturales

Is this a local or national custom?

¿Ésto es una costumbre local o del país?	*es*·to es *oo*·na kos·*toom*·bre lo·*kal* o del pa·*ees*

I don't want to offend you.

No quiero ofenderle/ ofenderte. pol/inf	no *kye*·ro o·fen·*der*·le/ o·fen·*der*·te

I'm not used to this.

No estoy acostumbrado/a a ésto. m/f	no es·*toy* a·kos·toom·*bra*·do/a a *es*·to

I'd rather not join in.

Prefiero no participar.	pre·*fye*·ro no par·tee·see·*par*

I'll try it.

Lo voy a probar.	lo voy a pro·*bar*

I didn't mean to do/say anything wrong.

No era mi intención hacer/decir algo malo.	no *e*·ra mee een·ten·*syon* a·*ser*/de·*seer al*·go *ma*·lo

I'm sorry, it's against my ...	*Lo siento, pero éso va en contra de ...*	lo *syen*·to *pe*·ro *e*·so va en *kon*·tra de ...
beliefs	*mis creencias*	mees kre·*en*·syas
religion	*mi religión*	mee re·lee·*khyon*

This is ...	*Ésto es ...*	*es*·to es ...
different	*diferente*	dee·fe·*ren*·te
fun	*divertido*	dee·ver·*tee*·do
interesting	*interesante*	een·te·re·*san*·te

mind your p's

As Roman Catholicism is the dominant religion in Costa Rica, be careful not to confuse *la papa* la *pa*·pa (with a lower case 'p'), which means 'potato', with *el Papa* el *pa*·pa (with an upper case 'P'), meaning 'Pope'. Best not to mix up your tubers and your pontiffs if you don't want to cause an unholy row.

In this chapter, phrases are given in the informal *tú* and *vos* forms. For more details on polite and informal forms, see the **phrasebuilder**, page 23.

When's the gallery open?
¿Cuándo está abierta la galería? — *kwan*·do es·*ta* a·*byer*·ta la ga·le·*ree*·a

When's the museum open?
¿Cuándo está abierto el museo? — *kwan*·do es·*ta* a·*byer*·to el moo·*se*·o

What's in the collection?
¿Qué hay en la colección? — ke ai en la ko·lek·*syon*

It's an exhibition of ...
Es una exhibición de ... — es *oo*·na ek·see·bee·*syon* de ...

What do you think of ...?
¿Qué opinas de ...? — ke o·*pee*·nas de ...

I like the works of ...
Me gusta la obra de ... — me *goos*·ta la *o*·bra de ...

It reminds me of ...
Me recuerda a ... — me re·*kwer*·da a ...

What kind of art are you interested in?
¿Qué tipo de arte te gusta? — ke *tee*·po de *ar*·te te *goos*·ta

I'm interested in ... art.	*Me interesa el arte ...*	me een·te·*re*·sa el *ar*·te ...
graphic	*gráfico*	*gra*·fee·ko
impressionist	*impresionista*	eem·pre·syo·*nees*·ta
indigenous	*autóctono*	ow·*tok*·to·no
modern	*moderno*	mo·*der*·no
performance	*de desempeño*	de de·sem·*pe*·nyo
Renaissance	*renacentista*	re·na·sen·*tees*·ta
traditional	*tradicional*	tra·dee·syo·*nal*
tropical art	*tropical*	tro·pee·*kal*

architecture	*arquitectura* **f**	ar·kee·tek·*too*·ra
art	*arte* **m**	*ar*·te
artwork	*obra de arte* **f**	*o*·bra de *ar*·te
curator	*curador* **m**	koo·ra·*dor*
exhibit n	*exhibición* **f**	ek·see·bee·*syon*
installation	*instalación* **f**	eens·ta·la·*syon*
painter	*pintor/pintora* **m/f**	peen·*tor*/peen·*to*·ra
painting (artwork)	*cuadro* **m**	*kwa*·dro
painting (technique)	*pintura* **f**	peen·*too*·ra
period	*periodo* **m**	pe·*ryo*·do
collection	*colección* **f**	ko·lek·*syon*
pottery	*alfarería* **f**	al·fa·re·*ree*·a
print n	*impresión* **f**	eem·pre·*syon*
sculptor	*escultor/escultora* **m/f**	es·kool·*tor*/es·kool·*to*·ra
sculpture	*escultura* **f**	es·kool·*too*·ra
statue	*estatua* **f**	es·*ta*·too·a
studio	*estudio* **m**	es·*too*·dyo
style n	*estilo* **m**	es·*tee*·lo

talking *tiquismos*

Ticos (Costa Ricans) colour their speech with a healthy smattering of distinctively Costa Rican expressions and slang words called *tiquismos* tee·*kees*·mos. These two phrases are ubiquitous:

¡Pura vida! *poo*·ra *vee*·da

This expression embodies Costa Rican life. Meaning literally 'pure life', it's really a more profound concept encompassing wellbeing, positivity and harmony. It can variously be translated as 'great, cool, right on' etc.

¡Tuanis! too·*a*·nees

A very popular phrase with younger folk, similar in meaning to *pura vida*. It's thought to have come from the English expression 'too nice'.

For more *tiquismos*, see the box **talking like a *tico***, page 31.

In this chapter, phrases are given in the informal *tú* and *vos* forms. For more details on polite and informal forms, see the **phrasebuilder**, page 23.

sporting interests

intereses deportivos

What sport do you ...?	*¿Qué deporte ...?*	ke de·*por*·te ...
follow	*te gusta*	te *goos*·ta
play	*practicas*	prak·*tee*·kas
I follow ...	*Me gusta el ...*	me *goos*·ta el ...
I play/do ...	*Yo juego/ hago el ...*	yo *khwe*·go/ *a*·go el ...
athletics	*atletismo*	at·le·*tees*·mo
football/soccer	*fútbol*	*foot*·bol
scuba diving	*buceo*	boo·*se*·o
volleyball	*voleibol*	vo·lay·*bol*
I ...	*Yo ...*	yo ...
cycle (for fun)	*ando en bicicleta*	*an*·do en bee·see·*kle*·ta
cycle (in races)	*practico ciclismo*	prak·*tee*·ko see·*klees*·mo
run	*corro*	*ko*·ro

Do you like (surfing)?
¿Te gusta (surfear)? — te *goos*·ta (soor·fe·*ar*)

Yes, very much.
Sí, mucho. — see *moo*·cho

Not really.
No, en realidad no. — no en re·a·lee·*dad* no

I like watching it.
Me gusta verlo. — me *goos*·ta *ver*·lo

Who's your favourite athlete/player?
¿Quién es tu atleta/ jugador preferido? — kyen es too at·*le*·ta/ khoo·ga·*dor* pre·fe·*ree*·do

What's your favourite team?
¿Cuál es tu equipo preferido? — kwal es too e·*kee*·po pre·fe·*ree*·do

For more sports, see the **dictionary**.

going to a game

para ir a un partido

Would you like to go to a game?
¿Querés ir a un partido? — ke·*res* eer a oon par·*tee*·do

Who are you supporting?
¿Con quién vas? — kon kyen vas

Who's ...?	*¿Quién ...?*	kyen ...
playing	*está jugando*	es·*ta* khoo·*gan*·do
winning	*va ganando*	va ga·*nan*·do

That was a ... game!	*¡Qué partido más ...!*	ke par·*tee*·do mas ...
bad	*malo*	*ma*·lo
boring	*aburrido*	a·boo·*ree*·do
great	*bueno*	*bwe*·no

scoring

What's the score?	*¿Cuánto van?*	*kwan*·to van
draw/even	*empate* m	em·*pa*·te
love/nil (zero)	*cero* m	*se*·ro
match-point	*punto de juego* m	*poon*·to de *khwe*·go

sports talk

What a …!	*¡Qué …!*	ke …
goal	*golazo*	go·*la*·so
hit	*tiro*	*tee*·ro
kick	*patada*	pa·*ta*·da
pass	*pase*	*pa*·se
performance	*buena presentación*	*bwe*·na pre·sen·ta·*syon*

playing sport

practicando deporte

Do you want to play?
¿Querés jugar? — ke·*res* khoo·*gar*

Can I join in?
¿Puedo jugar? — *pwe*·do khoo·*gar*

Sure.
Claro. — *kla*·ro

Yes, I'd love to.
Si, me encantaría. — see me en·kan·ta·*ree*·a

I can't.
No puedo. — no *pwe*·do

I have an injury.
Estoy lesionado/a. m/f — es·*toy* le·syo·*na*·do/a

Your/My point.
Punto mío/tuyo. — *poon*·to *mee*·o/*too*·yo

Kick/Pass it to me!
¡Pasámela! — pa·*sa*·me·la

You're a good player.
Jugás bien. — khoo·*gas* byen

Thanks for the game.
Gracias por el partido. — *gra*·syas por el par·*tee*·do

Where's a good place to ...?	*¿Dónde hay un buen lugar para ...?*	*don*·de ai oon bwen loo·*gar pa*·ra ...
fish	*pescar*	pes·*kar*
go horse riding	*montar a caballo*	mon·*tar* a ka·*ba*·yo
run	*correr*	ko·*rer*
snorkel	*esnorclear*	e·snor·kle·*ar*
surf	*surfear*	soor·fe·*ar*
Where's the nearest ...?	*¿Dónde está ... más cercano/a?* m/f	*don*·de es·*ta* ... mas ser·*ka*·no/a
golf course	*el campo de golf* m	el *kam*·po de golf
gym	*el gimnasio* m	el kheem·*na*·syo
swimming pool	*la piscina* f	la pee·*see*·na
tennis court	*la cancha de tenis* m	la *kan*·cha de *te*·nees

What's the charge per ...?	*¿Cuánto cobra por ...?*	*kwan*·to *ko*·bra por ...
day	*día*	*dee*·a
game	*juego*	*khwe*·go
hour	*hora*	*o*·ra
visit	*visita*	vee·*see*·ta
Can I hire a ...?	*¿Puedo alquilar una ...?*	*pwe*·do al·kee·*lar* *oo*·na ...
ball	*bola*	*bo*·la
bicycle	*bicicleta*	be·see·*kle*·ta
court	*cancha*	*kan*·cha
racquet	*raqueta*	ra·*ke*·ta

Do I have to be a member to attend?
¿Tengo que ser miembro para ir? — *ten*·go ke ser *myem*·bro *pa*·ra eer

Is there a women-only session?
¿Hay alguna sesión sólo para mujeres? — ai al·*goo*·na se·*syon* *so*·lo *pa*·ra moo·*khe*·res

Where are the changing rooms?
¿Dónde están los vestidores? — *don*·de es·*tan* los ves·tee·*do*·res

diving

buceo

Where's a good diving site?
¿Dónde hay un buen sitio para bucear? — *don*·de ai oon bwen *see*·tyo *pa*·ra boo·se·*ar*

Is the visibility good?
¿La visibilidad es buena? — la vee·see·bee·lee·*dad* es *bwe*·na

How deep is the dive?
¿Qué tan hondo es el buzo? — ke tan *on*·do es el *boo*·so

Is it a boat dive?
¿Es un buzo desde un bote? — es oon *boo*·so *des*·de oon *bo*·te

Is it a shore dive?
¿Es un buzo desde la orilla? — es oon *boo*·so *des*·de la o·*ree*·ya

I'd like to ...	*Me gustaría ...*	me goos·ta·*ree*·a ...
explore caves/ wrecks	*explorar cuevas/ruinas*	eks·plo·*rar* *kwe*·vas/*rwee*·nas
go night diving	*bucear de noche*	boo·se·*ar* de *no*·che
go scuba diving	*ir a bucear*	eer a boo·se·*ar*
go snorkelling	*ir a esnorclear*	eer a es·nor·kle·*ar*
join a diving tour	*ir a bucear con un tour*	eer a boo·se·*ar* kon oon toor
learn to dive	*aprender a bucear*	a·pren·*der* a boo·se·*ar*

Are there ...?	*¿Hay ...?*	ai ...
currents	*corrientes*	ko·*ryen*·tes
sharks	*tiburones*	tee·boo·*ro*·nes
whales	*ballenas*	ba·*ye*·nas

I want to hire (a) ...	*Quiero alquilar ...*	*kye*·ro al·kee·*lar* ...
buoyancy vest	*un chaleco salvavidas*	oon cha·*le*·ko sal·va·*vee*·das
diving equipment	*equipo de buceo*	e·*kee*·po de boo·*se*·o
fins	*unas patas de rana*	*oo*·nas *pa*·tas de *ra*·na
mask	*una mascarilla*	*oo*·na mas·ka·*ree*·ya
regulator	*un regulador*	oon re·goo·la·*dor*
snorkel	*un esnórquel*	oon e·*snor*·kel
tank	*un tanque*	oon *tan*·ke
weight belt	*un cinturón de pesas*	oon seen·too·*ron* de *pe*·sas
wetsuit	*un traje de buzo*	oon *tra*·khe de *boo*·so

buddy	*compañero/a* m/f	kom·pa·*nye*·ro/a
cave n	*cueva* f	*kwe*·va
dive n	*buceo* m	boo·*se*·o
dive v	*bucear*	boo·se·*ar*
diving boat	*bote de buceo* m	*bo*·te de boo·*se*·o
diving course	*curso de buceo* m	*koor*·so de boo·*se*·o
night dive	*buceo nocturno* m	boo·*se*·o nok·*toor*·no
wreck n	*ruinas* f pl	*rwee*·nas

SOCIAL

extreme sports

deportes extremos

I'd like to go ...	*Quiero ...*	*kye*·ro ...
bungee jumping	*tirarme de bungee*	tee·*rar*·me de *boon*·gee
caving	*ir a explorar cavernas*	eer a eks·plo·*rar* ka·*ver*·nas
canopying	*ir al canopy*	eer al ka·no·*pee*
game fishing	*ir de pesca*	eer de *pes*·ka
mountain biking	*practicar ciclismo de montaña*	prak·tee·*kar* see·*klees*·mo de mon·*ta*·nya
sea-kayaking	*andar en kayak en el mar*	an·*dar* en ka·*yak* en el mar
sky-diving	*tirarme en paracaídas*	tee·*rar*·me en *pa*·ra·ka·*ee*·das
white-water rafting	*ir a los rápidos*	eer a los *ra*·pee·dos

Is the equipment secure?
¿Está bien puesto el equipo? — es·*ta* byen *pwes*·to el e·*kee*·po

Is this safe?
¿Ésto es seguro? — *es*·to es se·*goo*·ro

This is insane.
Ésto es de locos. — *es*·to es de *lo*·kos

football/soccer

fútbol

Who plays for (Saprissa)?
¿Quién juega con (Saprissa)? — kyen *khwe*·ga kon (sa·*pree*·sa)

He's a great (player).
Él es un (jugador) buenísimo. — el es oon (khoo·ga·*dor*) bwe·*nee*·see·mo

He played brilliantly in the match against (Brazil).

Jugó muy bien en el partido contra (Brasil).	khoo·*go* mooy byen en el par·*tee*·do *kon*·tra (bra·*seel*)

Which team is at the top of the league?

¿Cuál equipo está de primero en la tabla?	kwal e·*kee*·po es·*ta* de pree·*me*·ro en la *ta*·bla

What a great/terrible team!

¿Qué equipo más bueno/malo!	ke e·*kee*·po mas *bwe*·no/*ma*·lo

ball	*bola* **f**	*bo*·la
coach n	*entrenador* **m**	en·tre·na·*dor*
corner (kick) n	*tiro de esquina* **m**	*tee*·ro de es·*kee*·na
fan	*aficionado/a* **m/f**	a·fee·syo·*na*·do/a
foul n	*falta* **f**	*fal*·ta
free kick	*tiro libre* **m**	*tee*·ro *lee*·bre
goal	*gol* **m**	gol
goalkeeper	*portero/a* **m/f**	por·*te*·ro/a
manager	*director* **m**	dee·rek·*tor*
offside	*posición prohibida* **f**	po·see·*syon* pro·ee·*bee*·da
penalty	*penal* **m**	pe·*nal*
red card	*tarjeta roja* **f**	tar·*khe*·ta *ro*·kha
referee	*árbitro* **m**	*ar*·bee·tro
throw in v	*meter*	me·*ter*

Off to see a match? Check out **going to a game**, page 136.

surfing

surfeo

How do I get to the surf beaches?

¿Cómo llego a las playas de surfear?	*ko*·mo *ye*·go a las *pla*·yas de soor·fe·*ar*

Which beach has the best conditions today?

¿Cuál playa tiene las mejores condiciones hoy?	kwal *pla*·ya *tye*·ne las me·*kho*·res kon·dee·*syo*·nes oy

Where's the nearest beach/point break?
¿Dónde está el beach/ point break más cerca? — *don*·de es·*ta* el beech/ poynt brek mas *ser*·ka

Where's the best beach/point break?
¿Dónde está el mejor beach/point break? — *don*·de es·*ta* el me·*khor* beech/poynt brek

What are the best times to surf there?
¿Cuál es la mejor hora para surfear ahí? — kwal es la me·*khor* *o*·ra *pa*·ra soor·fe·*ar* a·*ee*

Is the swell big?
¿Son grandes las olas? — son *gran*·des las *o*·las

Does it barrel?
¿Hay tubos? — ai *too*·bos

Does it work at high/low tide?
¿Sirve en marea alta/baja? — *seer*·ve en ma·*re*·a *al*·ta/*ba*·kha

Do you know any secret spots?
¿Conocés algún lugar secreto? — ko·no·*ses* al·*goon* loo·*gar* se·*kre*·to

Where can I find a surf shop?
¿Dónde hay una tienda de surf? — *don*·de ai *oo*·na *tyen*·da de soorf

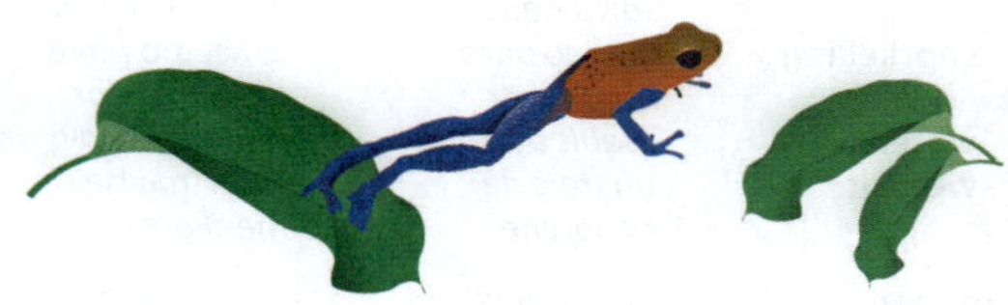

Where can I ... (equipment)?	*¿Dónde puedo ... (equipo)?*	*don*·de *pwe*·do ... (e·*kee*·po)
buy	*comprar*	kom·*prar*
rent	*alquilar*	al·kee·*lar*
repair	*arreglar*	a·re·*glar*

board bag	*bolsa para la tabla* f	*bol*·sa *pa*·ra la *ta*·bla
body board	*bodyboard* m	bo·dee·*bord*
fin(s)	*pata(s) de rana* f	*pa*·ta(s) de *ra*·na
sailboarding	*tabla de vela* f	*ta*·bla de *ve*·la
sailing boat	*bote de vela* m	*bo*·te de *ve*·la
set n	*set* m	set
surfing n	*surf* m	soorf
surf v	*surfear*	soor·fe·*ar*
surfboard	*tabla de surf* f	*ta*·bla de soorf
wave n	*ola* f	*o*·la
wax n	*cera* f	*se*·ra

water sports

deportes acuáticos

Can I book a lesson?
¿Puedo apuntarme en una clase? — *pwe*·do a·poon·*tar*·me en *oo*·na *kla*·se

Can I hire (a) ...?	*¿Puedo alquilar ...?*	*pwe*·do al·kee·*lar* ...
boat	*un bote*	oon *bo*·te
canoe	*una canoa*	*oo*·na ka·*no*·a
kayak	*un kayak*	oon ka·*yak*
life jacket	*un chaleco salvavidas*	oon cha·*le*·ko sal·va·*vee*·das
snorkelling gear	*equipo para esnorclear*	e·*kee*·po *pa*·ra e·snor·kle·*ar*
water-skis	*esquís de agua*	es·*kees* de *a*·gwa
wetsuit	*un traje de neoprene*	oon *tra*·khe de ne·o·*pre*·ne

Are there any ...?	*¿Hay algunos/algunas ...?* m/f	ai al·*goo*·nos/algunas ...
reefs	*arrecifes* m	a·re·*see*·fes
rips	*corrientes* f	ko·*ryen*·tes

guide n	*guía* m	*gee*·a
motorboat	*bote de motor* m	*bo*·te de mo·*tor*
oars	*paletas* f pl	pa·*le*·tas

hiking

caminatas

Where can I ...?	*¿Dónde puedo ...?*	*don*·de *pwe*·do ...
buy supplies	*comprar provisiones*	kom·*prar* pro·vee·*syo*·nes
find someone who knows this area	*encontrar a alguien que conozca la zona*	en·kon·*trar* a *al*·gyen ke ko·*nos*·ka la *so*·na
get a map	*conseguir un mapa*	kon·se·*geer* oon *ma*·pa
hire hiking gear	*alquilar equipo para la caminata*	al·kee·*lar* e·*kee*·po *pa*·ra la ka·mee·*na*·ta

How ...?	*¿Qué tan ...?*	ke tan ...
high is the climb	*alta es la subida*	*al*·ta es la soo·*bee*·da
long is the trail	*largo es el sendero*	*lar*·go es el sen·*de*·ro

Is the route scenic?
¿Es panorámica la ruta? es pa·no·*ra*·mee·ka la *roo*·ta

Do we need a guide?
¿Ocupamos un guía? o·koo·*pa*·mos oon *gee*·a

Are there guided treks?
¿Hay caminatas con guía? ai ka·mee·*na*·tas kon *gee*·a

Is it safe?
¿Es seguro? es se·*goo*·ro

Is there a hut?
¿Hay un rancho? ai oon *ran*·cho

When does it get dark?
¿A qué hora oscurece? a ke *o*·ra os·koo·*re*·se

Do we need to take ...?	*¿Tenemos que llevar ...?*	te·*ne*·mos ke ye·*var* ...
bedding	*ropa de cama*	*ro*·pa de *ka*·ma
food	*comida*	ko·*mee*·da
water	*agua*	*a*·gwa
Is the track ...?	*¿El sendero está ...?*	el sen·*de*·ro es·*ta* ...
(well) marked	*(bien) marcado*	(byen) mar·*ka*·do
open	*abierto*	a·*byer*·to
Which is the ... route?	*¿Cuál es el camino más ...?*	kwal es el ka·*mee*·no mas ...
easiest	*fácil*	*fa*·seel
shortest	*corto*	*kor*·to
Where can I find the ...?	*¿Dónde queda/ quedan ...?* sg/pl	*don*·de *ke*·da/ *ke*·dan ...
camping ground	*la zona para acampar* sg	la *so*·na *pa*·ra a·kam·*par*
showers	*las duchas* pl	las *doo*·chas
toilets	*los baños* pl	los *ba*·nyos

SOCIAL

Where have you come from?
¿De dónde viene/vienen? sg/pl — de *don*·de *vye*·ne/*vye*·nen

How long did it take you?
¿Cuánto duró/duraron en llegar? sg/pl — *kwan*·to doo·*ro*/doo·*ra*·ron en ye·*gar*

Does this path go to (Arenal)?
¿Este camino llega a (Arenal)? — *es*·te ka·*mee*·no *ye*·ga a (a·re·*nal*)

Can I go through here?
¿Puedo pasar por aquí? — *pwe*·do pa·*sar* por a·*kee*

Is the water OK to drink?
¿Se puede beber el agua? — se *pwe*·de be·*ber* el *a*·gwa

I'm lost.
Estoy perdido/a. m/f — es·*toy* per·*dee*·do/a

beach

playa

Where's the ... beach?	*¿Dónde está la ...?*	*don*·de es·*ta* la ...
best	*mejor playa*	me·*khor pla*·ya
nearest	*playa más cercana*	*pla*·ya mas ser·*ka*·na
How much to rent a/an ...?	*¿Cuánto cuesta alquilar ...?*	*kwan*·to *kwes*·ta al·kee·*lar* ...
chair	*una silla*	*oo*·na *see*·ya
hut	*un rancho*	oon *ran*·cho
umbrella	*una sombrilla*	*oo*·na som·*bree*·ya

signs

Prohibido Hacer Clavados	pro·ee·*bee*·do a·*ser* kla·*va*·dos	**No Diving**
Prohibido Nadar	pro·ee·*bee*·do na·*dar*	**No Swimming**

Is it dangerous to dive/swim here?

¿Será peligroso bucear/ nadar aquí? — se·*ra* pe·lee·*gro*·so boo·se·*ar*/ na·*dar* a·*kee*

What time is high/low tide?

¿A qué hora es la marea alta/baja? — a ke *o*·ra es la ma·*re*·a *al*·ta/*ba*·kha

listen for ...

¡Cuidado con las corrientes de resaca!
kwee·*da*·do kon las ko·*ryen*·tes de re·*sa*·ka — **Be careful of the undertow!**

¡Es peligroso!
es pe·lee·*gro*·so — **It's dangerous!**

weather

tiempo

What's the weather like?

¿Cómo está el tiempo? — *ko*·mo es·*ta* el *tyem*·po

It's ...	*Está ...*	es·*ta* ...
cloudy	*nublado*	noo·*bla*·do
cold	*frío*	*free*·o
hot	*haciendo mucho calor*	a·*syen*·do *moo*·cho ka·*lor*
raining	*lloviendo*	yo·*vyen*·do
sunny	*haciendo sol*	a·*syen*·do sol
warm	*caliente*	ka·*lyen*·te
windy	*ventoso*	ven·*to*·so
Where can I buy a/an ...?	*¿Dónde puedo comprar una ...?*	*don*·de *pwe*·do kom·*prar* *oo*·na ...
rain jacket	*capa*	*ka*·pa
umbrella	*sombrilla*	som·*bree*·ya
dry season	*estación seca* **f**	es·ta·*syon* *se*·ka
wet season	*estación lluviosa* **f**	es·ta·*syon* yoo·*vyo*·sa

ecotourism

ecoturismo

Costa Rica boasts some of the most diverse flora and fauna in the world, and opportunities for wildlife enthusiasts are endless. The country is known for its serious approach to conservation and protection of the environment, which includes one of the best park systems in the Western Hemisphere. Costa Rica also has numerous privately owned parks and ecotourism projects.

What … is that?	*¿Qué es …?*	ke es …
animal	*ese animal*	*e*·se a·nee·*mal*
flower	*esa flor*	*e*·sa flor
plant	*esa mata*	*e*·sa *ma*·ta
tree	*ese árbol*	*e*·se *ar*·bol

What's it used for?
¿Para qué se usa? — *pa*·ra ke se *oo*·sa

Can you eat the fruit?
¿Esa fruta se come? — *e*·sa *froo*·ta se *ko*·me

Is it …?	*¿Es …?*	es …
dangerous	*peligroso/a* **m/f**	pe·lee·*gro*·so/a
poisonous	*venenoso/a* **m/f**	ve·ne·*no*·so/a
Is it …?	*¿Está …?*	es·*ta* …
endangered	*en peligro de extinción*	en pe·*lee*·gro de eks·teen·*syon*
protected	*protegido/a* **m/f**	pro·te·*khee*·do/a
Is this a protected …?	*¿Este/Esta es … protegido/a?* **m/f**	*es*·te/*es*·ta es … pro·te·*khee*·do/a
park	*un parque* **m**	oon *par*·ke
species	*una especie* **f**	*oo*·na es·*pe*·sye

What time is best for seeing ...?

¿Cuál es la mejor hora para ver ...?	kwal es la me·*khor* o·ra *pa*·ra ver ...

Can I see ... here?

¿Puedo ver ... aquí?	*pwe*·do ver ... a·*kee*

Are there active volcanoes in this area?

¿Hay volcanes activos en esta zona?	ai vol·*ka*·nes ak·*tee*·vos en *es*·ta *so*·na

Is that an active volcano?

¿Es un volcán activo?	es oon vol·*kan* ak·*tee*·vo

wildlife & habitat

flora, fauna y hábitat

geography

cave	*cueva* f	*kwe*·va
cliff	*acantilado* m	a·kan·tee·*la*·do
estuary	*estuario* m	es·too·*a*·ryo
forest	*bosque* m	*bos*·ke
hill	*colina* f	ko·*lee*·na
island	*isla* f	*ees*·la
lake	*lago* m	*la*·go
lava	*lava* f	*la*·va
mountain	*montaña* f	mon·*ta*·nya
mountain range	*sierra* f	*sye*·ra
ocean	*océano* m	o·*se*·a·no
river	*río* m	*ree*·o
sea	*mar* m	mar
swamp	*pantano* m	pan·*ta*·no
valley	*valle* m	*va*·ye
volcano	*volcán* m	vol·*kan*
waterfall	*salto* m	*sal*·to
wildlife	*flora y fauna silvestre* f	*flo*·ra ee *fow*·na seel·*ves*·tre

flora

ceiba (silk cotton tree)	*ceiba* f	*say*·ba
cloud forest	*bosque nuboso* m	*bos*·ke noo·*bo*·so
guanacaste tree (national tree)	*árbol de guanacaste* m	*ar*·bol de gwa·na·*kas*·te
jungle	*selva* f	*sel*·va
mangrove	*manglar* m	man·*glar*
orchid	*orquídea* f	or·*kee*·de·a
palm tree	*palma* f	*pal*·ma
purple orchid (national flower)	*guaria morada* f	*gwa*·ree·a mo·*ra*·da
rain forest	*bosque lluvioso* m	*bos*·ke yoo·*vyo*·so
tropical dry forest	*bosque seco tropical* m	*bos*·ke *se*·ko tro·pee·*kal*
tropical plains	*llanura tropical* f	ya·*noo*·ra tro·pee·*kal*

mammals

agouti	*guatusa* f	gwa·*too*·sa
anteater	*oso hormiguero* m	*o*·so or·mee·*ge*·ro
armadillo	*armadillo* m	ar·ma·*dee*·yo
capuchin monkey	*mono capuchín* m	*mo*·no ka·poo·*cheen*
coati	*pizote* m	pee·*so*·te
howler monkey	*mono congo* m	*mo*·no *kon*·go
jaguar	*jaguar* m	kha·*gwar*
kinkajou	*martilla* f	mar·*tee*·ya
monkey	*mono* m	*mo*·no
opossum	*zorro* m	*so*·ro
paca	*tepezcuintle* m	te·pes·*kweent*·le
peccary	*chancho del monte* m	*chan*·cho del *mon*·te
sloth	*oso perezoso* m	*o*·so pe·re·*so*·so
spider monkey	*mono araña* m	*mo*·no a·*ra*·nya
squirrel	*ardilla* f	ar·*dee*·ya
squirrel monkey	*mono tití* m	*mo*·no tee·*tee*
tapir	*danta* f	*dan*·ta

outdoors

insects & birds

ant	*hormiga* **f**	or·*mee*·ga
butterfly	*mariposa* **f**	ma·ree·*po*·sa
eagle	*águila* **m**	*a*·gee·la
heron	*garza* **f**	*gar*·sa
hummingbird	*colibrí* **m**	ko·lee·*bree*
jacana	*jacana* **f**	kha·*ka*·na
macaw	*lapa* **f**	*la*·pa
morpho butterfly	*morfo* **m**	*mor*·fo
mosquito	*zancudo* **m**	san·*koo*·do
parakeet	*perico* **m**	pe·*ree*·ko
pelican	*pelícano* **m**	pe·*lee*·ka·no
pigeon	*paloma* **f**	pa·*lo*·ma
quetzal	*quetzal* **m**	ket·*sal*
toucan	*tucán* **m**	too·*kan*
vulture	*buitre* **m**	*bwee*·tre
yigüirro (national bird)	*yigüirro* **m**	yee·*gwee*·ro

reptiles

bushmaster (snake)	*cascabel muda* **f**	kas·ka·*bel moo*·da
crocodile	*cocodrilo* **m**	ko·ko·*dree*·lo
fer-de-lance (snake)	*terciopelo* **m**	ter·syo·*pe*·lo
iguana	*iguana* **f**/*garrobo* **m**	ee·*gwa*·na/ga·*ro*·bo
lizard	*lagarto* **m**	la·*gar*·to
snake	*culebra* **f**	koo·*le*·bra

marine life

dolphin	*delfín* **m**	del·*feen*
fish	*pes* **m**	pes
frog	*rana* **f**	*ra*·na
manatee	*manatí* **m**	ma·na·*tee*
otter	*nutria* **f**	noo·*tree*·a
turtle	*tortuga* **f**	tor·*too*·ga
whale	*ballena* **f**	ba·*ye*·na

FOOD > eating out
saliendo para comer

basics

lo básico

breakfast	*desayuno* **m**	de·sa·*yoo*·no
lunch	*almuerzo* **m**	al·*mwer*·so
dinner	*cena* **f**	*se*·na
snack n	*merienda* **f**	me·*ryen*·da
eat v	*comer*	ko·*mer*
drink v	*beber*	be·*ber*
I'd like …	*Me gustaría …* **pol**	me goos·ta·*ree*·a …
	Quiero … **inf**	*kye*·ro …
Please.	*Por favor.*	por fa·*vor*
Thank you.	*Gracias.*	*gra*·syas
Enjoy your meal.	*(Buen) Provecho.*	(bwen) pro·*ve*·cho
Cheers!	*¡Salud!*	sa·*lood*

a match made in heaven

The traditional lunch and dinner are variations on the famous *casado* ka·*sa*·do (lit: married couple). This match-made-in-heaven is a hearty combination plate of rice, beans, shredded cabbage salad, vegetable or fruit *picadillo* pee·ka·*dee*·yo (mince) and a meat of choice (beef, fish, pork or chicken). The whole is garnished with fried plantains, tortillas and a slice or two of tomato. It's cheap and more than enough to keep body and soul together! Specify what meat you want by asking for *bife* *bee*·fe (beef), *pescado* pes·*ka*·do (fish), *puerco* *pwer*·ko (pork) or *pollo* *po*·yo (chicken).

finding a place to eat

buscando un lugar para comer

Can you recommend a …?	*¿Podría recomendar …?*	po·*dree*·a re·ko·men·*dar* …
bar	*un bar*	oon bar
café	*un café*	oon ka·*fe*
lunch counter	*una soda*	*oo*·na *so*·da
(Chinese) restaurant	*un restaurante (chino)*	oon res·tow·*ran*·te (*chee*·no)
Where would you go for (a) …?	*¿Dónde podría ir para …?*	*don*·de po·*dree*·a eer *pa*·ra …
celebration	*una celebración*	*oo*·na se·le·bra·*syon*
cheap meal	*comer barato*	ko·*mer* ba·*ra*·to
local specialities	*comer comida local*	ko·*mer* ko·*mee*·da lo·*kal*
I'd like to reserve a table for …	*Quiero reservar una mesa para …*	*kye*·ro re·ser·*var* *oo*·na *me*·sa *pa*·ra …
(two) people	*(dos) personas*	(dos) per·*so*·nas
(eight) o'clock	*las (ocho)*	las (*o*·cho)

at the counter

If it's snacks you're after, you should be on the lookout for a *soda* *so*·da. You shouldn't have to look too far because they abound and come in various guises ranging from a lean-to or shack with a couple of makeshift tables to a small café-style restaurant.

Sodas dispense drinks and *casados* ka·*sa*·dos (combination plates of rice and meat or vegetables) in addition to snacks. They usually also sell *empanadas* em·pa·*na*·das (turnovers), *gallos* *ga*·yos (tortilla sandwiches) or *enchiladas* en·chee·*la*·das (pastries with spicy meat). Grilled beef or pork kebabs known as *pinchos* *peen*·chos are also a popular snack on the go. For more on these items and Costa Rican cuisine generally, see the **menu decoder**.

Are you still serving food?

¿Todavía están sirviendo comida?	to·da·*vee*·a es·*tan* seer·*vyen*·do ko·*mee*·da

How long is the wait?

¿Cuánto tengo que esperar?	*kwan*·to *ten*·go ke es·pe·*rar*

listen for …

Está cerrado.	es·*ta* se·*ra*·do	**We're closed.**
Está lleno.	es·*ta* *ye*·no	**We're full.**
Un momento.	oon mo·*men*·to	**One moment.**

at the restaurant

en el restaurante

I'd like (a/the) …	*Quisiera …, por favor.*	kee·*sye*·ra … por fa·*vor*
(non)smoking section	*el área de (no) fumado*	el *a*·re·a de (no) foo·*ma*·do
table for (five)	*una mesa para (cinco)*	*oo*·na *me*·sa *pa*·ra (*seen*·ko)
that dish	*ese plato*	*e*·se *pla*·to

What would you recommend?

¿Qué me recomienda?	ke me re·ko·*myen*·da

What's in that dish?

¿Ese plato qué trae?	*e*·se *pla*·to ke *tra*·e

What's that called?

¿Éso cómo se llama?	*e*·so *ko*·mo se *ya*·ma

I'll have that.

Yo quiero éso.	yo *kye*·ro *e*·so

Does it take long to prepare?

¿Se dura mucho preparándolo?	se *doo*·ra *moo*·cho pre·pa·*ran*·do·lo

Is it self-serve?

¿Es de auto-servicio?	es de ow·to·ser·*vee*·syo

Is there a cover/service charge?
¿Hay que pagar entrada/servicio? — ai ke pa·*gar* en·*tra*·da/ser·*vee*·syo

Is service included in the bill?
¿El servicio está incluído? — el ser·*vee*·syo es·*ta* een·kloo·*ee*·do

Are these complimentary?
¿Son gratis? — son *gra*·tees

Could I see the wine list?
¿Podría ver la lista de vinos, por favor? — po·*dree*·a ver la *lees*·ta de *vee*·nos por fa·*vor*

Bring me a/the …, please.	*Tráigame …, por favor.*	*trai*·ga·me … por fa·*vor*
children's menu	*el menú para niños*	el me·*noo* *pa*·ra *nee*·nyos
drink list	*la lista de tragos*	la *lees*·ta de *tra*·gos
half portion	*media porción*	*me*·dya por·*syon*
local speciality	*una especialidad local*	*oo*·na es·pe·sya·lee·*dad* lo·*kal*
menu (in English)	*el menú (en inglés)*	el me·*noo* (en een·*gles*)

listen for …

¿Cómo lo/la quiere? **m/f**
ko·mo lo/la *kye*·re — **How would you like that?**

¿Dónde se quiere sentar?
don·de se *kye*·re sen·*tar* — **Where would you like to sit?**

¿Qué le puedo traer?
ke le *pwe*·do tra·*er* — **What can I get for you?**

¡Aquí está!	a·*kee* es·*ta*	**Here you go!**
Buen provecho.	bwen pro·*ve*·cho	**Enjoy your meal.**
¿Le gusta …?	le *goos*·ta …	**Do you like …?**
Le recomiendo …	le re·ko·*myen*·do …	**I suggest the …**

I'd like it with/ without …	*Lo quiero con/sin …*	lo *kye*·ro kon/seen …
cheese	*queso*	*ke*·so
chilli sauce	*salsa picante*	*sal*·sa pee·*kan*·te
garlic	*ajo*	*a*·kho
ketchup	*ketchup*	ke·*tchoop*
nuts	*nueces*	*nwe*·ses
oil	*aceite*	a·*say*·te
pepper	*pimienta*	pee·*myen*·ta
Salsa Lizano	*Salsa Lizano*	*sal*·sa lee·*sa*·no
salt	*sal*	sal
vinegar	*vinagre*	vee·*na*·gre

For other specific meal requests, see **vegetarian & special meals**, page 169.

at the table

en la mesa

Please bring (a/the) …	*Por favor tráigame …*	por fa·*vor* *trai*·ga·me …
bill	*la cuenta*	la *kwen*·ta
cutlery	*los cubiertos*	los koo·*byer*·tos
glass	*un vaso*	oon *va*·so
serviette	*una servilleta*	*oo*·na ser·vee·*ye*·ta

There's a mistake in the bill.
Hay un error en la cuenta. ai oon e·*ror* en la *kwen*·ta

I didn't order this.
No pedí esto. no pe·*dee* *es*·to

talking food

hablando de comida

I'm starving!
¡Me estoy muriendo de hambre! — me es·*toy* moo·*ryen*·do de *am*·bre

The food is very good.
La comida está muy rica. — la ko·*mee*·da es·*ta* mooy *ree*·ka

I love the local cuisine.
Me encanta la comida de aquí. — me en·*kan*·ta la ko·*mee*·da de a·*kee*

I love this dish.
Me encanta este plato. — me en·*kan*·ta *es*·te *pla*·to

That was delicious!
¡Estuvo delicioso! — es·*too*·vo de·lee·*syo*·so

I'm full.
Estoy lleno/a. m/f — es·*toy* *ye*·no/a

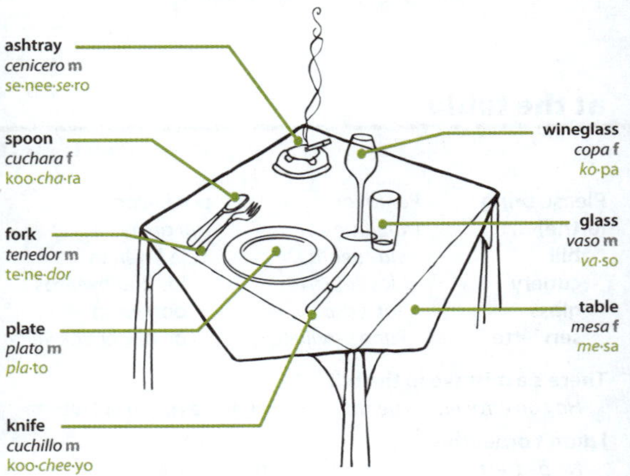

FOOD

This is ...	*Está ...*	es·*ta* ...
burnt	*quemado*	ke·*ma*·do
cold	*frío*	*free*·o
hot	*caliente*	ka·*lyen*·te
(too) spicy	*(demasiado) condimentado*	(de·ma·*sya*·do) kon·dee·men·*ta*·do

look for ...

Aperitivos	a·pe·ree·*tee*·vos	Appetisers
Sopas	*so*·pas	Soups
Entradas	en·*tra*·das	Entrées
Ensaladas	en·sa·*la*·das	Salads
Platos Fuertes	*pla*·tos *fwer*·tes	Main Courses
Guarniciónes	gwar·nee·*syo*·nes	Side Dishes (at restaurants)
Acompañamientos	a·kom·pa·nya·*myen*·tos	Side Dishes (at bars & lunch counters)
Postres	*pos*·tres	Desserts
Bebidas	be·*bee*·das	Drinks
Refrescos	re·*fres*·kos	Soft Drinks
Cocteles	kok·*te*·les	Spirits
Cervezas	ser·*ve*·sas	Beers
Vinos ...	*vee*·nos ...	... Wines
Blancos	*blan*·kos	White
Digestivos	dee·khes·*tee*·vos	Dessert
Espumantes	es·poo·*man*·tes	Sparkling
Tintos	*teen*·tos	Red

For more words you might see on a menu, see the **menu decoder**, page 171.

eating out

methods of preparation

métodos de preparación

I'd like it …	*Lo quiero …*	lo *kye*·ro …
I don't want it …	*No lo quiero …*	no lo *kye*·ro …
boiled	*hervido*	er·*vee*·do
broiled	*asado*	a·*sa*·do
fried	*frito*	*free*·to
grilled	*a la parrilla*	a la pa·*ree*·ya
mashed	*en puré*	en poo·*re*
medium	*término medio*	*ter*·mee·no *me*·dyo
rare	*crudo*	*kroo*·do
reheated	*recalentado*	re·ka·len·*ta*·do
steamed	*al vapor*	al va·*por*
well-done	*bien cocinado*	byen ko·see·*na*·do
with the dressing on the side	*con el aderezo al lado*	kon el a·de·*re*·so al *la*·do
without …	*sin …*	seen …

nonalcoholic drinks

bebidas sin alcohol

boiled water	*agua hervida* **f**	*a*·gwa er·*vee*·da
bottled water	*agua embotellada* **f**	*a*·gwa em·bo·te·*ya*·da
freshly-squeezed fruit drink	*fresco* **m**	*fres*·ko
fruit shake	*batido* **m**	ba·*tee*·do
hot water	*agua caliente* **f**	*a*·gwa ka·*lyen*·te
iced tea	*té con hielo* **m**	te kon *ye*·lo
(orange) juice	*jugo (de naranja)* **m**	*khoo*·go (de na·*ran*·kha)
mineral water	*agua mineral* **f**	*a*·gwa mee·ne·*ral*
soft drink	*gaseosa* **f**	ga·se·*o*·sa
sparkling mineral water	*soda* **f**	*so*·da
with/without ice	*con/sin hielo*	kon/seen *ye*·lo

(cup of) coffee …	*(taza de) café …*	(*ta*·sa de) ka·*fe* …
(cup of) tea …	*(taza de) té …*	(*ta*·sa de) te …
with (milk)	*con (leche)*	kon (*le*·che)
without (sugar)	*sin (azúcar)*	seen (a·*soo*·kar)

… coffee	*café …*	ka·*fe* …
black	*negro*	*ne*·gro
decaffeinated	*descafeinado*	des·ka·fay·*na*·do
strong	*fuerte*	*fwer*·te
weak	*ralo*	*ra*·lo
white	*con leche*	kon *le*·che

juicy treats

There are many delicious ways to quench your thirst in Costa Rica. Top of the list are the seemingly infinite varieties of *refrescos naturales* re·*fres*·kos na·too·*ra*·les, usually known simply as *frescos* *fres*·kos. These consist of almost any kind of fruit squeezed or blended with water and sugar or milk. You can specify whether you want water or milk by saying *con agua* kon *a*·gwa (with water) or *con leche* kon *le*·che (with milk). When ordering, simply refer to the flavour you want, eg *mora con leche* *mo*·ra kon *le*·che (blackberry with milk). Also popular are *batidos* ba·*tee*·dos (fruit shakes) which are essentially the same as *frescos* but thicker. Below are some of the most popular fruit flavours for both *frescos* and *batidos*:

barley	*cebada* **f**	se·*ba*·da
blackberry	*mora* **f**	*mo*·ra
cantaloupe	*melón* **m**	me·*lon*
carrot	*zanahoria* **f**	sa·na·*o*·rya
cas	*cas* **m**	kas
mango	*mango* **m**	*man*·go
naranjilla	*naranjilla* **f**	na·ran·*khee*·ya
papaya	*papaya* **f**	pa·*pa*·ya
pineapple	*piña* **f**	*pee*·nya
soursop	*guanábana* **f**	gwa·*na*·ba·na
star fruit	*carambola* **f**	ka·ram·*bo*·la
strawberry	*fresa* **f**	*fre*·sa
tamarind	*tamarindo* **m**	ta·ma·*reen*·do
watermelon	*sandía* **f**	san·*dee*·a

necesito cafecito

Coffee is the most popular beverage in the country and wherever you go, someone is likely to offer you a *cafecito* ka·fe·*see*·to (an affectionate term for a cup of coffee). Traditionally it's served strong and mixed with hot milk to taste. This is known as a *café con leche* ka·*fe* kon *le*·che. Some prefer a *café negro* ka·*fe ne*·gro (black coffee), but those who want a little milk can ask for *leche al lado le*·che al *la*·do (milk on the side). Many trendier places also serve capuccinos and espressos which you can ask for by these names.

alcoholic drinks

bebidas alcohólicas

a bottle/glass of … wine	*una botella/copa de vino …*	*oo*·na bo·*te*·ya/*ko*·pa de *vee*·no …
dessert	*digestivo*	dee·khes·*tee*·vo
red	*tinto*	*teen*·to
rosé	*rosado*	ro·*sa*·do
sparkling	*espumante*	es·poo·*man*·te
white	*blanco*	*blan*·ko
a … of beer	*… de cerveza*	… de ser·*ve*·sa
glass	*un vaso*	oon *va*·so
jug	*una jarra*	*oo*·na *kha*·ra
large bottle	*una botella grande*	*oo*·na bo·*te*·ya *gran*·de
pitcher	*un pichel*	oon pee·*chel*
small bottle	*una botella pequeña*	*oo*·na bo·*te*·ya pe·*ke*·nya
champagne	*champán* m	cham·*pan*
cocktail	*coctél* m	kok·*tel*
gin	*ginebra* f	khee·*ne*·bra
rum	*ron* m	ron
tequila	*tequila* f	te·*kee*·la
vodka	*vodka* m	*vod*·ka
whisky	*whisky* m	*wee*·skee

in the bar

en el bar

Most bars offer bar snacks called *bocas* bo·kas (lit: mouths). Typical offerings include black beans, *ceviche* se·*vee*·che (marinated shrimp or raw fish), chicken stew, potato chips, varieties of tacos or pieces of beef.

Excuse me!	*¡Con permiso!*	kon per·*mee*·so
I'm next.	*Sigo yo.*	*see*·go yo
I'll have (*Cacique*).	*Quiero (Cacique).*	*kye*·ro (ka·*see*·ke)
No ice, thanks.	*Sin hielo, gracias.*	seen *ye*·lo *gra*·syas

Same again, please.
Lo mismo, por favor. — lo *mees*·mo por fa·*vor*

I'll buy you a drink.
Te invito a un trago. — te en·*vee*·to a oon *tra*·go

It's my round.
Me toca. — me *to*·ka

What would you like?
¿Que querés? — ke ke·*res*

I don't drink alcohol.
Yo no tomo. — yo no *to*·mo

Do you serve meals here?
¿Sirven comida aquí? — *seer*·ven ko·*mee*·da a·*kee*

down the hatch

The most popular alcoholic drinks are *cerveza* ser·*ve*·sa (beer) and the cane alcohol *guaro* *gwa*·ro which has the kick of a mule and a hangover to match. Beer is served *cruda* *kroo*·da (as a draft), in a *jarra* *kha*·ra (jug) or in a *pichel* pee·*chel* (pitcher). *Guaro* comes in a shot or is mixed with a soft drink or juice. The most popular brand of *guaro* is *Cacique* ka·*see*·ke (meaning 'chief').

listen for...

Creo que ya tomaste suficiente. kre·o ke ya to·*mas*·te soo·fee·*syen*·te	**I think you've had enough.**
¿Que vas a pedir? ke vas a pe·*deer*	**What are you having?**
Última orden. *ool*·tee·ma *or*·den	**Last orders.**

drinking up

tomando

Cheers! *¡Salud!*	sa·*lood*
I feel fantastic! *¡Me siento fenomenal!*	me *syen*·to fe·no·me·*nal*
I think I've had one too many. *Ya me llegaron.*	ya me ye·*ga*·ron
I'm feeling drunk. *Estoy tapis.*	es·*toy ta*·pees
I'm pissed. *Estoy hasta el culo.*	es·*toy as*·ta el *koo*·lo
I feel ill. *Me siento mal.*	me *syen*·to mal
Where's the toilet? *¿Dónde está el baño?*	*don*·de es·*ta* el *ba*·nyo
I'm tired, I'd better go home. *Estoy cansado/a, mejor me voy.* **m/f**	es·*toy* kan·*sa*·do/a me·*khor* me voy
I don't think you should drive. *No deberías manejar.*	no de·be·*ree*·as ma·ne·*khar*
Can you call a taxi for me? *¿Me podrías llamar un taxi?*	me po·*dree*·as ya·*mar* oon *tak*·see

FOOD

buying food

comprando comida

What's the local speciality?
¿Cuál es la especialidad local? — kwal es la es·pe·sya·lee·*dad* lo·*kal*

What's that?
¿Qué es éso? — ke es *e*·so

Can I taste it?
¿Puedo probarlo? — *pwe*·do pro·*bar*·lo

How much is (a kilo of cheese)?
¿Cuánto cuesta (un kilo de queso)? — *kwan*·to *kwes*·ta (oon *kee*·lo de *ke*·so)

Can I have a bag, please?
¿Me da una bolsa, por favor? — me da *oo*·na *bol*·sa por fa·*vor*

I don't need a bag, thanks.
No necesito bolsa, gracias. — no ne·se·*see*·to *bol*·sa *gra*·syas

I'd like …	*Quiero …*	*kye*·ro …
(200) grams	*(doscientos) gramos*	(do·*syen*·tos) *gra*·mos
a kilo	*un kilo*	oon *kee*·lo
half a kilo	*medio kilo*	*me*·dyo *kee*·lo
(two) kilos	*(dos) kilos*	(dos) *kee*·los
a dozen	*una docena*	*oo*·na do·*se*·na
half a dozen	*media docena*	*me*·dya do·*se*·na
a bottle	*una botella*	*oo*·na bo·*te*·ya
a jar	*una jarra*	*oo*·na *kha*·ra
a packet	*un paquete*	oon pa·*ke*·te
a piece	*un pedazo*	oon pe·*da*·so
(three) pieces	*(tres) pedazos*	(tres) pe·*da*·sos
a slice	*una tajada*	*oo*·na ta·*kha*·da
(six) slices	*(seis) tajadas*	(says) ta·*kha*·das

I'd like …	*Quiero …*	*kye*·ro …
a little	*un poquitito*	oon po·kee·*tee*·to
some (of …)	*un poco (de …)*	oon *po*·ko (de …)
more	*más*	mas
that one	*ése/a* **m/f**	*e*·se/a
this one	*éste/a* **m/f**	*es*·te/a

Less.	*Menos.*	*me*·nos
A bit more.	*Un poquito más.*	oon po·*kee*·to mas
Enough.	*Suficiente.*	soo·fee·*syen*·te

Do you have …?	*¿Tiene …?*	*tye*·ne …
anything cheaper	*algo más barato*	*al*·go mas ba·*ra*·to
other kinds	*otros tipos*	o·tros *tee*·pos

Where can I find the … section?	*¿Dónde está/ están …* **sg/pl**	*don*·de es·*ta*/ es·*tan* …
dairy	*los lácteos* **pl**	los *lak*·te·yos
fish	*el pescado* **sg**	el pes·*ka*·do
frozen goods	*las comidas congeladas* **pl**	las ko·*mee*·das kon·khe·*la*·das
fruit and vegetable	*las frutas y verduras* **pl**	las *froo*·tas ee ver·*doo*·ras
meat	*las carnes* **pl**	las *kar*·nes
poultry	*las aves* **pl**	las *a*·ves

For food items, see the **menu decoder**, page 171.

food stuff

cooked	*cocinado/a* **m/f**	ko·see·*na*·do/a
cured	*adobado/a* **m/f**	a·do·*ba*·do/a
dried	*seco/a* **m/f**	*se*·ko/a
fresh	*fresco/a* **m/f**	*fres*·ko/a
frozen	*congelado/a* **m/f**	kon·khe·*la*·do/a
raw	*crudo/a* **m/f**	*kroo*·do/a
smoked	*ahumado/a* **m/f**	a·oo·*ma*·do/a

listen for ...

¿Algo más? al·go mas	**Anything else?**
¿Le puedo ayudar en algo? le *pwe*·do a·yoo·*dar* en *al*·go	**Can I help you with something?**
No hay. no ai	**There isn't any.**
¿Qué quiere? ke *kye*·re	**What would you like?**

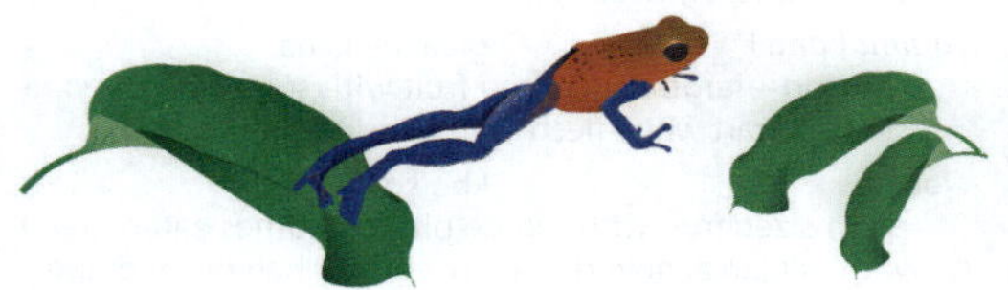

cooking utensils

utensilios de cocina

Can I borrow a ...?	*¿Podría prestarme ...?*	po·*dree*·a pres·*tar*·me ...
I need a ...	*Necesito ...*	ne·se·*see*·to ...
can opener	*un abrelatas*	oon a·bre·*la*·tas
chopping board	*una tabla para picar*	*oo*·na *ta*·bla *pa*·ra pee·*kar*
corkscrew	*un sacacorchos*	oon sa·ka·*kor*·chos
cup	*una taza*	*oo*·na *ta*·sa
frying pan	*un sartén*	oon sar·*ten*
knife	*un cuchillo*	oon koo·*chee*·yo
saucepan	*un sartén hondo*	oon sar·*ten on*·do
spoon	*una cuchara*	*oo*·na koo·*cha*·ra

For more cooking implements, see the **dictionary**.

tropical treats

One of the joys of a trip to Costa Rica is to sample some of the delicious varieties of healthy tropical fruits on offer. Some of these you'll discover in the guise of refreshing drinks called *frescos* fres·kos (see the box **juicy treats**, page 161). Note that not all local fruits have names in English.

caimito m — kai·*mee*·to
star apple – similar to a star fruit but has a purplish skin and soft sweet flesh

cas m — kas
small sour guava-like fruit which is whitish on the inside and frequently used in *frescos*

guanábana f — gwa·*na*·ba·na
soursop – large dark green fruit with spines on the outside and tart white flesh on the inside

jocote m — kho·*ko*·te
plum-sized fruit with a large pit, sometimes eaten green with salt (an acquired taste) or eaten when red and ripe – popular street snack

manzana de agua f — man·*sa*·na de *a*·gwa
'water apple' (relative of the rose apple) – has a crisp white juicy apple-like flesh

manzana rosa f — man·*sa*·na *ro*·sa
'rose apple' – round whitish-green to apricot-yellow fruit with a rose perfume and a sweet crispy and juicy flesh

naranjilla f — na·ran·*khee*·ya
orange tomato-like fruit with a juicy acidic pulp used in drinks and sherbets

zapote m — sa·*po*·te
sapote – fruit with a pinky-red flesh that has a sweet pumpkin-like flavour

zapote negro m — sa·*po*·te *ne*·gro
'black sapote' – fruit with a delicious jelly-like flesh, similar in flavour to a chocolate pudding (unrelated to sapote)

vegetarian & special meals
comidas vegetarianas y especiales

ordering food

ordenando comida

If you don't mind rice and beans, Costa Rica is a relatively comfortable place for vegetarians to travel. Most restaurants will do *casados vegetarianos* ka·*sa*·dos ve·khe·ta·*rya*·nos (ie vegetarian *casados*) on request – see the box **a match made in heaven**, page 153, for more information on this dish.

Is there a ... restaurant near here?	*¿Hay un restaurante ... cerca de aquí?*	ai oon res·tow·*ran*·te ... *ser*·ka de a·*kee*
Do you have ... food?	*¿Tienen comida ...?*	*tye*·nen ko·*mee*·da ...
halal	*halal*	a·*lal*
kosher	*kosher*	*ko*·sher
vegetarian	*vegetariana*	ve·khe·ta·*rya*·na

I don't eat ...	*No como ...*	no *ko*·mo ...
Is it cooked with ...?	*¿Está cocinado con ...?*	es·*ta* ko·see·*na*·do kon ...
butter	*mantequilla*	man·te·*kee*·ya
eggs	*huevos*	*we*·vos
fish (stock)	*(caldo de) pescado*	(*kal*·do de) pes·*ka*·do
meat (stock)	*(caldo de) carne*	(*kal*·do de) *kar*·ne
oil	*aceite*	a·*say*·te
pork	*cerdo*	*ser*·do
poultry	*ave*	*a*·ve
red meat	*carne roja*	*kar*·ne *ro*·kha

Could you prepare a meal without ...?

¿Podría preparar un plato sin ...?	po·*dree*·a pre·pa·*rar* oon *pla*·to seen ...

Does it contain animal produce?

¿Tiene productos animales?	*tye*·ne pro·*dook*·tos a·nee·*ma*·les

Is this ...?	*¿Es ...?*	es ...
decaffeinated	*descafeinado*	des·ka·fay·*na*·do
genetically modified	*genéticamente modificado*	khe·*ne*·tee·ka·men·te mo·dee·fee·*ka*·do
gluten-free	*sin gluten*	seen *gloo*·ten
low-fat	*de poca grasa*	de *po*·ka *gra*·sa
low in sugar	*de poca azúcar*	de *po*·ka a·*soo*·kar
organic	*orgánico*	or·*ga*·nee·ko
salt-free	*sin sal*	seen sal

special diets & allergies

dietas especiales y alergias

I'm on a special diet.

Estoy en una dieta especial.	es·*toy* en *oo*·na *dye*·ta es·pe·*syal*

I'm a vegan.

Soy vegano/a. m/f	soy ve·*ga*·no/a

I'm allergic to ...	*Soy alérgico/a ...* m/f	soy a·*ler*·khee·ko/a ...
dairy produce	*a los lácteos*	a los *lak*·te·os
eggs	*a los huevos*	a los *we*·vos
gelatine	*a la gelatina*	a la khe·la·*tee*·na
gluten	*al gluten*	al *gloo*·ten
honey	*a la miel*	a la myel
MSG	*al GMS*	al khe *e*·me *e*·se
nuts	*a las nueces*	a las *nwe*·ses
peanuts	*al maní*	al ma·*nee*
seafood	*a los mariscos*	a los ma·*rees*·kos
shellfish	*a las conchas*	a las *kon*·chas

To explain your dietary restrictions with reference to religious beliefs, see **beliefs & cultural differences**, page 131.

menu decoder
léxico culinario

This miniguide to Costa Rican cuisine lists ingredients in Spanish alphabetical order (see the box **spanish alphabet**, page 13). It's designed to help you navigate menus and get the most out of your gastronomic experience in Costa Rica. *¡Buen provecho!*

A

aceitunas ⓕ pl a·say·*too*·nas *olives*
— **negras** *ne*·gras *black olives*
— **rellenas** re·*ye*·nas *stuffed olives*
— **verdes** *ver*·des *green olives*
adobo ⓜ a·*do*·bo *garlic, oregano, paprika, peppercorn, salt, olive, lime juice & vinegar paste for seasoning meat*
agua ⓜ *a*·gwa *water*
— **del tubo** del *too*·bo *tap water*
— **de manantial** de ma·nan·*tyal* *spring water*
— **mineral** mee·ne·*ral* *mineral water*
— **sin gas** seen gas *still water*
aguacate ⓜ a·gwa·*ka*·te *avocado*
ahumado/a ⓜ/ⓕ a·oo·*ma*·do/a *smoked*
ají ⓜ a·*khee* *red chilli pepper*
ajillo, al a·*khee*·yo, al *cooked in garlic*
ajo ⓜ *a*·kho *garlic*
albahaca ⓕ al·ba·*a*·ka *basil*
albaricoque ⓜ al·ba·ree·*ko*·ke *apricot*
albóndigas ⓕ pl al·*bon*·dee·gas *meatballs*
alcachofa ⓕ al·ka·*cho*·fa *artichoke*
alcaparra ⓕ al·ka·*pa*·ra *caper*
alita ⓕ a·*lee*·ta *wing (poultry)*
almejas ⓕ pl al·*me*·khas *clams*
almendra ⓕ al·*men*·dra *almond*
alubias ⓕ pl a·*loo*·byas *red kidney beans*
anchoas ⓕ pl an·*cho*·as *anchovies*
anguila ⓕ an·*gee*·la *eel*
anís ⓜ a·*nees* *anise • aniseed*
apio ⓜ *a*·pyo *celery*
arreglado ⓜ a·re·*gla*·do *sandwich or tiny puff pastry stuffed with beef cheese or chicken*
arrollado/a ⓜ/ⓕ a·ro·*ya*·do/a *rolled*
arroz ⓜ a·*ros* *rice*
— **con atún** kon a·*toon* *rice & tuna*
— **con camarones** kon ka·ma·*ro*·nes *rice with shrimps*
— **con leche** kon *le*·che *milky sweet rice pudding with a hint of cinnamon*
— **con pollo** kon *po*·yo *rice & chicken*
— **guacho** gwa·*cho* *rice with onion, garlic, pork & cilantro (coriander)*
— **y frijoles** ee free·*kho*·les *rice with black beans*
arvejas ⓕ pl ar·*ve*·khas *peas (also known as* **petipoas***)*
— **secas** *se*·kas *split peas*
asado ⓜ a·*sa*·do *mixed grill*
atún ⓜ a·*toon* *tuna*
ave ⓜ *a*·ve *poultry*
avellana ⓕ a·ve·*ya*·na *hazelnut*
avena ⓕ a·*ve*·na *oats*
ayote ⓜ a·*yo*·te *gourd • squash*
azafrán ⓜ a·sa·*fran* *saffron*
azúcar ⓜ a·*soo*·kar *sugar*

B

bacalao ⓜ ba·ka·*low* *cod*
— **seco** *se*·ko *dried salted cod*
bagre ⓜ *ba*·gre *catfish*
banano ⓜ ba·*na*·no *banana*
batido ⓜ ba·*tee*·do *fresh fruit shake made with water (***con agua***) or milk (***con leche***)* – *see the box* **juicy treats***, page 161, for popular flavours*
berberechos ⓜ pl be·be·*re*·chos *cockles*
berenjena ⓕ be·ren·*khe*·na *aubergine • eggplant*
berro ⓜ *be*·ro *watercress*
bien asado/a ⓜ/ⓕ byen a·*sa*·do/a *well done*
bien cocido/a ⓜ/ⓕ byen ko·*see*·do/a *well done*

bien hecho/a ⓜ/ⓕ byen e·cho/a *well done*
bistec ⓜ bees·tek *steak*
— **con papas** kon pa·pas *steak & chips*
bocadillo ⓜ bo·ka·dee·yo *snack*
bocas ⓕ pl bo·kas
bar snacks such as black beans, **ceviche**, *chicken stew, potato chips, varieties of* **tacos**, *or pieces of beef – served with drinks*
bollos ⓜ pl bo·yos *bread rolls*
brócoli ⓜ bro·ko·lee *broccoli*
budín ⓜ boo·deen *pudding*
buey ⓜ bwey *ox*

C

cabra ⓕ ka·bra *goat*
cacho ⓜ ka·cho *sweet horn-shaped pastry filled with* **dulce de leche**
caimito ⓜ kai·mee·to
star apple – similar to a star fruit but has a purplish skin & a soft sweet flesh
cajeta ⓕ ka·khe·ta *thick caramel fudge*
calabaza ⓕ ka·la·ba·sa *pumpkin*
calamares ⓜ pl ka·la·ma·res *squid*
— **a la romana** a la ro·ma·na
squid rings fried in butter
caldo ⓜ kal·do *broth • consommé • stock*
camarón ⓜ ka·ma·ron *shrimp*
— **grande** gran·de *large prawn*
camote ⓜ ka·mo·te *sweet potato*
canela ⓕ ka·ne·la *cinnamon*
canelones ⓜ pl ka·ne·lo·nes *cannelloni*
cangrejo ⓜ kan·gre·kho *crab*
caracol ⓜ ka·ra·kol *snail*
carambola ⓕ ka·ram·bo·la
star fruit – mild sweet tropical fruit eaten fresh or juiced in **frescos**
carbón, al kar·bon, al *chargrilled*
carne ⓕ kar·ne
meat – usually synonymous with beef
— **de caballo** de ka·ba·yo *horsemeat*
— **de res** de res *beef*
— **de vaca** de va·ka *beef*
— **dorada al horno** do·ra·da al or·no *roast meat*
— **fría** free·ya *cold meat*
— **molida** mo·lee·da *ground meat*
— **picada** pee·ka·da *minced meat*
— **rotisada** ro·tee·sa·da *roast meat*
carpa ⓕ kar·pa *carp*
cas ⓜ kas *tropical fruit – relative of the guava but very sour & whitish on the inside*
casado ⓜ ka·sa·do *set platter with rice, black beans, fried plantains, chopped cabbage, tomato & usually a choice of beef, chicken or fish (often an egg, a lime or an avocado are included)*
— **vegetariano** ve·khe·ta·rya·no
casado *without the meat*
castaña ⓕ kas·ta·nya *chestnut*
caza ⓕ ka·sa *game (meat)*
— **de temporada** de tem·po·ra·da
game in season
cazuela ⓕ ka·swe·la *casserole*
cebada ⓕ se·ba·da *barley*
cebolla ⓕ se·bo·ya *onion*
cebollín ⓜ se·bo·yeen *shallot • spring onion*
cele ⓜ se·le
green mango – usually eaten with salt
cerdo ⓜ ser·do *pork*
cereza ⓕ se·re·sa *cherry*
cerveza ⓕ ser·ve·sa *beer*
— **en botella** en bo·te·ya *bottled beer*
ceviche ⓜ se·vee·che *raw fish, shrimp or conch marinated in lemon juice, chilli, cilantro (coriander) & onions*
chancho ⓜ chan·cho *pork*
chayote ⓜ cha·yo·te *pear-shaped vegetable similar in flavour to a squash*
chicharrón ⓜ chee·cha·ron
fried pork crackling – popular as ingredient
chifrijo ⓜ chee·free·kho
beans & **chicharrón** *with minced tomato, onion, cilantro (coriander) & lime juice*
chile ⓜ chee·le *chilli pepper*
chirimoya ⓕ chee·ree·mo·ya *custard apple*
chivo ⓜ chee·vo *kid*
choclo ⓜ cho·klo *corn • maize (off the cob)*
chorizo ⓜ cho·ree·so
spicy red or white pork sausage
— **al horno** al or·no
spicy sausage baked in the oven
chorreadas ⓕ pl cho·re·a·das
fried pancakes of fresh corn mash served with sour cream
chuleta ⓕ choo·le·ta *chop • cutlet*
— **de cerdo** de ser·do *pork cutlet*
churrasco ⓜ choo·ras·ko *rib steak*
chuzo ⓜ choo·so
kebab – also know as **pincho**

ciruela ⓕ see·*rwe*·la *plum*
cocinado/a ⓜ/ⓕ ko·see·*na*·do/a *cooked*
coco ⓜ *ko*·ko *coconut*
coctel ⓜ kok·*tel* *appetiser in sauce • cocktail*
codorniz ⓕ ko·dor·*nees* *quail*
coles de bruselas ⓜ pl *ko*·les de broo·*se*·las *Brussels sprouts*
coliflor ⓜ ko·lee·*flor* *cauliflower*
con agua kon *a*·gwa *'with water' – refers to the preparation of a* **batido** *or* **refresco natural** *with water*
conejo ⓜ ko·*ne*·kho *rabbit*
con leche kon *le*·che *'with milk' – refers to the preparation of a* **batido** *or* **refresco natural** *with milk*
corazón ⓜ ko·ra·*son* *heart*
cordero ⓜ kor·*de*·ro *lamb*
corvina ⓕ kor·*vee*·na *bass*
costilla ⓕ kos·*tee*·ya *loin • spare rib*
costillas de cordero ⓜ kos·*tee*·yas de kor·*de*·ro *rack of lamb*
crema ⓕ *kre*·ma *cream*
— **chantillí** chan·tee·*lee* *whipped cream*
crudo/a ⓜ/ⓕ *kroo*·do/a *raw*
crustáceos ⓜ pl kroos·*ta*·se·os *shellfish*
cuajada ⓕ kwa·*kha*·da *milk junket with honey*
culantro ⓜ koo·*lan*·tro *cilantro • coriander*

D

dátil ⓜ *da*·teel *date*
dorado ⓕ do·*ra*·do *sea bass*
dorado/a ⓜ/ⓕ do·*ra*·do/a *seared*
dulce ⓜ&ⓕ *dool*·se *sweet* a
dulce de leche ⓜ *dool*·se de *le*·che *caramelised condensed milk used as a filling for pastries or eaten on bread*

E

ejote ⓜ e·*kho*·te *string bean*
elote ⓜ e·*lo*·te *corn • maize (on the cob)*
— **asado** a·*sa*·do *corn roasted on the cob*
— **hervido** er·*vee*·do *boiled corn*
empanada ⓕ em·pa·*na*·da *baked or fried turnover usually containing fried meat & vegetables though it can have fruit fillings*
enchilada ⓕ en·chee·*la*·da *pastry stuffed with potatoes & cheese & sometimes meat*

eneldo ⓜ e·*nel*·do *dill*
ensalada ⓕ en·sa·*la*·da *salad*
— **de remolacha** de re·mo·*la*·cha *beetroot salad*
— **mixta** *mee*·sta *mixed salad*
— **rusa** *roo*·sa *'Russian salad' – vegetable salad with mayonnaise*
— **verde** *ver*·de *green salad*
espagueti ⓜ es·pa·*ge*·tee *spaghetti*
espárragos ⓜ pl es·*pa*·ra·gos *asparagus*
espinaca ⓕ es·pee·*na*·ka *spinach*
estofado ⓜ es·to·*fa*·do *stew*
estofado/a ⓜ/ⓕ es·to·*fa*·do/a *braised*

F

faisán ⓜ fai·*san* *pheasant*
fideos ⓜ pl fee·*de*·os *noodles*
filete ⓜ fee·*le*·te *fillet*
— **de carne** de *kar*·ne *beef fillet*
— **de pescado** de pes·*ka*·do *fish fillet*
flan ⓜ flan *crème caramel • egg custard*
frambuesa ⓕ fram·*bwe*·sa *raspberry*
fresa ⓕ *fre*·sa *strawberry*
fresco ⓜ *fres*·ko *fresh fruit drink – short for* **refresco natural**
frijol ⓜ free·*khol* *bean*
— **blanco** *blan*·ko *large butter bean*
frijoles ⓜ pl free·*kho*·les *beans*
— **con arroz** kon a·*ros* *beans & rice*
frito ⓜ *free*·to *scraps of fried or roast pork*
frito/a ⓜ/ⓕ *free*·to/a *fried*
— **al sartén** al sar·*ten* *pan-fried*
fruta ⓕ *froo*·ta *fruit*
frutilla ⓕ froo·*tee*·ya *berry*

G

galleta ⓕ ga·*ye*·ta *biscuit • cookie*
— **salada** sa·*la*·da *cracker*
gallo ⓜ *ga*·yo **tortilla** *sandwich containing a meat, bean, cheese or* **picadillo** *filling*
— **de queso con cebolla** de *ke*·so kon se·*bo*·ya *soft cheese & onions folded in a* **tortilla**
— **pinto** *peen*·to *'spotted rooster' – lighty spiced mixture of rice & black beans traditionally served for breakfast, sometimes with sour cream or fried eggs (Costa Rica's signature dish)*

ganso ⓜ *gan·so goose*
garbanzo ⓜ gar·*ban*·so *chickpea • garbanzo bean*
gazpacho ⓜ gas·*pa*·cho *cold tomato & vegetable soup*
granadilla ⓕ gra·na·*dee*·ya *pomegranate*
grasa ⓕ *gra*·sa *fat • grease (also called* **manteca***)*
gratinado ⓜ gra·tee·*na*·do *dish cooked au gratin*
guacamole ⓜ gwa·ka·*mo*·le *mashed avocado combined with onion, chilli, lemon & tomato*
guanábana ⓕ gwa·*na*·ba·na *prickly custard apple • soursop (fruit with a tart pulp)*
guaro ⓜ *gwa*·ro *local firewater made from sugar cane*
guayaba ⓕ gwa·*ya*·ba *guava*
guineo ⓜ gee·*ne*·o *small banana similar to a plantain*
guisantes ⓜ pl gee·*san*·tes *peas*
guiso ⓜ *gee*·so *stew*

H

haba ⓕ *a*·ba *broad bean*
hamburguesa ⓕ am·boor·*ge*·sa *hamburger*
harina ⓕ a·*ree*·na *flour*
helado ⓜ e·*la*·do *ice cream*
helado/a ⓜ/ⓕ e·*la*·do/a *chilled • iced*
hervido/a ⓜ/ⓕ er·*vee*·do/a *boiled*
— **a fuego lento** a *fwe*·go *len*·to *simmered*
hielo ⓜ *ye*·lo *ice*
hierba ⓕ *yer*·ba *herb*
hígado ⓜ *ee*·ga·do *liver*
higo ⓜ *ee*·go *fig*
hocico ⓜ o·*see*·ko *snout*
hongo ⓜ *on*·go *button mushroom*
hongos al ajillo ⓜ pl *on*·gos al a·*khee*·yo *garlic mushrooms*
horchata ⓕ or·*cha*·ta *rice-based drink flavoured with cinnamon*
horneado/a ⓜ/ⓕ or·ne·*a*·do/a *baked*
horno, al *or*·no, al *baked*
hueso ⓜ *we*·so *bone*
huevos ⓜ pl *we*·vos *eggs*
— **de tortuga** de tor·*too*·ga *turtle eggs – be aware that turtles are an endangered species*
— **duros** *doo*·ros *hard-boiled eggs*
— **fritos** *free*·tos *fried eggs*
— **hervidos** er·*vee*·dos *boiled eggs*
— **pateados** pa·te·*a*·dos *scrambled eggs*
— **revueltos** re·*vwel*·tos *scrambled eggs*

J

jabalí ⓜ kha·ba·*lee* *wild boar*
jalea ⓕ kha·*le*·a *jam*
jamón ⓜ kha·*mon* *ham*
— **dulce** *dool*·se *boiled ham*
— **serrano** se·*ra*·no *cured ham*
jarrete ⓜ kha·*re*·te *bone marrow • knuckle • shank*
jengibre ⓜ khen·*khee*·bre *ginger*
jocote ⓜ kho·*ko*·te *plum-sized fruit with a large pit, sometimes eaten green with salt (an acquired taste) or eaten when red & ripe*
jugo ⓜ *khoo*·go *juice*
— **de naranja** de na·*ran*·kha *orange juice*
— **natural** na·too·*ral* *freshly-squeezed juice*
— **puro** *poo*·ro *pure juice*

L

langosta ⓕ lan·*gos*·ta *spiny lobster*
langostino ⓜ lan·gos·*tee*·no *crawfish • crayfish*
leche ⓕ *le*·che *milk*
— **descremada** des·kre·*ma*·da *skimmed milk*
— **de soya** de *so*·ya *soya milk*
lechón ⓜ le·*chon* *suckling pig*
lechuga ⓕ le·*choo*·ga *lettuce*
legumbre ⓕ le·*goom*·bre *pulse*
lengua ⓕ *len*·gwa *tongue*
lenguado ⓜ len·*gwa*·do *dab • lemon sole*
lentejas ⓕ len·*te*·khas *lentils*
limón ⓜ lee·*mon* *lemon • lime*
lomo ⓜ *lo*·mo *sirloin*

M

macarela ⓕ ma·ka·*re*·la *mackerel*
macarrones ⓜ pl ma·ka·*ro*·nes *macaroni*
maduro/a ⓜ/ⓕ ma·*doo*·ro/a *ripe*
maíz ⓜ ma·*ees* *corn • maize*

mandarina Ⓕ man·da·*ree*·na
mandarin • tangerine
mango Ⓜ *man*·go *mango*
maní Ⓜ ma·*nee* *peanut*
manteca Ⓕ man·*te*·ka
grease • fat (also known as **grasa***)*
mantequilla Ⓕ man·te·*kee*·ya *butter*
manzana Ⓕ man·*sa*·na *apple*
— **de agua** de *a*·gwa
'water apple' (relative of the rose apple) – has a crisp, white, juicy, apple-like flesh
— **rosa** *ro*·sa *'rose apple' – fruit with an apple-like taste but with a rose perfume*
maracuyá Ⓕ ma·ra·koo·*ya* *passionfruit*
margarina Ⓕ mar·ga·*ree*·na *margarine*
marinado/a Ⓜ/Ⓕ ma·ree·*na*·do/a
marinated
mariscos Ⓜ pl ma·*rees*·kos
seafood • shellfish
mayonesa Ⓕ ma·yo·*ne*·sa *mayonnaise*
mazapán Ⓜ ma·sa·*pan*
almond paste • marzipan
medio crudo/a Ⓜ/Ⓕ *me*·dyo *kroo*·do/a
rare
mejilla Ⓕ me·*khee*·ya *cheek*
mejillones Ⓜ pl me·khee·*yo*·nes *mussels*
— **al vapor** al va·*por* *steamed mussels*
melocotón Ⓜ me·lo·ko·*ton* *peach*
melón Ⓜ me·*lon* *melon*
menta Ⓜ *men*·ta *mint*
menudo de pollo Ⓜ me·*noo*·do de *po*·yo
gizzard • poultry entrails
menudos Ⓜ pl me·*noo*·dos *giblets*
merluza Ⓕ mer·*loo*·sa *hake*
— **a la plancha** a la *plan*·cha *fried hake*
mermelada Ⓕ mer·me·*la*·da *marmalade*
miel Ⓕ myel *honey*
milanesa Ⓕ mee·la·*ne*·sa
schnitzel – pounded, breaded & fried meat
mil hojas Ⓕ pl meel *o*·khas
'thousand leaves' – layers of thin pastry filled with an almond & honey paste
mojarra Ⓕ mo·*kha*·ra *perch*
mondongo Ⓜ mon·*don*·go *tripe*
mora Ⓕ *mo*·ra *blackberry*
morcilla Ⓕ mor·*see*·ya *black pudding • blood sausage – common* **asado** *dish*
mostaza Ⓕ mos·*ta*·sa *mustard*
muslo Ⓜ *moo*·slo *thigh*
muy cocinado/a Ⓜ/Ⓕ
mooy ko·see·*na*·do/a *well done*

N

nabo Ⓜ *na*·bo *turnip*
naranja Ⓕ na·*ran*·kha *orange*
naranjilla Ⓕ na·ran·*khee*·ya
orange-coloured, tomato-like fruit with a juicy acidic pulp used in drinks & sherbets
nata Ⓕ *na*·ta *cream*
natilla Ⓕ na·*tee*·ya *sour cream*
natural Ⓜ na·too·*ral*
fresh fruit drink – short for **refresco natural**
nuez Ⓜ nwes *nut • walnut*

O

olla de carne Ⓕ *o*·ya de *kar*·ne
hearty soup containing beef, potatoes, corn, **chayote***, plantains & cassava*
omelet Ⓜ o·me·*let*
omelette (also known as **torta de huevo***)*
oreja Ⓕ o·*re*·kha
'ear' – sweet biscuit of flaky pastry
ostión Ⓜ os·tee·*on* *scallop*
ostra Ⓕ *os*·tra *oyster*
oveja Ⓕ o·*ve*·kha *ewe*

P

paleta Ⓕ pa·*le*·ta *shoulder*
palmitos Ⓜ pl pal·*mee*·tos *palm hearts – usually served in a vinegar dressing*
paloma Ⓕ pa·*lo*·ma *pigeon*
pan Ⓜ pan *bread*
— **dulce** *dool*·se *sweet bread*
panqueque Ⓜ pan·*ke*·ke *pancake*
papas Ⓕ pl *pa*·pas *potatoes*
— **fritas** *free*·tas *chips • French fries*
papaya Ⓕ pa·*pa*·ya *papaya*
papitas Ⓕ pl pa·*pee*·tas *crisps • potato chips*
pargo Ⓜ *par*·go *red snapper*
parrilla Ⓕ pa·*ree*·ya *grill*
parrilla, a la pa·*ree*·ya, a la
grilled over charcoal
parrillada Ⓕ pa·ree·*ya*·da
mixed grill – huge slabs of grilled meat prepared over hot coals & served with spicy sauces & vegetables
pasa Ⓜ *pa*·sa *raisin*
pasado/a al agua Ⓜ/Ⓕ pa·*sa*·do/a al *a*·gwa
boiled

pasta ⓕ *pas·ta pasta*
pastel ⓜ *pas·tel cake • pastry*
pata ⓕ *pa·ta leg*
patacones ⓜ pl *pa·ta·ko·nes*
fried green plantains cut into thin pieces, salted & then pressed & fried – popular on the Caribbean coast
patita de cerdo/chancho ⓕ
pa·tee·ta de ser·do/chan·cho pig's trotter
pato ⓜ *pa·to duck*
pavo ⓜ *pa·vo turkey*
pechuga ⓕ *pe·choo·ga breast meat*
pejibaye ⓜ *pe·khee·ba·ye*
starchy palm fruit boiled & frequently eaten with mayonnaise
pepinillo ⓜ *pe·pee·nee·yo pickle*
pepino ⓜ *pe·pee·no cucumber*
pera ⓕ *pe·ra pear*
perejil ⓜ *pe·re·kheel parsley*
pescado ⓜ *pes·ka·do fish*
— **ahumado** *a·oo·ma·do smoked fish*
— **al ajillo** *al a·khee·yo fish in garlic sauce*
— **de agua dulce** *de a·gwa dool·se freshwater fish*
— **de mar** *de mar saltwater fish*
pescaíto ⓜ *pes·ka·ee·to tiny fried fish*
petipoas ⓕ pl *pe·tee·po·as*
peas – another word for **arvejas**
pez espada ⓜ *pes es·pa·da swordfish*
pez hoja ⓜ *pes o·kha bottom fish • flounder*
picadillo ⓜ *pee·ka·dee·yo*
'minced' – side dish of minced vegetables and/or fruit & ground meat (usually beef)
picante ⓜ&ⓕ *pee·kan·te spicy*
pimentón ⓜ *pee·men·ton*
bell pepper • capsicum
pimienta ⓕ *pee·myen·ta pepper*
pincho ⓜ *peen·cho*
kebab – also know as **chuzo**
piña ⓕ *pee·nya pineapple*
pipa ⓕ *pee·pa*
green coconut – picked for its milk which is often drunk straight from the shell
pistacho ⓜ *pees·ta·cho pistachio nut*
plancha ⓕ *plan·cha grill • hot plate*
plancha, a la *plan·cha, a la grilled*
plátano ⓜ *pla·ta·no*
plantain – savoury banana-like fruit that's cooked & often served with main dishes
poco cocido/a ⓜ/ⓕ *po·ko ko·see·do/a rare*
poco hecho/a ⓜ/ⓕ *po·ko e·cho/a rare*
pollo ⓜ *po·yo chicken*
polvo ⓜ *pol·vo powder*
postre ⓜ *pos·tre dessert*
prestiño ⓜ *pres·tee·nyo*
very thin fried pastry eaten with syrup
puerco ⓜ *pwer·ko pork*
pulpo ⓜ *pool·po octopus*
— **a la gallega** *a la ga·ye·ga*
octopus in a garlicky wine & tomato sauce with bell pepper & potatoes thrown in
punto, a *poon·to, a medium (steak)*

Q

queque ⓜ *ke·ke cake • pastry*
— **seco** ⓜ *se·ko pound cake*
queso ⓜ *ke·so cheese*

R

rábano ⓜ *ra·ba·no radish*
rabo ⓜ *ra·bo tail*
rape ⓜ *ra·pe monkfish*
refresco ⓜ *re·fres·ko soft drink*
— **natural** *na·too·ral*
frequently referred to simply as **frescos** *or* **naturales**, *these are fruit juices made to order* **con agua** *(with water) or* **con leche** *(with milk) – see the box* **juicy treats**, *page 161, for common flavours*
relleno/a ⓜ/ⓕ *re·ye·no/a stuffed*
remolacha ⓕ *re·mo·la·cha beetroot*
repollo ⓜ *re·po·yo cabbage*
res, carne de ⓕ *res, kar·ne de beef*
riñón ⓜ *ree·nyon kidney*
romero ⓜ *ro·me·ro rosemary*
rosado ⓜ *ro·sa·do rosé*
rostisado/a ⓜ/ⓕ *ros·tee·sa·do/a roasted*
— **al espiedo** *al es·pye·do spit-roasted*
— **a la parilla** *a la pa·ree·ya grilled*
— **al horno** *al or·no oven roasted*

S

sal ⓕ *sal salt*
salado/a ⓜ/ⓕ *sa·la·do/a salted • salty*
salchichas ⓕ pl *sal·chee·chas*
sausages similar to hot dogs
salmón ⓜ *sal·mon salmon*

salsa ⓕ sal·sa sauce
— **de carne** de kar·ne gravy
— **picante** pee·kan·te chilli sauce
Salsa Lizano ⓕ sal·sa lee·sa·no the secret sauce of Costa Rica (added to everything, especially **gallo pinto**) – a tangy, yet somewhat sweet concoction, with tamarind as the main ingredient
salteado/a ⓜ/ⓕ sal·te·a·do/a sautéed
salvaje ⓜ&ⓕ sal·va·khe wild
sandía ⓕ san·dee·a watermelon
sandwich ⓜ sand·weech sandwich
sandwiche ⓜ sand·wee·che alternate spelling of **sandwich**
sangre ⓕ san·gre blood
sangría ⓕ san·gree·a sangria (red-wine punch)
sardina ⓕ sar·dee·na sardine
secado/a ⓜ/ⓕ se·ka·do/a dried
seco/a ⓜ/ⓕ se·ko/a dry • dried
semilla de marañón ⓕ se·mee·ya de ma·ra·nyon cashew
semolina ⓕ se·mo·lee·na semolina
sepia ⓕ se·pya cuttlefish
sésamo ⓜ se·sa·mo sesame
sesos ⓜ pl se·sos brains
sidra ⓕ see·dra cider
sin grasa seen gra·sa lean
sopa ⓕ so·pa soup
— **de albóndigas** de al·bon·dee·gas meatball soup
— **de espinacas** de es·pee·na·kas spinach soup
— **de frijoles negros** de free·kho·les ne·gros black bean soup
— **de mariscos** de ma·rees·kos shellfish soup
— **de mondongo** de mon·don·go tripe soup
— **de pescado** de pes·ka·do fish soup
— **de pollo** de po·yo chicken soup
— **negra** ne·gra creamy black bean soup, often with a hard-boiled egg & vegetables soaking in the bean broth
soya ⓕ so·ya soy
suflé ⓜ soo·fle soufflé

T

tacos ⓜ pl ta·kos Costa Rican-style tacos (**tortillas** filled with meat, beans & other ingredients) – deep-fried & served with shredded cabbage, mayonnaise & ketchup
tajadas ⓕ pl ta·kha·das slices
tallarines ⓜ pl ta·ya·ree·nes noodles mixed with pork, chicken, beef or vegetables
tamales ⓜ pl ta·ma·les cornmeal dough filled with spiced beef or pork, vegetables & potatoes, then wrapped in a maize husk or banana leaf & fried, grilled or baked
— **asado** a·sa·do sweet cornmeal cake
tamarindo ⓜ ta·ma·reen·do tamarind
té ⓜ te tea
término medio ter·mee·no me·dyo medium
ternera ⓕ ter·ne·ra veal
tiburón ⓜ tee·boo·ron shark
tinto ⓜ teen·to red (wine)
tocineta ⓕ to·see·ne·ta bacon
— **ahumada** a·oo·ma·da smoked bacon
tocino ⓜ to·see·no cold bacon
— **con queso** ⓜ kon ke·so cold bacon & cheese
tomate ⓜ to·ma·te tomato
toronja ⓕ to·ron·kha grapefruit
— **rellena** ⓕ re·ye·na caramelised grapefruit peel filled with milk **cajeta**
torta ⓕ tor·ta cake • tart
— **de huevo** de we·vo plain omelette also known as **omelet**
— **española** es·pa·nyo·la egg & potato omelette
tortilla ⓕ tor·tee·ya thin round of pressed corn (or sometimes wheat) dough cooked on a griddle • another name for an **omelet**
— **con queso** kon ke·so **tortilla** with cheese
tortuga ⓕ tor·too·ga turtle – be aware that turtles are an endangered species
tostada ⓕ tos·ta·da toast
tres leches ⓜ tres le·ches moist cake prepared with cream, condensed & evaporated milk
tripas ⓕ pl tree·pas offal
trucha ⓕ troo·cha trout
trufa ⓕ troo·fa truffle
turrón ⓜ too·ron almond nougat

U

ubre ⓕ oo·bre udder
uva ⓕ oo·va grape

V

vaca, carne de ⓕ *va·ka, kar·ne de beef*
vainilla ⓕ vai·nee·ya *vanilla*
vapor ⓜ va·*por* steam
vapor, al va·*por*, al *steamed*
vegetal ⓜ ve·khe·*tal* *vegetable* n
vegetales ⓜ pl ve·khe·*ta*·les *vegetables*
venado ⓜ ve·*na*·do *venison*
verdes ⓜ pl *ver*·des *greens*
verduras ⓕ pl ver·*doo*·ras *green vegetables*
vieira ⓕ *vyay*·ra *scallop*
vigorón ⓜ vee·go·*ron* *boiled cassava top served with cabbage salad,* **chicharrón**, *tomatoes, onions & lime juice*
vinagre ⓜ vee·*na*·gre *vinegar*
vino ⓜ *vee*·no *wine*
 — **blanco** *blan*·ko *white wine*
 — **espumoso** es·poo·*mo*·so *sparkling wine*
 — **rosado** ro·*sa*·do *rosé*
 — **tinto** *teen*·to *red wine*
vualve a la vida caribeño ⓜ *vwal*·ve a la *vee*·da ka·ree·*be*·nyo *thick seafood-based soup blended with coconut milk*

Y

yogur ⓜ yo·*gur* *yogurt*
yuca ⓕ *yoo*·ka *cassava – common staple in Latin American cuisine*

Z

zanahoria ⓕ sa·na·o·rya *carrot*
zapote ⓜ sa·*po*·te *sapote – fruit with a pinky red flesh & a pumpkin-like flavour*

emergencies

emergencias

Help!	*¡Socorro!*	so·*ko*·ro
Stop!	*¡Pare!*	*pa*·re
Go away!	*¡Váyase!*	*va*·ya·se
Thief!	*¡Ladrón!*	la·*dron*
Fire!	*¡Incendio!*	een·*sen*·dyo
Watch out!	*¡Cuidado!*	kwee·*da*·do
Call …	*Llame a …*	*ya*·me a …
an ambulance	*una ambulancia*	*oo*·na am·boo·*lan*·sya
a doctor	*un doctor*	oon dok·*tor*
the police	*la policía*	la po·lee·*see*·a

It's an emergency.
Es una emergencia. es *oo*·na e·mer·*khen*·sya

There's been an accident.
Hubo un accidente. *oo*·bo oon ak·see·*den*·te

Could you please help me/us?
¿Me/Nos podría ayudar, por favor? me/nos po·*dree*·a a·yoo·*dar* por fa·*vor*

signs

Emergencias	e·mer·*khen*·syas	**Emergency Department**
Estación Policial	es·ta·*syon* po·lee·*syal*	**Police Station (city)**
Guardia Rural	*gwar*·dya roo·*ral*	**Police Station (rural)**
Hospital	os·pee·*tal*	**Hospital**
Policía	po·lee·*see*·a	**Police**

Can I use your phone?		
¿Usted me prestaría el teléfono?	oos·*ted* me pres·ta·*ree*·a el te·*le*·fo·no	
I'm lost.		
Estoy perdido/a. m/f	es·*toy* per·*dee*·do/a	
Where are the toilets?		
¿Dónde está el baño?	*don*·de es·*ta* el *ba*·nyo	

Is it dangerous ...?	*¿Es peligroso ...?*	es pe·lee·*gro*·so ...
at night	*en la noche*	en la *no*·che
for gay people	*para homosexuales*	*pa*·ra o·mo·sek·*swa*·les
for travellers	*para turistas*	*pa*·ra too·*rees*·tas
for women	*para mujeres*	*pa*·ra moo·*khe*·res
on your own	*si uno va solo/a* m/f	see *oo*·no va *so*·lo/a

police

policía

Where's the police station?	
¿Dónde está la estación de policía?	*don*·de es·*ta* la es·ta·*syon* de po·lee·*see*·a
Please telephone the police.	
Por favor, llame a la policía.	por fa·*vor* *ya*·me a la po·lee·*see*·a
I want to report an offence.	
Quiero reportar un delito.	*kye*·ro re·por·*tar* oon de·*lee*·to
It was him/her.	
Fue él/ella.	fwe el/*e*·ya

I've been ...	*Me ...*	me ...
He/She has been ...	*Lo/La ...*	lo/la ...
assaulted	*asaltaron*	a·sal·*ta*·ron
raped	*violaron*	vyo·*la*·ron
robbed	*robaron*	ro·*ba*·ron

My … was/ were stolen.	*Me robaron …*	me ro·*ba*·ron …
I've lost my …	*Perdí …*	per·*dee* …
backpack	*mi mochila*	mee mo·*chee*·la
credit card	*mi tarjeta de crédito*	mee tar·*khe*·ta de *kre*·dee·to
handbag	*mi bolso*	mee *bol*·so
jewellery	*mis joyas*	mees *kho*·yas
money	*mi plata*	mee *pla*·ta
papers	*mis documentos*	mees do·koo·*men*·tos
passport	*mi pasaporte*	mee pa·sa·*por*·te
travellers cheques	*mis cheques de viajero*	mee *che*·kes de vya·*khe*·ro
wallet	*mi billetera*	mee bee·ye·*te*·ra

the police may say …

Es una multa por …	es *oo*·na *mool*·ta por …	**It's a … fine.**
exceso de velocidad	ek·*se*·so de ve·lo·see·*dad*	**speeding**
parquear donde no se permite	par·ke·*ar don*·de no se per·*mee*·te	**parking**
A usted se le acusa de …	a oos·*ted* se le a·*koo*·sa de …	**You're charged with …**
asaltar a alguien	a·sal·*tar* a *al*·gyen	**assault**
no tener visa	no te·*ner vee*·sa	**not having a visa**
permanecer ilegalmente en el país con documentos vencidos	per·ma·ne·*ser* ee·le·gal·*men*·te en el pa·*ees* kon do·koo·*men*·tos ven·*see*·dos	**overstaying a visa**
robo	*ro*·bo	**theft**
tenencia (de sustancias ilegales)	te·*nen*·sya (de soos·*tan*·syas ee·lee·*ga*·les)	**possession (of illegal substances)**

What am I accused of?
¿De que me están acusando? de ke me es·*tan* a·koo·*san*·do

I apologise.
Lo siento. lo *syen*·to

I didn't realise I was doing anything wrong.
No sabía que estaba haciendo algo malo. no sa·*bee*·a ke es·*ta*·ba a·*syen*·do *al*·go *ma*·lo

I didn't do it.
Yo no fui. yo no fwee

Can I pay an on-the-spot fine?
¿Puedo pagar la multa aquí mismo? *pwe*·do pa·*gar* la *mool*·ta a·*kee* *mees*·mo

I have insurance.
Tengo seguro. *ten*·go se·*goo*·ro

Do you have this form in (English)?
¿Tiene este formulario en (inglés)? *tye*·ne *es*·te for·moo·*la*·ryo en (een·*gles*)

I want to contact my embassy/consulate.
Quiero contactar a mi embajada/consulado. *kye*·ro kon·tak·*tar* a mee em·ba·*kha*·da/kon·soo·*la*·do

Can I make a phone call?
¿Puedo hacer una llamada telefónica? *pwe*·do a·*ser* *oo*·na ya·*ma*·da te·le·*fo*·nee·ka

Can I have a lawyer (who speaks English)?
¿Me pueden traer un abogado (que hable inglés)? me *pwe*·den tra·*er* oon a·bo·*ga*·do (ke *a*·ble een·*gles*)

I want to speak to a female police officer.
Quiero hablar con una mujer policía. *kye*·ro ab·*lar* kon *oo*·na moo·*kher* po·lee·*see*·a

I have a prescription for this drug.
Tengo receta para este medicamento. *ten*·go re·*se*·ta *pa*·ra *es*·te me·dee·ka·*men*·to

This drug is for personal use.
Esta droga es de uso personal. *es*·ta *dro*·ga es de *oo*·so per·so·*nal*

doctor

doctor

Where's the nearest ...?	*¿Dónde está ... más cercano/a?* **m/f**	*don*·de es·*ta* ... mas ser·*ka*·no/a
dentist	*el dentista* **m**	el den·*tees*·ta
doctor	*el doctor* **m**	el dok·*tor*
emergency department	*la sección de emergencias* **f**	la sek·*syon* de e·mer·*khen*·syas
hospital	*el hospital* **m**	el os·pee·*tal*
medical centre	*la clínica* **f**	la *klee*·nee·ka
optometrist	*el optometrista* **m**	el op·to·me·*trees*·ta
(24-hour) pharmacist	*la farmacia (abierta 24 horas)* **f**	la far·*ma*·sya (a·*byer*·ta vayn·tee·*kwa*·tro *o*·ras)

I need a doctor (who speaks English).
Necesito un doctor (que hable inglés). — ne·se·*see*·to oon dok·*tor* (ke *a*·ble een·*gles*)

Could I see a female doctor?
¿Podría atenderme una doctora? — po·*dree*·a a·ten·*der*·me *oo*·na dok·*to*·ra

Could the doctor come here?
¿El doctor podría venir acá? — el dok·*tor* po·*dree*·a ve·*neer* a·*ka*

Is there an after-hours emergency number?
¿Hay un número de emergencias fuera de horas hábiles? — ai oon *noo*·me·ro de e·mer·*khen*·syas *fwe*·ra de *o*·ras *a*·bee·les

I've run out of my medication.
Se me acabó mi medicamento. — se me a·ka·*bo* mee me·dee·ka·*men*·to

This is my usual medicine.

Esta es mi medicina normal.	es·ta es mee me·dee·*see*·na nor·*mal*

My son/daughter weighs (20 kilos).

Mi hijo/hija pesa (20 kilos).	me *ee*·kho/*ee*·kha *pe*·sa (*vayn*·te *kee*·los)

What's the correct dosage?

¿Cuál es la dosis correcta?	kwal es la *do*·sees ko·*rek*·ta

I don't want a blood transfusion.

No quiero que me hagan una transfusión.	no *kye*·ro ke me *a*·gan *oo*·na trans·foo·*syon*

Please use a new syringe.

Por favor, use una jeringa nueva.	por fa·*vor oo*·se *oo*·na khe·*reen*·ga *nwe*·va

I have my own syringe.

Yo tengo mi propia jeringa.	yo *ten*·go mee *pro*·pya khe·*reen*·ga

the doctor may say ...

¿Cuál es el problema? kwal es el pro·*ble*·ma	**What's the problem?**
¿Dónde le duele? *don*·de le *dwe*·le	**Where does it hurt?**
¿Qué tiene? ke *tye*·ne	**What do you have?**
¿Tiene fiebre? *tye*·ne *fye*·bre	**Do you have a temperature?**
¿Cuánto tiene de estar así? *kwan*·to *tye*·ne de es·*tar* a·*see*	**How long have you been like this?**
¿Ha tenido esto mismo antes? ha te·*nee*·do *es*·to *mees*·mo *an*·tes	**Have you had this before?**
¿Es usted alérgico/a a algo? m/f es oos·*ted* a·*ler*·khee·ko/a a *al*·go	**Are you allergic to anything?**

SAFE TRAVEL

the doctor may say ...

¿Está usted tomando algún medicamento?	
es·*ta* oos·*ted* to·*man*·do al·*goon* me·dee·ka·*men*·to	**Are you on medication?**
¿Usted es sexualmente activo/a? **m/f**	
oos·*ted* es sek·swal·*men*·te ak·*tee*·vo/a	**Are you sexually active?**
¿Ha tenido relaciones sexuales sin protección?	
ha te·*nee*·do re·la·*syo*·nes sek·*swa*·les seen pro·tek·*syon*	**Have you had unprotected sex?**
¿Usted fuma?	
oos·*ted foo*·ma	**Do you smoke?**
¿Usted toma licor?	
oos·*ted to*·ma lee·*kor*	**Do you drink?**
¿Usted usa drogas?	
oos·*ted oo*·sa *dro*·gas	**Do you take drugs?**
¿Por cuánto tiempo es su viaje?	
por *kwan*·to *tyem*·po es soo *vya*·khe	**How long are you travelling for?**
Debería ir a revisarse eso cuando llegue a su casa.	
de·be·*ree*·a eer a re·vee·*sar*·se *e*·so *kwan*·do *ye*·ge a soo *ka*·sa	**You should have it checked when you go home.**
Debería devolverse a su casa para que le den tratamiento.	
de·be·*ree*·a de·vol·*ver*·se a soo *ka*·sa *pa*·ra ke le den tra·ta·*myen*·to	**You should return home for treatment.**
Vamos a tener que internarlo en el hospital.	
va·mos a te·*ner* ke een·ter·*nar*·lo en el os·pee·*tal*	**You need to be admitted to hospital.**
Usted es hipocondríaco.	
oos·*ted* es ee·po·kon·*dree*·a·ko	**You're a hypochondriac.**

I've been vaccinated against …	*Yo estoy vacunado/a contra …* **m/f**	yo es·*toy* va·koo·*na*·do/a *kon*·tra …
He/She has been vaccinated against …	*El/Ella está vacunado/a contra …*	el/e·ya es·*ta* va·koo·*na*·do/a *kon*·tra …
hepatitis A/B/C	*hepatitis A/B/C*	e·pa·*tee*·tees a/be/se
tetanus	*tétano*	*te*·ta·no
typhoid	*fiebre tifoidea*	*fye*·bre tee·foy·*de*·a
I need new …	*Necesito … nuevos/as.* **m/f**	ne·se·*see*·to … *nwe*·vos/as
contact lenses	*lentes de contacto* **f**	*len*·tes de kon·*tak*·to
glasses	*anteojos* **m**	an·te·*o*·khos

My prescription is …
Mi receta está … — mee re·*se*·ta es·*ta* …

How much will it cost?
¿Cuánto me va a costar? — *kwan*·to me va a kos·*tar*

Can I have a receipt for my insurance?
¿Me podría dar una factura para mi seguro médico? — me po·*dree*·a dar *oo*·na fak·*too*·ra *pa*·ra mee se·*goo*·ro *me*·dee·ko

symptoms & conditions

condiciones y síntomas

I'm sick.
Estoy enfermo/a. **m/f** — es·*toy* en·*fer*·mo/a

My friend is (very) sick.
Mi amigo/a está (muy) enfermo/a. **m/f** — mee a·*mee*·go/a es·*ta* (mooy) en·*fer*·mo/a

My son/daughter is (very) sick.
Mi hijo/hija está (muy) enfermo/a. — mee *ee*·kho/*ee*·kha es·*ta* (mooy) en·*fer*·mo/a

I've been injured.
Estoy herido/a. m/f — es·*toy* e·*ree*·do/a

He/She has been injured.
El/Ella está herido/a. — el/e·ya es·*ta* e·*ree*·do/a

I've been vomiting.
He estado vomitando. — e es·*ta*·do vo·mee·*tan*·do

He/She has been vomiting.
El/Ella ha estado vomitando. — el/e·ya a es·*ta*·do vo·mee·*tan*·do

She's having a baby.
Está teniendo el bebé. — es·*ta* te·*nyen*·do el be·*be*

He/She is having a/an …	*Le está dando …*	le es·*ta* *dan*·do …
allergic reaction	*una reacción alérgica*	*oo*·na re·ak·*syon* a·*ler*·khee·ka
asthma attack	*un ataque de asma*	oon a·*ta*·ke de *as*·ma
epileptic fit	*un ataque epiléptico*	oon a·*ta*·ke e·pee·*lep*·tee·ko
heart attack	*un ataque cardíaco*	oon a·*ta*·ke kar·*dee*·a·ko

I feel …	*Me siento …*	me *syen*·to …
anxious	*ansioso/a* m/f	an·*syo*·so/a
better	*mejor* m&f	me·*khor*
depressed	*deprimido/a* m/f	de·pree·*mee*·do/a
dizzy	*mareado/a* m/f	ma·re·*a*·do/a
hot and cold	*con calor y con frío*	kon ka·*lor* ee kon *free*·o
strange	*raro/a* m/f	*ra*·ro/a
weak	*débil* m&f	*de*·beel
worse	*peor* m&f	pe·*or*

I feel nauseous.
Tengo náuseas. — *ten*·go *now*·se·as

I feel shivery.
Tengo escalofríos. — *ten*·go es·ka·lo·*free*·os

It hurts here.
Me duele aquí. — me *dwe*·le a·*kee*

I'm dehydrated.
Estoy deshidratado/a. m/f — es·*toy* de·see·dra·*ta*·do/a

I can't sleep.
No puedo dormir. — no *pwe*·do dor·*meer*

I think it's the medication I'm on.
Creo que son las medicinas que estoy tomando. — *kre*·o ke son las me·dee·*see*·nas ke es·*toy* to·*man*·do

I'm on medication for ...
Estoy tomando medicinas para ... — es·*toy* to·*man*·do me·dee·*see*·nas *pa*·ra ...

He/She is on medication for ...
Él/Ella está tomando medicinas para ... — el/*e*·ya es·*ta* to·*man*·do me·dee·*see*·nas *pa*·ra ...

I have (a/an) ...
Tengo (un/una) ... m/f — *ten*·go (oon/*oo*·na) ...

He/She has (a/an) ...
Él/Ella tiene (un/una) ... m/f — el/*e*·ya *tye*·ne (oon/*oo*·na) ...

asthma	*asma* f	*as*·ma
cold n	*resfrío* m	res·*free*·o
constipation	*estreñimiento* m	es·tre·nyee·*myen*·to
cough n	*tos* m	tos
diabetes	*diabetes* m	dee·a·*be*·tees
diarrhoea	*diarrea* f	dee·a·*re*·a
fever	*fiebre* f	*fye*·bre
flu	*gripe* f	*gree*·pe
headache	*dolor de cabeza* m	do·*lor* de ka·*be*·sa
migraine	*migraña* f	mee·*gra*·nya
nausea	*náuseas* f pl	*now*·se·as
pain n	*dolor* m	do·*lor*
sore throat	*dolor de garganta* m	do·*lor* de gar·*gan*·ta

women's health

salud de la mujer

(I think) I'm pregnant.
(Creo que) Estoy embarazada. (*kre*·o ke) es·*toy* em·ba·ra·*sa*·da

I'm on the pill.
Estoy tomando pastillas anticonceptivas. es·*toy* to·*man*·do pas·*tee*·yas an·tee·kon·sep·*tee*·vas

I haven't had my period for (six) weeks.
No me ha bajado la regla en (seis) semanas. no me a ba·*kha*·do la *re*·gla en (says) se·*ma*·nas

I've noticed a lump here.
Noté una pelota aquí. no·*te* *oo*·na pe·*lo*·ta a·*kee*

Do you have something for (period pain)?
¿Tiene algo para (dolores menstruales)? *tye*·ne *al*·go *pa*·ra (do·*lo*·res mens·*trwa*·les)

I have a ...	*Tengo una ...*	*ten*·go *oo*·na ...
urinary tract infection	*infección urinaria*	een·fek·*syon* oo·ree·*na*·rya
yeast infection	*infección vaginal*	een·fek·*syon* va·khee·*nal*
I need (a/the) ...	*Necesito ...*	ne·se·*see*·to ...
contraception	*un anti-conceptivo*	oon an·tee·kon·sep·*tee*·vo
morning-after pill	*una pastilla del día siguiente*	*oo*·na pas·*tee*·ya del *dee*·a see·*gyen*·te
pregnancy test	*una prueba de embarazo*	*oo*·na *prwe*·ba de em·ba·*ra*·so

the doctor may say ...

¿Cuándo fue la última vez que tuvo la regla?	
kwan·do fwe la ool·tee·ma ves ke too·vo la re·gla	**When did you last have your period?**
¿ Está con la regla?	
es·ta kon la reg·la	**Are you menstruating?**
¿Está embarazada?	
es·ta em·ba·ra·sa·da	**Are you pregnant?**
Está embarazada.	
es·ta em·ba·ra·sa·da	**You're pregnant.**
¿Está usando algún anticonceptivo?	
es·ta oo·san·do al·goon an·tee·kon·sep·tee·vo	**Are you using contraception?**

allergies

alergias

I'm allergic to ...	*Soy alérgico/ alérgica ...* m/f	soy a·ler·khee·ko/ a·ler·khee·ka ...
He/She is allergic to ...	*Él/Ella es alérgico/a ...*	el/e·ya es a·ler·khee·ko/a ...
antibiotics	*a los antibióticos*	a los an·tee·byo·tee·kos
anti-inflammatories	*a los anti-inflamatorios*	a los an·tee·een·fla·ma·to·ryos
aspirin	*a la aspirina*	a la as·pee·ree·na
bees	*a las abejas*	a las a·be·khas
codeine	*a la codeína*	a la ko·de·ee·na
penicillin	*a la penicilina*	a la pe·nee·see·lee·na
pollen	*al polen*	al po·len
sulphur-based drugs	*a los medicamentos a base de azufre*	a los me·dee·ka·men·tos a ba·se de a·soo·fre

I have a skin allergy.
Tengo una alergia en la piel. — ten·go *oo*·na a·*ler*·khee·a en la pyel

antihistamines	*antihistamínicos* **m pl**	an·tee·ees·ta·*mee*·nee·kos
inhaler	*inhalador* **m**	een·a·la·*dor*
injection	*inyección* **f**	een·yek·*syon*

For phrases on food-related allergies, see **special diets & allergies**, page 170.

alternative treatments

tratamientos alternativos

I don't use (Western medicine).
Yo no uso (la medicina occidental). — yo no *oo*·so (la me·dee·*see*·na ok·see·den·*tal*)

I prefer …	*Prefiero …*	pre·*fye*·ro …
Can I see someone who practises …?	*¿Podría ver a alguien que practique la …?*	po·*dree*·a ver a *al*·gyen ke prak·*tee*·ke la …
acupuncture	*acupuntura*	a·koo·poon·*too*·ra
aromatherapy	*aromaterapia*	a·ro·ma·te·*ra*·pee·a
homeopathy	*homeopatía*	o·me·o·pa·*tee*·a
meditation	*meditación*	me·dee·ta·*syon*
naturopathy	*neuropatía*	ne·oo·ro·pa·*tee*·a
reflexology	*reflexología*	re·flek·so·lo·*khee*·a

parts of the body

partes del cuerpo

My … hurts.
Me duele el/la … **m/f** — me *dwe*·le el/la …

I can't move my …
No puedo mover el/la … **m/f** — no *pwe*·do mo·*ver* el/la …
No puedo mover los/las … **m/f pl** — no *pwe*·do mo·*ver* los/las …

My … is swollen.
Tengo el/la … hinchado/a. **m/f** — *ten*·go el/la … een·*cha*·do/a

For other parts of the body, see the **dictionary**.

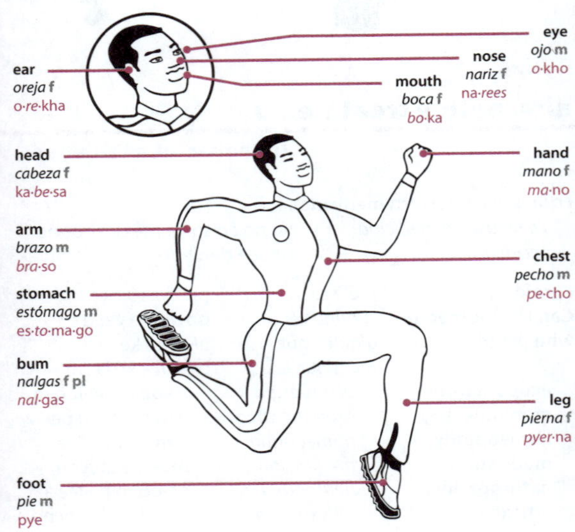

pharmacist

farmacéutico

I need something for (a headache).
Necesito algo para (el dolor de cabeza). ne·se·*see*·to *al*·go *pa*·ra (el do·*lor* de ka·*be*·sa)

Do I need a prescription for (antihistamines)?
¿Necesito una receta para (antihistamínicos)? ne·se·*see*·to *oo*·na re·*se*·ta *pa*·ra (an·tee·ees·ta·*mee*·nee·kos)

I have a prescription.
Tengo una receta. *ten*·go *oo*·na re·*se*·ta

How many times a day?
¿Cuántas veces al día? *kwan*·tas *ve*·ses al *dee*·a

Will it make me drowsy?
¿Me va a dar sueño? me va a dar *swe*·nyo

antiseptic n	*antiséptico* m	an·tee·*sep*·tee·ko
contraceptives	*anticonceptivo* m	an·tee·kon·sep·*tee*·vo
insect repellent	*repelente* m	re·pe·*len*·te
painkillers	*medicinas para el dolor* f pl	me·dee·*see*·nas *pa*·ra el do·*lor*
rehydration salts	*sales hidratantes* f pl	*sa*·les ee·dra·*tan*·tes
sunblock	*bloqueador* m	blo·ke·a·*dor*
thermometer	*termómetro* m	ter·*mo*·me·tro

the pharmacist may say ...

Antes de comer.	*an*·tes de ko·*mer*	**Before food.**
Con la comida.	kon la ko·*mee*·da	**With food.**
Después de comer.	des·*pwes* de ko·*mer*	**After food.**

Dos/Tres veces al día.
dos/tres *ve*·ses al *dee*·a **Twice/Three times a day.**

¿Ha tomado esto antes?
ha to·*ma*·do *es*·to *an*·tes **Have you taken this before?**

Tiene que terminar el tratamiento completo.
tye·ne ke ter·mee·*nar* el tra·ta·*myen*·to kom·*ple*·to **You must complete the course.**

dentist

dentista

I have a …	*Tengo …*	ten·go …
broken tooth	*un diente quebrado*	oon *dyen*·te ke·*bra*·do
cavity	*una caries*	*oo*·na *ka*·ryes
toothache	*un dolor de muela*	oon *do*·lor de *mwe*·la

I need a/an …	*Necesito …*	ne·se·*see*·to …
anaesthetic	*un anestésico*	oon a·nes·*te*·see·ko
filling	*una calza*	*oo*·na *kal*·sa

I've lost a filling.
Se me cayó una calza. — se me ka·*yo* *oo*·na *kal*·sa

My dentures are broken.
Mi dentadura está quebrada. — mee den·ta·*doo*·ra es·*ta* ke·*bra*·da

My gums hurt.
Me duelen las encías. — me *dwe*·len las en·*see*·as

I don't want it extracted.
No quiero que me la saque. — no *kye*·ro ke me la *sa*·ke

Ouch!
Ay! — ai

the dentist may say …

Abra grande.	*a*·bra *gran*·de	**Open wide.**
Enjuague.	en·*khwa*·ge	**Rinse.**
Esto no le va a doler.	*es*·to no le va a do·*ler*	**This won't hurt a bit.**
Muerda esto.	*mwer*·da *es*·to	**Bite down on this.**
No se mueva.	no se *mwe*·va	**Don't move.**
Vuelva, no he terminado.	*vwel*·va no e ter·mee·*na*·do	**Come back, I haven't finished.**

Spanish nouns in this dictionary have their gender indicated with ⓜ (masculine) and ⓕ (feminine). If adjectives and nouns have just one form for both genders, it's marked as ⓜ&ⓕ. Where adjectives and nouns have separate masculine and feminine forms, the endings are divided by a slash (eg *bello/a* ⓜ/ⓕ). In other cases we spell out the masculine and feminine forms in full for clarity of pronunciation (eg *embajador/embajadora* ⓜ/ⓕ). See the **phrasebuilder** for more on gender. Words are also marked as n (noun), a (adjective), adv (adverb), v (verb), pl (plural), sg (singular), inf (informal) and pol (polite) where necessary. Verbs are given in the infinitive – for details on how to change verbs for use in a sentence, see the **phrasebuilder**, page 28.

A

aboard *a bordo* a *bor*·do
abortion *aborto* ⓜ a·*bor*·to
about *sobre* *so*·bre
above *sobre* *so*·bre
abroad *en el extranjero* en el eks·tran·*khe*·ro
accident *accidente* ⓜ ak·see·*den*·te
accommodation *alojamiento* ⓜ a·lo·kha·*myen*·to
account (bill) *cuenta* ⓕ *kwen*·ta
acid *ácido* ⓜ *a*·see·do
across *a través* a tra·*ves*
activist *activista* ⓜ&ⓕ ak·tee·*vees*·ta
actor *actor/actriz* ⓜ/ⓕ ak·*tor*/ak·*trees*
acupuncture *acupuntura* ⓕ a·koo·poon·*too*·ra
adaptor *adaptador* ⓜ a·dap·ta·*dor*
addiction *adicción* ⓕ a·deek·*syon*
address *dirección* ⓕ dee·rek·*syon*
administration *administración* ⓕ ad·mee·nees·tra·*syon*
admission (price) *admisión* ⓕ ad·mee·*syon*
admit *admitir* ad·mee·*teer*
adult n&a *adulto/a* ⓜ/ⓕ a·*dool*·to/a
advertisement *anuncio* ⓜ a·*noon*·syo
advice *consejo* ⓜ kon·*se*·kho
aerobics *aeróbicos* ⓜ a·e·*ro*·bee·kos
aeroplane *avión* ⓜ a·*vyon*
Africa *África* ⓕ *a*·free·ka
after *después* des·*pwes*
afternoon *tarde* ⓕ *tar*·de
aftershave *loción para despues del afeitado* ⓕ lo·*syon* *pa*·ra des·*pwes* del a·fay·*ta*·do
again *otra vez* *o*·tra ves
age *edad* ⓕ e·*dad*
(three days) ago *hace (tres días)* *a*·se (tres *dee*·as)
agree *estar de acuerdo* es·*tar* de a·*kwer*·do
agriculture *agricultura* ⓕ a·gree·kool·*too*·ra
ahead *adelante* a·de·*lan*·te
AIDS *SIDA* ⓜ *see*·da
air *aire* ⓜ *ai*·re
air-conditioned *con aire acondicionado* kon *ai*·re a·kon·dee·syo·*na*·do
air conditioning *aire acondicionado* ⓜ *ai*·re a·kon·dee·syo·*na*·do
airline *aerolínea* ⓕ a·e·ro·*lee*·ne·a
airmail *correo aéreo* ⓜ ko·*re*·o a·e·re·o
airplane *avión* ⓜ a·*vyon*
airport *aeropuerto* ⓜ a·e·ro·*pwer*·to
airport tax *impuesto de salida* ⓜ eem·*pwes*·to de sa·*lee*·da
aisle (on plane) *pasillo* ⓜ pa·*see*·yo
alarm clock *reloj despertador* ⓜ re·*lokh* des·per·ta·*dor*
alcohol *alcohol* ⓜ al·*kol*
all *todo/a* ⓜ/ⓕ *to*·do/a
allergy *alergia* ⓕ a·ler·*khee*·a
all-terrain vehicle *camión de todo-terreno* ⓜ ka·*myon* de *to*·do te·*re*·no
almond *almendra* ⓕ al·*men*·dra
almost *casi* *ka*·see
alone *solo/a* ⓜ/ⓕ *so*·lo/a

already *ya* ya
also *también* tam·byen
altar *altar* ⓜ al·tar
altitude *altura* ⓕ al·too·ra
always *siempre* syem·pre
ambassador *embajador/embajadora* ⓜ/ⓕ em·ba·kha·dor/em·ba·kha·do·ra
ambulance *ambulancia* ⓕ am·boo·lan·sya
anaemia *anemia* ⓕ a·ne·mya
anarchist n&a *anarquista* ⓜ&ⓕ a·nar·kees·ta
ancient *antiguo/a* ⓜ/ⓕ an·tee·gwo/a
and *y* ee
angry *enfadado/a* ⓜ/ⓕ en·fa·da·do/a
animal *animal* ⓜ a·nee·mal
ankle *tobillo* ⓜ to·bee·yo
another *otro/a* ⓜ/ⓕ o·tro/a
answer *respuesta* ⓕ res·pwes·ta
answer v *responder* res·pon·der
ant *hormiga* ⓕ or·mee·ga
antibiotics *antibióticos* ⓜ pl an·tee·byo·tee·kos
antinuclear *antinuclear* an·tee·noo·kle·ar
antique *antigüedad* ⓕ an·tee·gwe·dad
antiseptic *antiséptico* ⓜ an·tee·sep·tee·ko
any *cualquier/cualquiera* ⓜ/ⓕ kwal·kyer/kwal·kye·ra
apartment *apartamento* ⓜ a·par·ta·men·to
appendix (body) *apéndice* ⓜ a·pen·dee·se
apple *manzana* ⓕ man·sa·na
appointment *cita* ⓕ see·ta
apricot *albaricoque* ⓜ al·ba·ree·ko·ke
April *abril* ⓜ a·breel
archaeological *arqueológico/a* ⓜ/ⓕ ar·ke·o·lo·khee·ko/a
architect *arquitecto/a* ⓜ/ⓕ ar·kee·tek·to/a
architecture *arquitectura* ⓕ ar·kee·tek·too·ra
argue *argumentar* ar·goo·men·tar
arm (body) *brazo* ⓜ bra·so
aromatherapy *aromaterapia* ⓕ a·ro·ma·te·ra·pya
arrest *arrestar* a·res·tar
arrivals *llegadas* ⓕ pl ye·ga·das
arrive *llegar* ye·gar
art *arte* ⓜ ar·te
art gallery *galería de arte* ⓕ ga·le·ree·a de ar·te
artist *artista* ⓜ&ⓕ ar·tees·ta
ashtray *cenicero* ⓜ se·nee·se·ro
Asia *Asia* ⓕ a·sya
ask (a question) *preguntar* pre·goon·tar
ask (for something) *pedir* pe·deer
asparagus *espárragos* ⓜ es·pa·ra·gos
aspirin *aspirina* ⓕ as·pee·ree·na
asthma *asma* ⓕ as·ma
at *en* en
athletics *atletismo* ⓜ at·le·tees·mo
Atlantic Ocean *Océano Atlántico* ⓜ o·se·a·no at·lan·tee·ko
ATM *cajero automático* ⓜ ka·khe·ro ow·to·ma·tee·ko
atmosphere *atmósfera* ⓕ at·mos·fe·ra
aubergine *berenjena* ⓕ be·ren·khe·na
August *agosto* ⓜ a·gos·to
aunt *tía* ⓕ tee·a
Australia *Australia* ⓕ ows·tra·lya
autumn *otoño* ⓜ o·to·nyo
avenue *avenida* ⓕ a·ve·nee·da
avocado *aguacate* ⓜ a·gwa·ka·te
awful *horrible* ⓜ&ⓕ o·ree·ble

B

B&W (film) a *blanco y negro* blan·ko ee ne·gro
baby *bebé* ⓜ&ⓕ be·be
baby food *comida de bebé* ⓕ ko·mee·da de be·be
baby powder *talcos* ⓜ pl tal·kos
babysitter *niñera* ⓕ nee·nye·ra
back (body) *espalda* ⓕ es·pal·da
back (position) *atrás* a·tras
backpack *mochila* ⓕ mo·chee·la
bacon *tocineta* ⓕ to·see·ne·ta
bad *malo/a* ⓜ/ⓕ ma·lo/a
bag *bolsa* ⓕ bol·sa
baggage *equipaje* ⓜ e·kee·pa·khe
baggage allowance *límite de equipaje* ⓜ lee·mee·te de e·kee·pa·khe
baggage claim *reclamo de equipaje* ⓜ re·kla·mo de e·kee·pa·khe
bakery *panadería* ⓕ pa·na·de·ree·a
balance (account) *saldo* ⓜ sal·do
balcony *balcón* ⓜ bal·kon
ball (sport) *bola* ⓕ bo·la
ballet *ballet* ⓜ ba·let
banana *banano* ⓜ ba·na·no
band (music) *grupo musical* ⓜ groo·po moo·see·kal

bandage *vendaje* ⓜ ven·*da*·khe
Band-Aid *curita* ⓕ koo·*ree*·ta
bank *banco* ⓜ *ban*·ko
bank account *cuenta bancaria* ⓕ *kwen*·ta ban·*ka*·rya
banknote *billete de banco* ⓜ bee·*ye*·te de *ban*·ko
baptism *bautismo* ⓜ bow·*tees*·mo
bar *bar* ⓜ bar
barber *barbero* ⓜ bar·*be*·ro
bar work *trabajo en el bar* ⓜ tra·*ba*·kho en el bar
baseball *béisbol* ⓜ *bays*·bol
basket *canasta* ⓕ ka·*nas*·ta
basketball *básquetbol* ⓜ *bas*·ket·bol
bath *baño* ⓜ *ba*·nyo
bathing suit *vestido de baño* ⓜ ves·*tee*·do de *ba*·nyo
bathroom *baño* ⓜ *ba*·nyo
battery *batería* ⓕ ba·te·*ree*·a
be (permanent) *ser* ser
be (temporary) *estar* es·*tar*
beach *playa* ⓕ *pla*·ya
beach volleyball *volibol de playa* ⓜ vo·lee·*bol* de *pla*·ya
bean *frijol* ⓜ free·*khol*
beansprout *frijol nacido* ⓜ free·*khol* na·*see*·do
beautician *estilista* ⓜ&ⓕ es·tee·*lees*·ta
beautiful *bello/a* ⓜ/ⓕ *be*·yo/a
beauty salon *salón de belleza* ⓜ sa·*lon* de be·*ye*·sa
because *porque* *por*·ke
bed *cama* ⓕ *ka*·ma
bedding *ropa de cama* ⓕ *ro*·pa de *ka*·ma
bed linen *sábana* ⓕ *sa*·ba·na
bedroom *cuarto* ⓜ *kwar*·to
bee *abeja* ⓕ a·*be*·kha
beef *carne de res/vaca* ⓕ *kar*·ne de res/*va*·ka
beer *cerveza* ⓕ ser·*ve*·sa
before *antes* *an*·tes
beggar *mendigo/a* ⓜ/ⓕ men·*dee*·go/a
behind *detrás* de·*tras*
Belgium *Bélgica* ⓕ *bel*·khee·ka
below *debajo* de·*ba*·kho
berth *litera* ⓕ lee·*te*·ra
beside *junto a* *khoon*·to a
(the) best *el/la mejor* ⓜ/ⓕ el/la me·*khor*
bet *apuesta* ⓕ a·*pwes*·ta
bet v *apostar* a·pos·*tar*
better *mejor* me·*khor*
between *entre* *en*·tre
Bible *Biblia* ⓕ *bee*·blya
bicycle *bicicleta* ⓕ bee·see·*kle*·ta
big *grande* ⓜ&ⓕ *gran*·de
bigger *más grande* ⓜ&ⓕ mas *gran*·de
(the) biggest *el/la más grande* ⓜ/ⓕ el/la mas *gran*·de
bike *bicicleta* ⓕ bee·see·*kle*·ta
bike chain *cadena de bicicleta* ⓕ ka·*de*·na de bee·see·*kle*·ta
bike lock *candado de bicicleta* ⓜ kan·*da*·do de bee·see·*kle*·ta
bike trail *sendero de bicicleta* ⓜ sen·*de*·ro de bee·see·*kle*·ta
bike shop *ciclo* ⓜ *see*·klo
bill (account/restaurant) *cuenta* ⓕ *kwen*·ta
binoculars *binoculares* ⓜ pl bee·no·koo·*la*·res
bird *pájaro* ⓜ *pa*·kha·ro
birth certificate *certificado de nacimiento* ⓜ ser·tee·fee·*ka*·do de na·see·*myen*·to
birthday *cumpleaños* ⓜ koom·ple·*a*·nyos
biscuit (savoury) *pancito* ⓜ pan·*see*·to
biscuit (sweet) *galleta* ⓕ ga·*ye*·ta
bite (dog) *mordida* ⓕ mor·*dee*·da
bite (insect) *picada* ⓕ pee·*ka*·da
bitter *amargo/a* ⓜ/ⓕ a·*mar*·go/a
black *negro/a* ⓜ/ⓕ *ne*·gro/a
black market *mercado negro* ⓜ mer·*ka*·do *ne*·gro
bladder *vejiga* ⓕ ve·*khee*·ga
blanket *cobija* ⓕ ko·*bee*·kha
blind *ciego/a* ⓜ/ⓕ *sye*·go/a
blister *ampolla* ⓕ am·*po*·ya
blocked *bloqueado/a* ⓜ/ⓕ blo·ke·*a*·do/a
blood *sangre* ⓕ *san*·gre
blood group *grupo sanguíneo* ⓜ *groo*·po san·*gee*·ne·o
blood pressure *presión sanguínea* ⓕ pre·*syon* san·*gee*·ne·a
blood test *prueba de sangre* ⓕ *prwe*·ba de *san*·gre
blue *azul* ⓜ&ⓕ a·*sool*
board (plane/ship) *abordar* a·bor·*dar*
boarding house *pensión* ⓕ pen·*syon*
boarding pass *tiquete de abordaje* ⓜ tee·*ke*·te de a·bor·*da*·khe
boat *barco* ⓜ *bar*·ko
body *cuerpo* ⓜ *kwer*·po

boiled *hervido/a* ⓜ/ⓕ er·*vee*·do/a

bone *hueso* ⓜ *we*·so

book *libro* ⓜ *lee*·bro

book (make a booking) *reservar* re·ser·*var*

booked out *sin espacio* seen es·*pa*·syo

book shop *librería* ⓕ lee·bre·*ree*·a

boots *botas* ⓕ pl *bo*·tas

border (geographic) *frontera* ⓕ fron·*te*·ra

bored *aburrido/a* ⓜ/ⓕ a·boo·*ree*·do/a

boring *aburrido/a* ⓜ/ⓕ a·boo·*ree*·do/a

borrow *pedir prestado* pe·*deer* pres·*ta*·do

botanic garden *jardín botánico* ⓜ khar·*deen* bo·*ta*·nee·ko

both *ambos/as* ⓜ/ⓕ pl *am*·bos/as

bottle *botella* ⓕ bo·*te*·ya

bottle opener *abridor* ⓜ a·bree·*dor*

bottle shop *licorera* ⓕ lee·ko·*re*·ra

bottom (body) *trasero* ⓜ tra·*se*·ro

bottom (position) *fondo* ⓜ *fon*·do

bowl *plato hondo* ⓜ *pla*·to *on*·do

box *caja* ⓕ *ka*·kha

boxer shorts *bóxer* ⓜ *bok*·ser

boxing *boxeo* ⓜ bok·*se*·o

boy *chico* ⓜ *chee*·ko

boyfriend *novio* ⓜ *no*·vyo

bra *bracier* ⓜ bra·*syer*

brakes *frenos* ⓜ pl *fre*·nos

brave *valiente* ⓜ&ⓕ va·*lyen*·te

bread *pan* ⓜ pan

bread rolls *bollos de pan* ⓜ pl *bo*·yos de pan

break (in general) *quebrar* ke·*brar*

break (smash) *romper* rom·*per*

break down (car) *quedarse varado* ke·*dar*·se va·*ra*·do

breakfast *desayuno* ⓜ de·sa·*yoo*·no

breast (body) *pecho* ⓜ *pe*·cho

breast (poultry) *pechuga* ⓕ pe·*choo*·ga

breasts (body) *senos* ⓜ pl *se*·nos

bribe *soborno* ⓜ so·*bor*·no

bribe v *sobornar* so·bor·*nar*

bridge (structure) *puente* ⓜ *pwen*·te

briefcase *valija* ⓕ va·*lee*·kha

bring *traer* tra·*er*

brochure *panfleto* ⓜ pan·*fle*·to

broken *quebrado/a* ⓜ/ⓕ ke·*bra*·do/a

broken down (car) *descompuesto/a* ⓜ/ⓕ des·kom·*pwes*·to/a

bronchitis *bronquitis* ⓕ bron·*kee*·tees

brother *hermano* ⓜ er·*ma*·no

brown *café* ⓜ&ⓕ ka·*fe*

bruise *moretón* ⓜ mo·re·*ton*

brush *cepillo* ⓜ se·*pee*·yo

bucket *balde* ⓜ *bal*·de

Buddhist n&a *budista* ⓜ&ⓕ boo·*dees*·ta

budget *presupuesto* ⓜ pre·soo·*pwes*·to

buffet *buffet* ⓜ boo·*fe*

bug *bicho* ⓜ *bee*·cho

build *construir* kons·troo·*eer*

builder *constructor/constructora* ⓜ/ⓕ kons·trook·*tor*/kons·trook·*to*·ra

building *edificio* ⓜ e·dee·*fee*·syo

burn *quemadura* ⓕ ke·ma·*doo*·ra

burnt *quemado/a* ⓜ/ⓕ ke·*ma*·do/a

bus *bus* ⓜ boos

bus station *estación de bus* ⓕ es·ta·*syon* de boos

bus stop *parada de bus* ⓕ pa·*ra*·da de boos

business *negocio* ⓜ ne·*go*·syo

business class *clase ejecutiva* ⓕ *kla*·se e·khe·koo·*tee*·va

businessman *hombre de negocios* ⓜ *om*·bre de ne·*go*·syos

businesswoman *mujer de negocios* ⓕ moo·*kher* de ne·*go*·syos

busker *artista callejero* ⓜ&ⓕ ar·*tees*·ta ka·ye·*khe*·ro

busy *ocupado/a* ⓜ/ⓕ o·koo·*pa*·do/a

but *pero* *pe*·ro

butcher *carnicero* ⓜ kar·nee·*se*·ro

butcher's shop *carnicería* ⓕ kar·nee·se·*ree*·a

butter *mantequilla* ⓕ man·te·*kee*·ya

butterfly *mariposa* ⓕ ma·ree·*po*·sa

button *botón* ⓜ bo·*ton*

buy *comprar* kom·*prar*

C

cabbage *repollo* ⓜ re·*po*·yo

cable car *teleférico* ⓜ te·le·*fe*·ree·ko

café *café* ⓜ ka·*fe*

cake *queque* ⓜ *ke*·ke

cake shop *pastelería* ⓕ pas·te·le·*ree*·a

calculator *calculadora* ⓕ kal·koo·la·*do*·ra

calendar *calendario* ⓜ ka·len·*da*·ryo

call (phone) *llamar* ya·*mar*

camera *cámara* ⓕ *ka*·ma·ra

camera shop *tienda de cámaras* ⓕ *tyen*·da de *ka*·ma·ras

camp *acampar* a·kam·*par*

camping ground *área de acampar* ⓕ a·re·a de a·kam·par
camping store *tienda de artículos para acampar* ⓕ tyen·da de ar·tee·koo·los pa·ra a·kam·par
camp site *sitio para acampar* ⓜ see·tyo pa·ra a·kam·par
can (be able/have permission) *poder* po·der
can (tin) *lata* ⓕ la·ta
Canada *Canadá* ⓕ ka·na·da
cancel *cancelar* kan·se·lar
cancer *cáncer* ⓜ kan·ser
candle *vela* ⓕ ve·la
candy *confite* ⓜ kon·fee·te
canoe *canoa* ⓕ ka·no·a
can opener *abrelatas* ⓜ a·bre·la·tas
cantaloupe *melón* ⓜ me·lon
capsicum *pimentón* ⓜ pee·men·ton
car *carro* ⓜ ka·ro
caravan *caravana* ⓕ ka·ra·va·na
cardiac arrest *ataque cardíaco* ⓜ a·ta·ke kar·dee·a·ko
cards (playing) *naipes* ⓜ pl nai·pes
care (for someone) *cuidar de* kwee·dar de
car hire *alquiler de carros* ⓜ al·kee·ler de ka·ros
Caribbean Sea *Mar Caribe* ⓜ mar ka·ree·be
car owner's title *título de propiedad* ⓜ tee·too·lo de pro·pee·e·dad
car park *parqueo* ⓜ par·ke·o
carpenter *carpintero* ⓜ kar·peen·te·ro
car registration *registro del carro* ⓜ re·khees·tro del ka·ro
carrot *zanahoria* ⓕ sa·na·o·rya
carry *llevar* ye·var
carton *cartón* ⓜ kar·ton
cash *efectivo* ⓜ e·fek·tee·vo
cash (a cheque) *cambiar (un cheque)* kam·byar (oon che·ke)
cashew *semilla de marañón* ⓕ se·mee·ya de ma·ra·nyon
cashier *cajero/a* ⓜ/ⓕ ka·khe·ro/a
cash register *caja* ⓕ ka·kha
casino *casino* ⓜ ka·see·no
cassette *cassette* ⓜ ka·se·te
castle *castillo* ⓜ kas·tee·yo
casual work *trabajo temporal* ⓜ tra·ba·kho tem·po·ral
cat *gato/a* ⓜ/ⓕ ga·to/a
cathedral *catedral* ⓕ ka·te·dral
Catholic n&a *católico/a* ⓜ/ⓕ ka·to·lee·ko/a
cave *cueva* ⓕ kwe·va
CD *CD* ⓜ se de
celebration *celebración* ⓕ se·le·bra·syon
cell phone *teléfono celular* ⓜ te·le·fo·no se·loo·lar
cemetery *cementerio* ⓜ se·men·te·ryo
cent *centavo* ⓜ sen·ta·vo
centimetre *centímetro* ⓜ sen·tee·me·tro
centre *centro* ⓜ sen·tro
ceramics *cerámica* ⓕ se·ra·mee·ka
cereal (breakfast) *cereal* ⓜ se·re·al
certificate *certificado* ⓜ ser·tee·fee·ka·do
chain *cadena* ⓕ ka·de·na
chair *silla* ⓕ see·ya
champagne *champaña* ⓕ cham·pa·nya
championships *campeonatos* ⓜ pl kam·pe·o·na·tos
chance *oportunidad* ⓕ o·por·too·nee·dad
change *cambio* ⓜ kam·byo
change (coins) *vuelto* ⓜ vwel·to
change (money) v *cambiar* kam·byar
changing room *vestidores* ⓜ pl ves·tee·do·res
charming *encantador/encantadora* ⓜ/ⓕ en·kan·ta·dor/en·kan·ta·do·ra
chat up (flirt) *ligar* lee·gar
cheap *barato/a* ⓜ/ⓕ ba·ra·to/a
cheat *tramposo/a* ⓜ/ⓕ tram·po·so/a
check v *revisar* re·vee·sar
check (banking) *cheque* ⓜ che·ke
check (bill) *cuenta* ⓕ kwen·ta
check-in (desk) *chequeo* ⓜ che·ke·o
checkpoint (border) *punto de control* ⓜ poon·to de kon·trol
cheese *queso* ⓜ ke·so
chef *chef* ⓜ shef
chemist (pharmacist) *farmacéutico/a* ⓜ/ⓕ far·ma·se·oo·tee·ko/a
chemist (pharmacy) *farmacia* ⓕ far·ma·sya
cheque (banking) *cheque* ⓜ che·ke
cherry *cereza* ⓕ se·re·sa
chess *ajedrez* ⓜ a·khe·dres
chest (body) *pecho* ⓜ pe·cho
chewing gum *chicle* ⓜ chee·kle
chicken *pollo* ⓜ po·yo
chicken pox *varicela* ⓕ va·ree·se·la
chickpea *garbanzo* ⓜ gar·ban·so
child *chiquito/a* ⓜ/ⓕ chee·kee·to/a

child-minding service *guardería* ⓕ gwar·de·*ree*·a
child seat *silla para niños* ⓕ *see*·ya *pa*·ra *nee*·nyos
children *niños/as* ⓜ/ⓕ pl *nee*·nyos/as
chilli *chile* ⓜ *chee*·le
chilli sauce *salsa picante* ⓕ *sal*·sa pee·*kan*·te
China *China* ⓕ *chee*·na
chiropractor *qiropráctico* ⓜ kee·ro·*prak*·tee·ko
chocolate *chocolate* ⓜ cho·ko·*la*·te
choose *escoger* es·ko·*kher*
chopping board *tabla para picar* ⓕ *ta*·bla *pa*·ra pee·*kar*
chopsticks *palillos chinos* ⓜ pl pa·*lee*·yos *chee*·nos
Christian n&a *cristiano/a* ⓜ/ⓕ krees·*tya*·no/a
Christian name *nombre cristiano* ⓜ *nom*·bre krees·*tya*·no
Christmas *Navidad* ⓕ na·vee·*dad*
Christmas Day *día de Navidad* ⓜ *dee*·a de na·vee·*dad*
Christmas Eve *víspera de Navidad* ⓕ *vees*·pe·ra de na·vee·*dad*
church *iglesia* ⓕ ee·*gle*·sya
cider *cidra* ⓕ *see*·dra
cigar *cigarro* ⓜ see·*ga*·ro
cigarette *cigarrillo* ⓜ see·ga·*ree*·yo
cigarette lighter *encendedor* ⓜ en·sen·de·*dor*
cinema *cine* ⓜ *see*·ne
circus *circo* ⓜ *seer*·ko
citizenship *ciudadanía* ⓕ syoo·da·da·*nee*·a
city *ciudad* ⓕ syoo·*dad*
city centre *centro de la ciudad* ⓜ *sen*·tro de la syoo·*dad*
civil rights *derechos civiles* ⓜ pl de·*re*·chos see·*vee*·les
clarinet *clarinete* ⓜ kla·ree·*ne*·te
class (category) *clase* ⓕ *kla*·se
class system *escalas sociales* ⓕ pl es·*ka*·las so·*sya*·les
classical *clásico/a* ⓜ/ⓕ *kla*·see·ko/a
clean *limpio/a* ⓜ/ⓕ *leem*·pyo/a
clean v *limpiar* leem·*pyar*
cleaning *limpieza* ⓕ leem·*pye*·sa
client *cliente* ⓜ klee·*en*·te
cliff *precipicio* ⓜ pre·see·*pee*·syo
climb v *escalar* es·ka·*lar*
cloakroom *guardaropa* ⓜ gwar·da·*ro*·pa
clock *reloj* ⓜ re·*lokh*
close (by) *cerca* *ser*·ka
close v *cerrar* se·*rar*
closed *cerrado/a* ⓜ/ⓕ se·*ra*·do/a
clothesline *tendedero* ⓜ ten·de·*de*·ro
clothing *ropa* ⓕ *ro*·pa
clothing store *tienda de ropa* ⓕ *tyen*·da de *ro*·pa
cloud *nube* ⓕ *noo*·be
cloud forest *bosque nuboso* ⓜ *bos*·ke noo·*bo*·so
cloudy *nublado/a* ⓜ/ⓕ noo·*bla*·do/a
clutch (car) *closh* ⓜ klosh
coach (bus) *bus* ⓜ boos
coach (trainer) *entrenador/entrenadora* ⓜ/ⓕ en·tre·na·*dor*/en·tre·na·*do*·ra
coach *entrenar* en·tre·*nar*
coast *costa* ⓕ *kos*·ta
coat *abrigo* ⓜ a·*bree*·go
cocaine *cocaína* ⓕ ko·ka·*ee*·na
cockroach *cucaracha* ⓕ koo·ka·*ra*·cha
cocktail *coctel* ⓜ kok·*tel*
cocoa *cacao* ⓜ ka·*kow*
coconut *coco* ⓜ *ko*·ko
coffee *café* ⓜ ka·*fe*
coins *monedas* ⓕ pl mo·*ne*·das
cold *frío/a* ⓜ/ⓕ *free*·o/a
cold (illness) *resfriado* ⓜ res·free·*a*·do
colleague *colega* ⓜ&ⓕ ko·*le*·ga
collect call *llamada a cobrar* ⓕ ya·*ma*·da a ko·*brar*
college (university) *universidad* ⓕ oo·nee·ver·see·*dad*
colour *color* ⓜ ko·*lor*
comb *peine* ⓜ *pay*·ne
come *venir* ve·*neer*
comedy *comedia* ⓕ ko·*me*·dya
comfortable *cómodo/a* ⓜ/ⓕ *ko*·mo·do/a
commission *conmoción* ⓕ kon·mo·*syon*
communications (profession) *comunicación* ⓕ ko·moo·nee·ka·*syon*
communion *comunión* ⓕ ko·moo·*nyon*
communist n&a *comunista* ⓜ&ⓕ ko·moo·*nees*·ta
companion *compañero/a* ⓜ/ⓕ kom·pa·*nye*·ro/a
company (firm) *compañía* ⓕ kom·pa·*nyee*·a
compass *brújula* ⓕ *broo*·khoo·la
complain *quejarse* ke·*khar*·se

C

DICTIONARY

complaint *queja* ⓕ *ke*·kha
complimentary (free) *gratis* ⓜ&ⓕ *gra*·tees
computer *computadora* ⓕ kom·poo·ta·*do*·ra
computer game *juego de computadora* ⓜ *khwe*·go de kom·poo·ta·*do*·ra
concert *concierto* ⓜ kon·*syer*·to
concussion *contusión* ⓕ kon·too·*syon*
conditioner (hair) *acondicionador* ⓜ a·kon·dee·syo·na·*dor*
condom *preservativo* ⓜ pre·ser·va·*tee*·vo
conference (big) *congreso* ⓜ kon·*gre*·so
conference (small) *conferencia* ⓕ kon·fe·*ren*·sya
confession (religious) *confesión* ⓕ kon·fe·*syon*
confirm (a booking) *confirmar* kon·feer·*mar*
congratulations *felicidades* fe·lee·see·*da*·des
conjunctivitis *conjuntivitis* ⓕ kon·khoon·tee·*vee*·tees
connection *conexión* ⓕ ko·nek·*syon*
conservative n&a *conservador/conservadora* ⓜ/ⓕ kon·ser·va·*dor*/kon·ser·va·*do*·ra
constipation *estreñimiento* ⓜ es·tre·nyee·*myen*·to
consulate *consulado* ⓜ kon·soo·*la*·do
contact lenses *lentes de contacto* ⓜ pl *len*·tes de kon·*tak*·to
contact lens solution *líquido para lentes de contacto* ⓜ *lee*·kee·do *pa*·ra *len*·tes de kon·*tak*·to
contraceptives *anticonceptivos* ⓜ pl an·tee·kon·sep·*tee*·vos
contract *contrato* ⓜ kon·*tra*·to
convenience store *súper* ⓜ *soo*·per
convent *convento* ⓜ kon·*ven*·to
cook *cocinero/a* ⓜ/ⓕ ko·see·*ne*·ro/a
cook *cocinar* ko·see·*nar*
cookie *galleta* ⓕ ga·*ye*·ta
cooking *cocina* ⓕ ko·*see*·na
cool (temperature) *fresco/a* ⓜ/ⓕ *fres*·ko/a
corkscrew *sacacorchos* ⓜ sa·ka·*kor*·chos
corn *maíz* ⓜ ma·*ees*
corner *esquina* ⓕ es·*kee*·na
cornflakes *cornflakes* ⓜ pl *korn*·fleks
corrupt *corrupto/a* ⓜ/ⓕ ko·*roop*·to/a
corruption *corrupción* ⓕ ko·roop·*syon*
cost (price) *precio* ⓜ *pre*·syo
cost v *costar* kos·*tar*
cotton *algodón* ⓜ al·go·*don*
cotton balls *bolitas de algodón* ⓕ pl bo·*lee*·tas de al·go·*don*
cotton buds (swabs) *aplicadores* ⓜ pl a·plee·ka·*do*·res
cough *tos* ⓕ tos
cough v *toser* to·*ser*
cough medicine *jarabe para la tos* ⓜ kha·*ra*·be *pa*·ra la tos
count *contar* kon·*tar*
counter (at bar) *barra* ⓕ *ba*·ra
country *país* ⓜ pa·*ees*
countryside *campo* ⓜ *kam*·po
coupon *cupón* ⓜ koo·*pon*
court (legal) *corte* ⓕ *kor*·te
court (tennis) *cancha de tenis* ⓕ *kan*·cha de *te*·nees
cover charge *entrada* ⓕ en·*tra*·da
cow *vaca* ⓕ *va*·ka
cracker *galleta salada* ⓕ ga·*ye*·ta sa·*la*·da
crafts *artesanías* ⓕ pl ar·te·sa·*nee*·as
crash *choque* ⓜ *cho*·ke
crazy *loco/a* ⓜ/ⓕ *lo*·ko/a
cream (food/lotion) *crema* ⓕ *kre*·ma
crèche *cuna* ⓕ *koo*·na
credit *crédito* ⓜ *kre*·dee·to
credit card *tarjeta de crédito* ⓕ tar·*khe*·ta de *kre*·dee·to
cricket (sport) *cricket* ⓜ *kree*·ket
cross (religious) *cruz* ⓕ kroos
crowded *lleno/a de gente* ⓜ/ⓕ *ye*·no/a de *khen*·te
cucumber *pepino* ⓜ pe·*pee*·no
cup *taza* ⓕ *ta*·sa
cupboard *armario* ⓜ ar·*ma*·ryo
currency exchange *cambio de moneda* ⓜ *kam*·byo de mo·*ne*·da
current (electricity) *corriente* ⓕ ko·*ryen*·te
current affairs *actualidad* ⓕ ak·twa·lee·*dad*
custom *costumbre* ⓕ kos·*toom*·bre
customs (immigration) *aduana* ⓕ a·*dwa*·na
cut *cortada* ⓕ kor·*ta*·da
cut v *cortar* kor·*tar*
cutlery *cubiertos* ⓜ pl koo·*byer*·tos
CV *currículum* ⓜ koo·*ree*·koo·loom
cycle (ride) *andar en bicicleta* an·*dar* en bee·see·*kle*·ta
cycling *ciclismo* ⓜ see·*klees*·mo
cyclist *ciclista* ⓜ&ⓕ see·*klees*·ta
cystitis *cistitis* ⓕ sees·*tee*·tees

D

dad *papá* ⓜ pa·pa
daily adv *todos los días* to·dos los dee·as
dance *baile* ⓜ bai·le
dance v *bailar* bai·lar
dangerous *peligroso/a* ⓜ/ⓕ pe·lee·gro·so/a
dark (colour/night) *oscuro/a* ⓜ/ⓕ os·koo·ro/a
date (appointment) *cita* ⓕ see·ta
date (day) *fecha* ⓕ fe·cha
date (go out with) *salir con* sa·leer kon
date of birth *fecha de nacimiento* ⓕ fe·cha de na·see·myen·to
daughter *hija* ⓕ ee·kha
dawn *amanecer* ⓜ a·ma·ne·ser
day *día* ⓜ dee·a
day after tomorrow *pasado mañana* ⓜ pa·sa·do ma·nya·na
day before yesterday *anteayer* ⓜ an·te·a·yer
dead *muerto/a* ⓜ/ⓕ mwer·to/a
deaf *sordo/a* ⓜ/ⓕ sor·do/a
deal (cards) *repartir* re·par·teer
December *diciembre* ⓜ dee·syem·bre
decide *decidir* de·see·deer
deep *hondo/a* ⓜ/ⓕ on·do/a
deforestation *deforestación* ⓕ de·fo·res·ta·syon
degrees (temperature) *grados* ⓜ pl gra·dos
delay *atraso* ⓜ a·tra·so
delicatessen *delicatessen* ⓕ de·lee·ka·te·sen
deliver *enviar* en·vyar
democracy *democracia* ⓕ de·mo·kra·sya
demonstration (display) *demostración* ⓕ de·mos·tra·syon
demonstration (rally) *manifestación* ⓕ ma·nee·fes·ta·syon
Denmark *Dinamarca* ⓕ dee·na·mar·ka
dental floss *hilo dental* ⓜ ee·lo den·tal
dentist *dentista* ⓜ&ⓕ den·tees·ta
deodorant *desodorante* ⓜ de·so·do·ran·te
depart *partir* par·teer
department store *tienda por departamentos* ⓕ tyen·da por de·par·ta·men·tos
departure *salida* ⓕ sa·lee·da
departure gate *puerta de salida* ⓕ pwer·ta de sa·lee·da
deposit (bank) *depósito* ⓜ de·po·see·to
descendent *descendiente* ⓜ de·sen·dyen·te
desert *desierto* ⓜ de·syer·to
design *diseño* ⓜ dee·se·nyo
dessert *postre* ⓜ pos·tre
destination *destino* ⓜ des·tee·no
details *detalles* ⓜ pl de·ta·yes
diabetes *diabetes* ⓕ dee·a·be·tes
dial tone *tono* ⓜ to·no
diaper *pañal* ⓜ pa·nyal
diaphragm (contraceptive) *diafragma* ⓜ dya·frag·ma
diarrhoea *diarrea* ⓕ dee·a·re·a
diary *agenda* ⓕ a·khen·da
dice *dados* ⓜ pl da·dos
dictionary *diccionario* ⓜ deek·syo·na·ryo
die *morir* mo·reer
diet *dieta* ⓕ dye·ta
different *diferente* ⓜ&ⓕ dee·fe·ren·te
difficult *difícil* ⓜ&ⓕ dee·fee·seel
digital *digital* ⓜ&ⓕ dee·khee·tal
dinner *cena* ⓕ se·na
direct *directo/a* ⓜ/ⓕ dee·rek·to/a
direct-dial *marcación directa* ⓕ mar·ka·syon dee·rek·ta
direction *dirección* ⓕ dee·rek·syon
director *director/directora* ⓜ/ⓕ dee·rek·tor/dee·rek·to·ra
dirty *sucio/a* ⓜ/ⓕ soo·syo/a
disabled *discapacitado/a* ⓜ/ⓕ dees·ka·pa·see·ta·do/a
disco *discoteca* ⓕ dees·ko·te·ka
discount *descuento* ⓜ des·kwen·to
discrimination *discriminación* ⓕ dees·kree·mee·na·syon
disease *enfermedad* ⓕ en·fer·me·dad
dish *plato* ⓜ pla·to
disk (CD-ROM) *CD-ROM* ⓜ se de rom
disk (floppy) *disquete* ⓜ dees·ke·te
diving *buceo* ⓜ boo·se·o
diving equipment *equipo de buceo* ⓜ e·kee·po de boo·se·o
divorced *divorciado/a* ⓜ/ⓕ dee·vor·sya·do/a
dizzy *mareado/a* ⓜ/ⓕ ma·re·a·do/a
do *hacer* a·ser
doctor *doctor/doctora* ⓜ/ⓕ dok·tor/dok·to·ra
documentary *documental* ⓜ do·koo·men·tal
dog *perro/a* ⓜ/ⓕ pe·ro/a
doll *muñeca* ⓕ moo·nye·ka
dollar *dólar* ⓜ do·lar

door *puerta* ⓕ pwer·ta
dope (drugs) *hierba* ⓕ • *mota* ⓕ yer·ba • mo·ta
double *doble* ⓜ&ⓕ do·ble
double bed *cama matrimonial* ⓕ ka·ma ma·tree·mo·nyal
double room *cuarto doble* ⓜ kwar·to do·ble
down *abajo* a·ba·kho
downhill *cuesta abajo* kwes·ta a·ba·kho
dozen *docena* ⓕ do·se·na
drama *drama* ⓜ dra·ma
dream *sueño* ⓜ swe·nyo
dress *vestido* ⓜ ves·tee·do
dried *seco/a* ⓜ/ⓕ se·ko/a
dried fruit *frutas secas* ⓕ pl froo·tas se·kas
drink *bebida* ⓕ be·bee·da
drink v *beber* • *tomar* be·ber • to·mar
drink (alcoholic) *trago* ⓜ tra·go
drive *conducir* kon·doo·seer
driving licence *licencia de conductor* ⓕ lee·sen·sya de kon·dook·tor
drug (illicit) *droga* ⓕ dro·ga
drug (medicine) *medicamento* ⓜ me·dee·ka·men·to
drug addiction *drogadicción* ⓕ dro·ga·deek·syon
drug dealer *narcotraficante* ⓜ&ⓕ nar·ko·tra·fee·kan·te
drug trafficking *narcotráfico* ⓜ nar·ko·tra·fee·ko
drug user *drogadicto/a* ⓜ/ⓕ dro·ga·deek·to/a
drum (instrument) *tambor* ⓜ tam·bor
drums (kit) *batería* ⓕ ba·te·ree·a
drunk *borracho/a* ⓜ/ⓕ bo·ra·cho/a
dry *seco/a* ⓜ/ⓕ se·ko/a
dry (clothes, etc) *secar* se·kar
dry (onself) *secarse* se·kar·se
duck *pato* ⓜ pa·to
dummy (pacifier) *chupeta* ⓕ choo·pe·ta
DVD *DVD* ⓜ de ve de

E

each *cada* ka·da
ear *oreja* ⓕ o·re·kha
early adv *temprano* tem·pra·no
earn *ganar* ga·nar
earplugs *tapones para los oídos* ⓜ pl ta·po·nes pa·ra los o·ee·dos
earrings *aretes* ⓜ pl a·re·tes
Earth *tierra* ⓕ tye·ra
earthquake *terremoto* ⓜ te·re·mo·to
east *este* ⓜ es·te
Easter *Pascua* ⓕ pas·kwa
easy *fácil* ⓜ&ⓕ fa·seel
eat *comer* ko·mer
economy class *clase económica* ⓕ kla·se e·ko·no·mee·ka
ecstacy (drug) *éxtasis* ⓜ eks·ta·sees
eczema *eczema* ⓕ ek·se·ma
education *educación* ⓕ e·doo·ka·syon
egg *huevo* ⓜ we·vo
eggplant *berenjena* ⓕ be·ren·khe·na
election *elección* ⓕ e·lek·syon
electrical store *tienda de electrónicos* ⓕ tyen·da de e·lek·tro·nee·kos
electrician *electricista* ⓜ&ⓕ e·lek·tree·sees·ta
electricity *electricidad* ⓕ e·lek·tree·see·dad
elevator *ascensor* ⓜ a·sen·sor
email *correo electrónico* ⓜ ko·re·o e·lek·tro·nee·ko
embarrassed *avergonzado/a* ⓜ/ⓕ a·ver·gon·sa·do/a
embassy *embajada* ⓕ em·ba·kha·da
emergency *emergencia* ⓕ e·mer·khen·sya
emotional *emocional* ⓜ&ⓕ e·mo·syo·nal
employee *empleado/a* ⓜ/ⓕ em·ple·a·do/a
employer *empleador/empleadora* ⓜ/ⓕ em·ple·a·dor/em·ple·a·do·ra
empty *vacío/a* ⓜ/ⓕ va·see·o/a
end *fin* ⓜ feen
endangered species *especie en peligro de extinción* ⓕ es·pe·sye en pe·lee·gro de eks·teen·syon
engaged (phone) *ocupado* o·koo·pa·do
engaged (to marry) *comprometido/a* ⓜ/ⓕ kom·pro·me·tee·do/a
engagement (to marry) *compromiso* ⓜ kom·pro·mee·so
engine *motor* ⓜ mo·tor
engineer *ingeniero/a* ⓜ/ⓕ een·khe·nye·ro/a
engineering *ingeniería* ⓕ een·khe·nye·ree·a
England *Inglaterra* ⓕ een·gla·te·ra
English (language) *inglés* ⓜ een·gles
English a *inglés/inglesa* ⓜ/ⓕ een·gles/een·gle·sa
enjoy (oneself) *disfrutar* dees·froo·tar
enough *suficiente* soo·fee·syen·te

enter *entrar* en·*trar*
entertainment guide *guía de entretenimiento* ⓕ gee·a de en·tre·te·nee·*myen*·to
entry *entrada* ⓕ en·*tra*·da
envelope *sobre* ⓜ *so*·bre
environment *medio ambiente* ⓜ *me*·dyo am·*byen*·te
epilepsy *epilepsia* ⓕ e·pee·*lep*·sya
equality *igualdad* ⓕ ee·gwal·*dad*
equal opportunity *igualdad de oportunidades* ⓕ ee·gwal·*dad* de o·por·too·nee·*da*·des
equipment *equipo* ⓜ e·*kee*·po
escalator *gradas* ⓕ pl *gra*·das
estate agent *agente de bienes raíces* ⓜ a·*khen*·te de *bye*·nes ra·*ee*·ses
estuary *estuario* ⓜ es·*twa*·ryo
euro *euro* ⓜ *e*·oo·ro
Europe *Europa* ⓕ e·oo·*ro*·pa
euthanasia *eutanasia* ⓕ e·oo·ta·*na*·sya
evening *noche* ⓕ *no*·che
every *todo/a* ⓜ/ⓕ *to*·do/a
everyone *todos/as* ⓜ/ⓕ pl *to*·dos/as
everything *todo* *to*·do
exactly *exactamente* ek·sak·ta·*men*·te
example *ejemplo* ⓜ e·*khem*·plo
excellent *excelente* ⓜ&ⓕ ek·se·*len*·te
excess baggage *exceso de equipaje* ⓜ ek·*se*·so de e·kee·*pa*·khe
exchange *cambio* ⓜ *kam*·byo
exchange (money) *cambiar* kam·*byar*
exchange rate *tipo de cambio* ⓜ *tee*·po de *kam*·byo
excluded *excluido/a* ⓜ/ⓕ eks·kloo·*ee*·do/a
exhaust (car) *escape* ⓕ es·*ka*·pe
exhibition *exhibición* ⓕ ek·see·bee·*syon*
exit *salida* ⓕ sa·*lee*·da
expensive *caro/a* ⓜ/ⓕ *ka*·ro/a
experience *experiencia* ⓕ eks·pe·*ryen*·sya
exploitation *explotación* ⓕ eks·plo·ta·*syon*
express *directo/a* ⓜ/ⓕ dee·*rek*·to/a
express mail *correo express* ⓜ ko·*re*·o eks·*pres*
extension (visa) *extensión* ⓕ eks·ten·*syon*
eyes *ojos* ⓜ pl *o*·khos
eye drops *gotas para los ojos* ⓕ pl *go*·tas *pa*·ra los *o*·khos

F

fabric *tela* ⓕ *te*·la
face *cara* ⓕ *ka*·ra
face cloth *paño para la cara* ⓜ *pa*·nyo *pa*·ra la *ka*·ra
factory *fábrica* ⓕ *fa*·bree·ka
fall (autumn) *otoño* ⓜ o·*to*·nyo
fall (down) v *caer* ka·*er*
family *familia* ⓕ fa·*mee*·lya
family name *apellido* ⓜ a·pe·*yee*·do
famous *famoso/a* ⓜ/ⓕ fa·*mo*·so/a
fan (hand-held) *abanico* ⓜ a·ba·*nee*·ko
fan (machine) *ventilador* ⓜ ven·tee·la·*dor*
fan (sport, etc) *aficionado/a* ⓜ/ⓕ a·fee·syo·*na*·do/a
fanbelt *faja del abanico* ⓕ *fa*·kha del a·ba·*nee*·ko
far (away) *lejos* *le*·khos
fare *tarifa* ⓕ ta·*ree*·fa
farm *finca* ⓕ *feen*·ka
farmer *finquero/a* ⓜ/ⓕ feen·*ke*·ro/a
fashion *moda* ⓕ *mo*·da
fast *rápido/a* ⓜ/ⓕ *ra*·pee·do/a
fat *gordo/a* ⓜ/ⓕ *gor*·do/a
father *padre* ⓜ *pa*·dre
father-in-law *suegro* ⓜ *swe*·gro
faucet *tubo* ⓜ *too*·bo
fault (someone's) *culpa* ⓕ *kool*·pa
faulty *defectuoso/a* ⓜ/ⓕ de·fek·*two*·so/a
fax machine *fax* ⓜ faks
February *febrero* ⓜ fe·*bre*·ro
feed *dar de comer* dar de ko·*mer*
feel (emotions) *sentir* sen·*teer*
feelings *sentimientos* ⓜ pl seen·tee·*myen*·tos
female *hembra* ⓕ *em*·bra
fence *cerca* ⓕ *ser*·ka
fencing (sport) *esgrima* ⓕ es·*gree*·ma
ferry *ferry* ⓜ *fe*·ree
festival *fiesta* ⓕ *fyes*·ta
fever *fiebre* ⓕ *fye*·bre
few *poco/a* ⓜ/ⓕ *po*·ko/a
fiancé *prometido* ⓜ pro·me·*tee*·do
fiancée *prometida* ⓕ pro·me·*tee*·da
fiction *ficción* ⓕ feek·*syon*
fig *higo* ⓜ *ee*·go
fight *pelea* ⓕ pe·*le*·a
fill *llenar* ye·*nar*
fillet *filete* ⓜ fee·*le*·te

film (cinema) *película* Ⓕ pe·*lee*·koo·la
film (for camera) *rollo* Ⓜ *ro*·yo
film speed *asa* Ⓜ *a*·sa
filtered *filtrado/a* Ⓜ/Ⓕ feel·*tra*·do/a
find *encontrar* en·kon·*trar*
fine adv *bien* byen
fine (payment) *multa* Ⓕ *mool*·ta
finger *dedo* Ⓜ *de*·do
finish *meta* Ⓕ *me*·ta
finish v *terminar* ter·mee·*nar*
Finland *Finlandia* Ⓕ feen·*lan*·dya
fire *fuego* Ⓜ *fwe*·go
firewood *leña* Ⓕ *le*·nya
first *primero/a* Ⓜ/Ⓕ pree·*me*·ro/a
first class *primera clase* Ⓕ pree·*me*·ra *kla*·se
first-aid kit *maletín de primeros auxilios* Ⓜ ma·le·*teen* de pree·*me*·ros owk·*see*·lyos
first name *nombre cristiano* Ⓜ *nom*·bre krees·*tya*·no
fish (animal) *pez* Ⓜ pes
fish (meat) *pescado* Ⓜ pes·*ka*·do
fishing *pesca* Ⓕ *pes*·ka
fishmonger *vendedor de pescado* Ⓜ ven·de·*dor* de pes·*ka*·do
fish shop *tienda de pesca* Ⓕ *tyen*·da de *pes*·ka
flag *bandera* Ⓕ ban·*de*·ra
flannel (face cloth) *franela* Ⓕ fra·*ne*·la
flash (camera) *flash* Ⓜ flash
flashlight (torch) *foco* Ⓜ *fo*·ko
flat *plano/a* Ⓜ/Ⓕ *pla*·no/a
flat (apartment) *apartamento* Ⓜ a·par·ta·*men*·to
flea *pulga* Ⓕ *pool*·ga
fleamarket *mercado de pulgas* Ⓜ mer·*ka*·do de *pool*·gas
flight *vuelo* Ⓜ *vwe*·lo
flood *inundación* Ⓕ ee·noon·da·*syon*
floor (ground) *suelo* Ⓜ *swe*·lo
floor (storey) *piso* Ⓜ *pee*·so
florist (shop) *floristería* Ⓕ flo·rees·te·*ree*·a
flour *harina* Ⓕ a·*ree*·na
flower *flor* Ⓕ flor
flu *gripe* Ⓕ *gree*·pe
flute *flauta* Ⓕ *flow*·ta
fly *mosca* Ⓕ *mos*·ka
fly v *volar* vo·*lar*
foggy *con neblina* kon ne·*blee*·na
follow *seguir* se·*geer*
food *comida* Ⓕ ko·*mee*·da
food supplies *provisiones* Ⓕ pl pro·vee·*syo*·nes
foot *pie* Ⓜ pye
football (soccer) *fútbol* Ⓜ *foot*·bol
footpath *sendero* Ⓜ sen·*de*·ro
foreign *extranjero/a* Ⓜ/Ⓕ eks·tran·*khe*·ro/a
forest *bosque* Ⓜ *bos*·ke
forever *para siempre* *pa*·ra *syem*·pre
forget *olvidar* ol·vee·*dar*
forgive *perdonar* per·do·*nar*
fork *tenedor* Ⓜ te·ne·*dor*
fortnight *quincena* Ⓕ keen·*se*·na
fortune teller *adivino/a* Ⓜ/Ⓕ a·dee·*vee*·no/a
foul (soccer) *faul* Ⓜ *fa*·ool
foyer *vestíbulo* Ⓜ ves·*tee*·boo·lo
fragile *frágil* Ⓜ&Ⓕ *fra*·kheel
France *Francia* Ⓕ *fran*·sya
free (available) *disponible* Ⓜ&Ⓕ dees·po·*nee*·ble
free (gratis) *gratis* Ⓜ&Ⓕ *gra*·tees
free (not bound) *libre* Ⓜ&Ⓕ *lee*·bre
freeze *congelar* kon·khe·*lar*
French (language) *francés* fran·*ses*
fresh *fresco/a* Ⓜ/Ⓕ *fres*·ko/a
Friday *viernes* Ⓜ *vyer*·nes
fridge *refri* Ⓜ *re*·free
fried *frito/a* Ⓜ/Ⓕ *free*·to/a
friend *amigo/a* Ⓜ/Ⓕ a·*mee*·go/a
from *de • desde* de • *des*·de
frost *escarcha* Ⓕ es·*kar*·cha
frozen *congelado/a* Ⓜ/Ⓕ kon·khe·*la*·do/a
fruit *fruta* Ⓕ *froo*·ta
fry *freír* fre·*eer*
frying pan *sartén* Ⓜ sar·*ten*
full *lleno/a* Ⓜ/Ⓕ *ye*·no/a
full time n *tiempo completo* Ⓜ *tyem*·po kom·*ple*·to
fun *divertido/a* Ⓜ/Ⓕ dee·ver·*tee*·do/a
funeral *funeral* Ⓜ foo·ne·*ral*
funny *vacilón/vacilona* Ⓜ/Ⓕ va·see·*lon*/va·see·*lo*·na
furniture *muebles* Ⓜ pl *mwe*·bles
future *futuro* Ⓜ foo·*too*·ro

G

game (sport) *partido* Ⓜ par·*tee*·do
garage *garaje* Ⓜ ga·*ra*·khe
garbage *basura* Ⓕ ba·*soo*·ra

garbage can *basurero* ⓜ ba·soo·*re*·ro
garden *jardín* ⓜ khar·*deen*
gardener *jardinero/a* ⓜ/ⓕ khar·dee·*ne*·ro/a
gardening *jardinería* ⓕ khar·dee·ne·*ree*·a
garlic *ajo* ⓜ *a*·kho
gas (cooking) *gas* ⓜ gas
gas (petrol) *gasolina* ⓕ ga·so·*lee*·na
gas cartridge *cilindro de gas* ⓜ see·*leen*·dro de gas
gas station *bomba* ⓕ *bom*·ba
gastroenteritis *gastritis* ⓕ gas·*tree*·tees
gate (airport, etc) *puerta* ⓕ *pwer*·ta
gauze *gasa* ⓕ *ga*·sa
gay n&a *gay* gay
gearbox *caja de cambios* ⓕ *ka*·kha de *kam*·byos
German (language) *alemán* a·le·*man*
Germany *Alemania* ⓕ a·le·*ma*·nya
get *obtener* ob·te·*ner*
get off (bus, train) *bajar* ba·*khar*
gift *regalo* ⓜ re·*ga*·lo
gig *chivo* ⓜ *chee*·vo
gin *ginebra* ⓕ khee·*ne*·bra
girl *chiquita* ⓕ chee·*kee*·ta
girlfriend *novia* ⓕ *no*·vya
give *dar* dar
given name *nombre cristiano* ⓜ *nom*·bre krees·*tya*·no
glandular fever *mononucleosis* ⓕ mo·no·noo·kle·*o*·sees
glass (drinking) *vaso* ⓜ *va*·so
glasses (spectacles) *anteojos* ⓜ pl an·te·*o*·khos
gloves *guantes* ⓜ pl *gwan*·tes
glue *pegamento* ⓜ pe·ga·*men*·to
go *ir* eer
go out (with) *salir (con)* sa·*leer* (kon)
go shopping *ir de compras* eer de *kom*·pras
goal (sport) *gol* ⓜ gol
goalkeeper *portero* ⓜ por·*te*·ro
goat *cabra* ⓕ *ka*·bra
god *dios* ⓜ dee·*os*
goggles (diving) *mascara* ⓕ mas·*ka*·ra
goggles (swimming) *mascarilla* ⓕ mas·ka·*ree*·ya
gold *oro* ⓜ *o*·ro
golf ball *bola de golf* ⓕ *bo*·la de golf
golf course *campo de golf* ⓜ *kam*·po de golf
good *bueno/a* ⓜ/ⓕ *bwe*·no/a
goodbye *adiós* a·*dyos*

government *gobierno* ⓜ go·*byer*·no
gram *gramo* ⓜ *gra*·mo
grandchild *nieto/a* ⓜ/ⓕ *nye*·to/a
grandfather *abuelo* ⓜ a·*bwe*·lo
grandmother *abuela* ⓕ a·*bwe*·la
grapes *uvas* ⓕ pl *oo*·vas
grass (lawn) *zacate* ⓜ sa·*ka*·te
grateful *agradecido/a* ⓜ/ⓕ a·gra·de·*see*·do/a
grave *tumba* ⓕ *toom*·ba
great (fantastic) *fantástico/a* ⓜ/ⓕ fan·*tas*·tee·ko
green *verde* ⓜ&ⓕ *ver*·de
greengrocer *verdurería* ⓕ ve·doo·re·*ree*·a
grey *gris* ⓜ&ⓕ grees
grocery store *súper* ⓜ *soo*·per
grow *crecer* kre·*ser*
guaranteed *garantizado/a* ⓜ/ⓕ ga·ran·tee·*sa*·do/a
guess *adivinar* a·dee·vee·*nar*
guesthouse *pensión* ⓕ pen·*syon*
guide (audio) *guía* ⓕ *gee*·a
guide (person) *guía* ⓜ&ⓕ *gee*·a
guidebook *guía turistica* ⓕ *gee*·a too·*rees*·tee·ka
guide dog *perro guía* ⓜ *pe*·ro *gee*·a
guided tour *tour con guía* ⓜ toor kon *gee*·a
guilty *culpable* ⓜ&ⓕ kool·*pa*·ble
guitar *guitarra* ⓕ gee·*ta*·ra
gum (chewing) *chicle* ⓜ *chee*·kle
gums (mouth) *encías* ⓕ pl en·*see*·as
gun *pistola* ⓕ pees·*to*·la
gym (place) *gimnasio* ⓜ kheem·*na*·syo
gymnastics *gimnasia* ⓕ kheem·*na*·sya
gynaecologist *ginecólogo/a* ⓜ/ⓕ khee·ne·*ko*·lo·go/a

H

hair *pelo* ⓜ *pe*·lo
hairbrush *cepillo* ⓜ se·*pee*·yo
haircut *corte de pelo* ⓜ *kor*·te de *pe*·lo
hairdresser *peluquero/a* ⓜ/ⓕ pe·loo·*ke*·ro/a
halal *halal* ⓜ&ⓕ a·*lal*
half *mitad* ⓕ mee·*tad*
hallucination *alucinación* ⓕ a·loo·see·na·*syon*
ham *jamón* ⓜ kha·*mon*
hammer *martillo* ⓜ mar·*tee*·yo

hammock *hamaca* ⓕ a·*ma*·ka
hand *mano* ⓕ *ma*·no
handbag *bolso* ⓜ *bol*·so
handball *balomano* ⓜ ba·lo·*ma*·no
handicraft *artesanías* ⓕ pl ar·te·sa·*nee*·as
handkerchief *pañuelo* ⓜ pa·*nywe*·lo
handlebars *manillar* ⓜ ma·nee·*yar*
handmade *hecho/a a mano* ⓜ/ⓕ e·cho/a a *ma*·no
handsome *guapo/a* ⓜ/ⓕ *gwa*·po/a
happy *feliz* ⓜ&ⓕ fe·*lees*
harassment *acoso* ⓜ a·*ko*·so
harbour *puerto* ⓜ *pwer*·to
hard (not soft) *duro/a* ⓜ/ⓕ *doo*·ro/a
hard-boiled (eggs) *duro/a* ⓜ/ⓕ *doo*·ro/a
hardware store *ferretería* ⓕ fe·re·te·*ree*·a
hashish *hachís* ⓜ a·*chees*
hat *sombrero* ⓜ som·*bre*·ro
have *tener* te·*ner*
have fun *divertirse* dee·ver·*teer*·se
hay fever *fiebre del heno* ⓕ *fye*·bre del *e*·no
hazelnut *avellana* ⓕ a·ve·*ya*·na
he *él* el
head *cabeza* ⓕ ka·*be*·sa
headache *dolor de cabeza* ⓜ do·*lor* de ka·*be*·sa
headlights *focos* ⓜ pl *fo*·kos
health *salud* ⓕ sa·*lood*
health-food store *macrobiótica* ⓕ ma·kro·*byo*·tee·ka
hear *oír* o·*eer*
hearing aid *audífono* ⓜ ow·*dee*·fo·no
heart *corazón* ⓜ ko·ra·*son*
heart attack *ataque al corazón* ⓜ a·*ta*·ke al ko·ra·*son*
heart condition *condición cardíaca* ⓕ kon·dee·*syon* kar·*dee*·a·ka
heat *calor* ⓜ ka·*lor*
heated *calentado/a* ⓜ/ⓕ ka·len·*ta*·do/a
heater *calentador* ⓜ ka·len·ta·*dor*
heating *calentamiento* ⓜ ka·len·ta·*myen*·to
heavy (weight) *pesado/a* ⓜ/ⓕ pe·*sa*·do/a
helmet *casco* ⓜ *kas*·ko
help *ayuda* ⓕ a·*yoo*·da
help v *ayudar* a·yoo·*dar*
hepatitis *hepatitis* ⓕ e·pa·*tee*·tees
her *ella* *e*·ya
her (possessive) *su* soo
herb *hierba* ⓕ *yer*·ba
herbalist *hierbero/a* ⓜ/ⓕ yer·*be*·ro/a
here *aquí* a·*kee*
heroin *heroína* ⓕ e·ro·*ee*·na
herring *arenque* ⓜ a·*ren*·ke
high (height) *alto/a* ⓜ/ⓕ *al*·to/a
highchair *silla de comer para niños* ⓕ *see*·ya de ko·*mer* *pa*·ra *nee*·nyos
high school *colegio* ⓜ ko·*le*·khyo
highway *autopista* ⓕ ow·to·*pees*·ta
hike *caminar* ka·mee·*nar*
hiking *caminata* ⓕ ka·mee·*na*·ta
hiking boots *botas para caminata* ⓕ *bo*·tas *pa*·ra ka·mee·*na*·ta
hiking route *sendero* ⓜ sen·*de*·ro
hill *loma* ⓕ *lo*·ma
him *él* el
Hindu n&a *hindú* ⓜ&ⓕ een·*doo*
hire (rent) *alquilar* al·kee·*lar*
his *su* soo
historical *histórico/a* ⓜ/ⓕ ees·*to*·ree·ko/a
history *historia* ⓕ ees·*to*·rya
hitchhike *pedir un aventón* pe·*deer* oon a·ven·*ton*
HIV *VIH* ⓜ ve ee *a*·che
hockey *hockey* ⓜ *o*·kee
holiday *feriado* ⓜ fe·ree·*a*·do
holidays *vacación* ⓕ va·ka·*syon*
home *hogar* ⓜ o·*gar*
homeless n&a *indigente* ⓜ&ⓕ een·dee·*khen*·te
homeopathy *homeopatía* ⓕ o·me·o·pa·*tee*·a
homesick *nostálgico/a* ⓜ/ⓕ nos·*tal*·khee·ko/a
homosexual n&a *homosexual* ⓜ&ⓕ o·mo·*sek*·swal
honey *miel* ⓕ myel
honeymoon *luna de miel* ⓕ *loo*·na de myel
horoscope *horóscopo* ⓜ o·*ros*·ko·po
horse *caballo* ⓜ ka·*ba*·yo
horse racing *carreras de caballo* ⓕ pl ka·*re*·ras de ka·*ba*·yo
horse riding *equitación* ⓕ e·kee·ta·*syon*
hospital *hospital* ⓜ os·pee·*tal*
hospitality *hospitalidad* ⓕ os·pee·ta·lee·*dad*
hot *caliente* ⓜ&ⓕ ka·*lyen*·te
hot water *agua caliente* ⓕ *a*·gwa ka·*lyen*·te
hotel *hotel* ⓜ o·*tel*
hour *hora* ⓕ *o*·ra
house *casa* ⓕ *ka*·sa

housework *trabajo de la casa* ⓜ tra·*ba*·kho de la *ka*·sa
how *cómo* *ko*·mo
how many *cuántos/as* ⓜ/ⓕ *kwan*·tos/as
how much *cuánto/a* ⓜ/ⓕ *kwan*·to/a
hug *abrazar* a·bra·*sar*
huge *enorme* ⓜ&ⓕ e·*nor*·me
humanities *humanidades* ⓕ pl oo·ma·nee·*da*·des
human resources *recursos humanos* ⓜ pl re·*koor*·sos oo·*ma*·nos
human rights *derechos humanos* ⓜ pl de·*re*·chos oo·*ma*·nos
hundred *cien* syen
hungry *hambriento/a* ⓜ/ⓕ am·bree·*yen*·to/a
hunting *caza* ⓕ *ka*·sa
hurt (be painful) *doler* do·*ler*
hurt (cause pain) *lastimar* las·tee·*mar*
husband *esposo* ⓜ es·*po*·so

I

I *yo* yo
ice *hielo* ⓜ *ye*·lo
ice cream *helado* ⓜ e·*la*·do
ice-cream parlour *heladería* ⓕ e·la·de·*ree*·a
ice hockey *hockey sobre hielo* ⓜ o·kee *so*·bre *ye*·lo
identification *identificación* ⓕ ee·den·tee·fee·ka·*syon*
identification card (ID) *cédula de identificación* ⓕ *se*·doo·la de ee·den·tee·fee·ka·*syon*
idiot *idiota* ⓜ&ⓕ ee·*dyo*·ta
if *si* see
ill *enfermo/a* ⓜ/ⓕ en·*fer*·mo/a
immigration *migración* ⓕ mee·gra·*syon*
important *importante* ⓜ&ⓕ eem·por·*tan*·te
impossible *imposible* ⓜ&ⓕ eem·po·*see*·ble
in *en* en
in a hurry *apurado/a* ⓜ/ⓕ a·poo·*ra*·do/a
included *incluido/a* ⓜ/ⓕ een·kloo·*ee*·do/a
income tax *impuesto* ⓜ eem·*pwes*·to
indicator *indicador* ⓜ een·dee·ka·*dor*
indigestion *indigestión* ⓕ een·dee·khes·*tyon*
indoor *adentro* a·*den*·tro
industry *industria* ⓕ een·*doos*·tree·a
infection *infección* ⓕ een·fek·*syon*
inflammation *inflamación* ⓕ een·fla·ma·*syon*
influenza *gripe* ⓕ *gree*·pe
information *información* ⓕ een·for·ma·*syon*
in front of *en frente de* en *fren*·te de
ingredient *ingrediente* ⓜ een·gre·*dyen*·te
inject *inyectar* een·yek·*tar*
injection *inyección* ⓕ een·yek·*syon*
injured *lastimado/a* ⓜ/ⓕ las·tee·*ma*·do/a
injury *herida* ⓕ e·*ree*·da
inner tube (tyre) *tubo interno* ⓜ *too*·bo een·*ter*·no
innocent *inocente* ⓜ&ⓕ ee·no·*sen*·te
insect *insecto* ⓜ een·*sek*·to
insect repellent *repelente* ⓜ re·pe·*len*·te
inside *dentro de* *den*·tro de
instructor *instructor/instructora* ⓜ/ⓕ eens·trook·*tor*/eens·trook·*to*·ra
insurance *seguro* ⓜ se·*goo*·ro
interesting *interesante* ⓜ&ⓕ een·te·re·*san*·te
intermission *intermedio* ⓜ een·ter·*me*·dyo
international *internacional* ⓜ&ⓕ een·ter·na·syo·*nal*
Internet *internet* ⓜ&ⓕ een·ter·*net*
Internet café *café internet* ⓜ ka·*fe* een·ter·*net*
interpreter *intérprete* ⓜ&ⓕ een·*ter*·pre·te
interview *entrevista* ⓕ en·tre·*vees*·ta
invite *invitar* een·vee·*tar*
Ireland *Irlanda* ⓕ eer·*lan*·da
iron (for clothes) *plancha* ⓕ *plan*·cha
island *isla* ⓕ *ees*·la
IT (information technology) *informática* ⓕ een·for·*ma*·tee·ka
Italy *Italia* ⓕ ee·*ta*·lya
itch *picazón* ⓕ pee·ka·*son*
itemised *detallado/a* ⓜ/ⓕ de·ta·*ya*·do/a
itinerary *itinerario* ⓜ ee·tee·ne·*ra*·ryo
IUD *DIU* ⓜ de ee oo

J

jacket *jacket* ⓕ *cha*·ket
jail *cárcel* ⓕ *kar*·sel
jam *jalea* ⓕ kha·*le*·a
January *enero* ⓜ e·*ne*·ro
Japan *Japón* ⓜ kha·*pon*
jar *frasco* ⓜ *fras*·ko
jaw *mandíbula* ⓕ man·*dee*·boo·la
jealous *celoso/a* ⓜ/ⓕ se·*lo*·so/a

jeans *jeans* ⓜ yeens
jeep *jeep* ⓜ yeep
jet lag *desfase de horario* ⓜ des·fa·se de o·ra·ryo
jewellery *joyas* ⓕ pl kho·yas
Jewish *judío/a* ⓜ/ⓕ khoo·dee·o/a
job *trabajo* ⓜ tra·ba·kho
jogging *trotar* ⓜ tro·tar
joke *chiste* ⓜ chees·te
journalist *periodista* ⓜ&ⓕ pe·ree·o·dees·ta
journey *viaje* ⓜ vya·khe
judge *juez/jueza* ⓜ/ⓕ khwes/khwe·sa
juice *jugo* ⓜ khoo·go
July *julio* ⓜ khoo·lyo
jump *saltar* sal·tar
jumper (sweater) *suéter* ⓜ swe·ter
jumper leads *jumpers* ⓜ pl chom·pers
June *junio* ⓜ khoo·nyo

K

kayak *kayak* ⓜ ka·yak
ketchup *ketchup* ⓜ ke·choop
key (door etc) *llave* ⓕ ya·ve
keyboard *teclado* ⓜ te·kla·do
kick *patear* pa·te·ar
kidney *riñón* ⓜ ree·nyon
kilogram *kilogramo* ⓜ kee·lo·gra·mo
kilometre *kilómetro* ⓜ kee·lo·me·tro
kind (nice) *amable* ⓜ&ⓕ a·ma·ble
kindergarten *kinder* ⓜ keen·der
king *rey* ⓜ ray
kiosk *quiosco* ⓜ kyos·ko
kiss *beso* ⓜ be·so
kiss v *besar* be·sar
kitchen *cocina* ⓕ ko·see·na
knee *rodilla* ⓕ ro·dee·ya
knife *cuchillo* ⓜ koo·chee·yo
know (someone) *conocer* ko·no·ser
know (something) *saber* sa·ber
kosher *kosher* ⓜ&ⓕ ko·sher

L

labourer *trabajador/trabajadora* ⓜ/ⓕ tra·ba·kha·dor/tra·ba·kha·do·ra
lake *lago* ⓜ la·go
lamb (meat) *cordero* ⓜ kor·de·ro
land *tierra* ⓕ tye·ra
landlady *dueña* ⓕ dwe·nya
landlord *dueño* ⓜ dwe·nyo
language *idioma* ⓜ ee·dyo·ma
laptop *laptop* ⓕ lap·top
large *grande* ⓜ&ⓕ gran·de
last (final) *último/a* ⓜ/ⓕ ool·tee·mo/a
last (previous) *pasado/a* ⓜ/ⓕ pa·sa·do/a
late adv *tarde* tar·de
later *más tarde* mas tar·de
laugh *reír* re·eer
launderette *lavandería* ⓕ la·van·de·ree·a
laundry (clothes) *ropa* ⓕ ro·pa
laundry (place) *lavandería* ⓕ la·van·de·ree·a
law (legislation) *ley* ⓕ lay
law (profession) *derecho* ⓜ de·re·cho
lawyer *abogado/a* ⓜ/ⓕ a·bo·ga·do/a
laxative *laxante* ⓜ lak·san·te
lazy *perezoso/a* ⓜ/ⓕ pe·re·so·so/a
leader *líder* ⓜ&ⓕ lee·der
leaf *hoja* ⓕ o·kha
learn *aprender* a·pren·der
leather *cuero* ⓜ kwe·ro
lecturer *presentador/presentadora* ⓜ/ⓕ pre·sen·ta·dor/pre·sen·ta·do·ra
ledge *borde* ⓜ bor·de
left (direction) *izquierda* ⓕ ees·kyer·da
left-luggage office *consigna* ⓕ kon·seeg·na
left-wing *izquierdista* ⓜ&ⓕ ees·kyer·dees·ta
leg (body) *pierna* ⓕ pyer·na
legal *legal* ⓜ&ⓕ le·gal
legislation *legislación* ⓕ le·khee·sla·syon
legume *legumbre* ⓕ le·goom·bre
lemon *limón* ⓜ lee·mon
lemonade *limonada* ⓕ lee·mo·na·da
lens (camera) *objetivo* ⓜ ob·khe·tee·vo
lentil *lenteja* ⓕ len·te·kha
lesbian n&a *lesbiana* ⓕ les·bya·na
less *menos* me·nos
letter (mail) *carta* ⓕ kar·ta
lettuce *lechuga* ⓕ le·choo·ga
liar *mentiroso/a* ⓜ/ⓕ men·tee·ro·so/a
librarian *bibliotecario/a* ⓜ/ⓕ bee·blee·o·te·ka·ryo/a
library *biblioteca* ⓕ bee·blee·o·te·ka
lice *piojos* ⓜ pl pyo·khos
licence *licencia* ⓕ lee·sen·sya
license plate number *número de placa* ⓜ noo·me·ro de pla·ka
lie (not stand) *acostarse* a·kos·tar·se
lie (not tell the truth) *mentir* men·teer
life *vida* ⓕ vee·da

life jacket *chaleco salvavidas* ⓜ cha·*le*·ko sal·va·*vee*·das
lift (elevator) *ascensor* ⓜ a·sen·*sor*
light *luz* ⓕ lus
light (colour) *claro/a* ⓜ/ⓕ *kla*·ro/a
light (weight) *liviano/a* ⓜ/ⓕ lee·*vya*·no/a
light bulb *bombillo* ⓜ bom·*bee*·yo
lighter (cigarette) *encendedor* ⓜ en·sen·de·*dor*
light meter *medidor de luz* ⓜ me·dee·*dor* de lus
like v *gustar* goos·*tar*
lime (fruit) *limón* ⓜ lee·*mon*
linen (material) *lino* ⓜ *lee*·no
linen (sheets) *sábanas* ⓕ pl *sa*·ba·nas
linguist *lingüista* ⓜ&ⓕ leen·*gwees*·ta
lip balm *brillo* ⓜ *bree*·yo
lips *labios* ⓜ pl *la*·byos
lipstick *pintura de labios* ⓕ peen·*too*·ra de *la*·byos
liquor store *licorera* ⓕ lee·ko·*re*·ra
listen *escuchar* es·koo·*char*
little (quantity) *poco/a* ⓜ/ⓕ *po*·ko/a
little (size) *pequeño/a* ⓜ/ⓕ pe·*ke*·nyo/a
live *vivir* vee·*veer*
liver *hígado* ⓜ *ee*·ga·do
lizard *lagartija* ⓕ la·gar·*tee*·kha
local *local* ⓜ&ⓕ lo·*kal*
lock *candado* ⓜ kan·*da*·do
lock v *cerrar con llave* se·*rar* kon *ya*·ve
locked *cerrado/a con llave* ⓜ/ⓕ se·*ra*·do/a kon *ya*·ve
long *largo/a* ⓜ/ⓕ *lar*·go/a
look *ver* ver
look after *cuidar* kwee·*dar*
look for *buscar* boos·*kar*
lookout *mirador* ⓜ mee·ra·*dor*
loose *flojo/a* ⓜ/ⓕ *flo*·kho/a
loose change *menudo* ⓜ me·*noo*·do
lose *perder* per·*der*
lost *perdido/a* ⓜ/ⓕ per·*dee*·do/a
lost property office *oficina de objetos perdidos* ⓕ o·fee·*see*·na de ob·*khe*·tos per·*dee*·dos
(a) lot *mucho/a* ⓜ/ⓕ *moo*·cho/a
loud *ruidoso/a* ⓜ/ⓕ rwee·*do*·so/a
love *amor* ⓜ a·*mor*
love v *amar* a·*mar*
lover *amante* ⓜ&ⓕ a·*man*·te
low *bajo/a* ⓜ/ⓕ *ba*·kho/a
lubricant *lubricante* ⓜ loo·bree·*kan*·te
luck *suerte* ⓕ *swer*·te
lucky *afortunado/a* ⓜ/ⓕ a·for·too·*na*·do/a
luggage *equipaje* ⓜ e·kee·*pa*·khe
luggage tag *etiqueta del equipaje* ⓕ e·tee·*ke*·ta del e·kee·*pa*·khe
lump *bulto* ⓜ *bool*·to
lunch *almuerzo* ⓜ al·*mwer*·so
lung *pulmón* ⓜ pool·*mon*
luxury *lujoso/a* ⓜ/ⓕ loo·*kho*·so/a

M

machine *máquina* ⓕ *ma*·kee·na
magazine *revista* ⓕ re·*vees*·ta
mail *correo* ⓜ ko·*re*·o
mail *enviar* en·*vyar*
mailbox *buzón* ⓜ boo·*son*
main *principal* ⓜ&ⓕ preen·see·*pal*
main road *calle principal* ⓕ *ka*·ye preen·se·*pal*
make *hacer* a·*ser*
make-up *maquillaje* ⓜ ma·kee·*ya*·khe
malaria *malaria* ⓕ ma·*la*·rya
mammogram *mamografía* ⓕ ma·mo·gra·*fee*·a
man *hombre* ⓜ *om*·bre
manager (business) *gerente* ⓜ&ⓕ khe·*ren*·te
manager (sport) *director/directora* ⓜ/ⓕ dee·rek·*tor*/dee·rek·*to*·ra
mandarin *mandarina* ⓕ man·da·*ree*·na
mango *mango* ⓜ *man*·go
mangrove *manglar* ⓜ man·*glar*
many *muchos/as* ⓜ/ⓕ pl *moo*·chos/as
map *mapa* ⓜ *ma*·pa
March *marzo* ⓜ *mar*·so
margarine *margarina* ⓕ mar·ga·*ree*·na
marijuana *marihuana* ⓕ ma·ree·*wa*·na
marital status *estado civil* ⓜ es·*ta*·do see·*veel*
market *mercado* ⓜ mer·*ka*·do
marriage *matrimonio* ⓜ ma·tree·*mo*·nyo
married *casado/a* ⓜ/ⓕ ka·*sa*·do/a
marry *casarse* ka·*sar*·se
martial arts *artes marciales* ⓕ *ar*·tes mar·*sya*·les
mass (Catholic) *misa* ⓕ *mee*·sa
massage *masaje* ⓜ ma·*sa*·khe

masseur *masajeador* (m) ma·sa·khe·a·dor
masseuse *masajeadora* (f) ma·sa·khe·a·do·ra
mat *colchoneta* (f) kol·cho·ne·ta
match (sports) *partido* (m) par·tee·do
matches (lighting) *fósforos* (m) pl fos·fo·ros
mattress *colchón* (m) kol·chon
May *mayo* (m) ma·yo
maybe *tal vez* tal ves
mayonnaise *mayonesa* (f) ma·yo·ne·sa
mayor *alcalde/alcaldesa* (m)/(f) al·kal·de/al·kal·de·sa
me *mí* mee
meal *comida* (f) ko·mee·da
measles *sarampión* (m) sa·ram·pyon
meat *carne* (f) kar·ne
mechanic *mecánico/a* (m)/(f) me·ka·nee·ko/a
media *medios* (m) pl me·dyos
medicine (medication) *medicamento* (m) me·dee·ka·men·to
medicine (profession) *medicina* (f) me·dee·see·na
meditation *meditación* (f) me·dee·ta·syon
meet (first time) *conocerse* ko·no·ser·se
meet (get together) *encontrarse* en·kon·trar·se
melon *melón* (m) me·lon
member *miembro/a* (m)/(f) myem·bro/a
memory card *tarjeta de memoria* (f) tar·khe·ta de me·mo·rya
menstruation *regla* (f) re·gla
menu *menú* (m) me·noo
message *mensaje* (m) men·sa·khe
metal *metal* (m) me·tal
metre *metro* (m) me·tro
microwave oven *horno microondas* (m) or·no mee·kro·on·das
midday *mediodía* (m) me·dyo·dee·a
midnight *medianoche* (f) me·dya·no·che
migraine *migraña* (f) mee·gra·nya
military *ejército* (m) e·kher·see·to
military service *servicio militar* (m) ser·vee·syo mee·lee·tar
milk *leche* (f) le·che
millimetre *milímetro* (m) mee·lee·me·tro
million *millón* (m) mee·yon
mince *picadillo* (m) pee·ka·dee·yo
mineral water *agua mineral* (f) a·gwa mee·ne·ral
minute *minuto* (m) mee·noo·to
mirror *espejo* (m) es·pe·kho
miscarriage *aborto natural* (m) a·bor·to na·too·ral
miss (feel absence of) *extrañar* eks·tra·nyar
miss (lose) *perder* per·der
mistake *error* (m) e·ror
mix *mezclar* mes·klar
mobile phone *teléfono celular* (m) te·le·fo·no se·loo·lar
modem *módem* (m) mo·dem
modern *moderno/a* (m)/(f) mo·der·no/a
moisturiser *humectante* (m) oo·mek·tan·te
monastery *monasterio* (m) mo·nas·te·ryo
Monday *lunes* (m) loo·nes
money *dinero* (m) dee·ne·ro
monk *monje* (m) mon·khe
monkey *mono* (m) mo·no
month *mes* (m) mes
monument *monumento* (m) mo·noo·men·to
moon *luna* (f) loo·na
more *más* mas
morning *mañana* (f) ma·nya·na
morning sickness *achaques* (m) pl a·cha·kes
mosque *mezquita* (f) mes·kee·ta
mosquito *zancudo* (m) san·koo·do
mosquito coil *espiral para mosquitos* (f) es·pee·ral pa·ra mos·kee·tos
mosquito net *mosquitero* (m) mos·kee·te·ro
motel *motel* (m) mo·tel
mother *madre* (f) ma·dre
mother-in-law *suegra* (f) swe·gra
motorbike *moto* (f) mo·to
motorboat *lancha* (f) lan·cha
motorcycle *moto* (f) mo·to
motorway (tollway) *autopista* (f) ow·to·pees·ta
mountain *montaña* (f) mon·ta·nya
mountain bike *bicicleta montañera* (f) bee·see·kle·ta mon·ta·nye·ra
mountaineering *montañismo* (m) mon·ta·nyees·mo
mountain path *camino de montaña* (m) ka·mee·no de mon·ta·nya
mountain range *cordillera* (f) kor·dee·ye·ra
mouse (animal) *ratón* (m) ra·ton
mouse (computer) *mouse* (m) mows
mouth *boca* (f) bo·ka
movie *película* (f) pe·lee·koo·la
mud *barro* (m) ba·ro
muesli *granola* (f) gra·no·la
mumps *paperas* (f) pl pa·pe·ras

murder *asesinato* ⓜ a·se·see·na·to
murder v *asesinar* a·se·see·nar
muscle *músculo* ⓜ moos·koo·lo
museum *museo* ⓜ moo·se·o
mushroom *hongo* ⓜ on·go
music *música* ⓕ moo·see·ka
music shop *tienda de música* ⓕ tyen·da de moo·see·ka
musician *músico/a* ⓜ/ⓕ moo·see·ko/a
Muslim *musulmán/musulmana* ⓜ/ⓕ moo·sool·man/moo·sool·ma·na
mussel *mejillón* ⓜ me·khee·yon
mustard *mostaza* ⓕ mos·ta·sa
mute *mudo/a* ⓜ/ⓕ moo·do/a
my *mi* mee

N

nail clippers *cortauñas* ⓜ kor·ta·oo·nyas
name *nombre* ⓜ nom·bre
napkin *servilleta* ⓕ ser·vee·ye·ta
nappy *pañal* ⓜ pa·nyal
nappy rash *salpullido* ⓜ sal·poo·yee·do
nationality *nacionalidad* ⓕ na·syo·na·lee·dad
national park *parque nacional* ⓜ par·ke na·syo·nal
nature *naturaleza* ⓕ na·too·ra·le·sa
naturopathy *neuropatía* ⓕ ne·oo·ro·pa·tee·a
nausea *náuseas* ⓕ pl now·se·as
near *cerca de* ser·ka de
nearby *cerca* ser·ka
nearest *más cerca* mas ser·ka
necessary *necesario/a* ⓜ/ⓕ ne·se·sa·ryo/a
neck *cuello* ⓜ kwe·yo
necklace *cadena* ⓕ ka·de·na
nectarine *nectarina* ⓕ nek·ta·ree·na
need *necesitar* ne·se·see·tar
needle (sewing) *aguja* ⓕ a·goo·kha
needle (syringe) *jeringa* ⓕ khe·reen·ga
negative *negativo/a* ⓜ/ⓕ ne·ga·tee·vo/a
negatives (photos) *negativos* ⓜ pl ne·ga·tee·vos
neither *ninguno/a* ⓜ/ⓕ neen·goo·no/a
net *red* ⓕ red
Netherlands *Holanda* ⓕ o·lan·da
network (phone/Internet) *red* ⓕ red
never *nunca* noon·ka
new *nuevo/a* ⓜ/ⓕ nwe·vo/a
news *noticias* ⓕ pl no·tee·syas
newsagency *agencia de noticias* ⓕ a·khen·sya de no·tee·syas
newspaper *periódico* ⓜ pe·ryo·dee·ko
newsstand *venta de periódicos* ⓕ ven·ta de pe·ryo·dee·kos
New Year's Day *día de Año Nuevo* ⓜ dee·a de a·nyo nwe·vo
New Year's Eve *víspera de Año Nuevo* ⓕ vees·pe·ra de a·nyo nwe·vo
New Zealand *Nueva Zelanda* ⓕ nwe·va se·lan·da
next (following) *próximo/a* ⓜ/ⓕ prok·see·mo/a
next to *junto a* khoon·to a
nice *bueno/a* ⓜ/ⓕ bwe·no/a
Nicaragua *Nicaragua* ⓕ nee·ka·ra·gwa
nickname *apodo* ⓜ a·po·do
night *noche* ⓕ no·che
nightclub *club nocturno* ⓜ kloob nok·toor·no
night out *salida de noche* ⓕ sa·lee·da de no·che
no *no* no
noisy *ruidoso/a* ⓜ/ⓕ rwee·do·so/a
none *ninguno/a* ⓜ/ⓕ neen·goo·no/a
nonsmoking *no fumado* no foo·ma·do
noodles *fideos* ⓜ pl fee·de·os
noon *mediodía* ⓜ me·dyo·dee·a
north *norte* ⓜ nor·te
Norway *Noruega* ⓕ no·rwe·ga
nose *nariz* ⓕ na·rees
not *no* no
notebook *cuaderno* ⓜ kwa·der·no
nothing *nada* na·da
November *noviembre* ⓜ no·vyem·bre
now *ahora* a·o·ra
nuclear energy *energía nuclear* ⓕ e·ner·khee·a noo·kle·ar
nuclear testing *pruebas nucleares* ⓕ pl prwe·bas noo·kle·a·res
nuclear waste *desechos nucleares* ⓜ pl de·se·chos noo·kle·a·res
number *número* ⓜ noo·me·ro
numberplate *placa* ⓕ pla·ka
nun *monja* ⓕ mon·kha
nurse *enfermero/a* ⓜ/ⓕ en·fer·me·ro/a
nut (food) *nuez* ⓕ nwes

O

oats *avena* ⓕ a·*ve*·na
ocean *océano* ⓜ o·*se*·a·no
October *octubre* ⓜ ok·*too*·bre
off (power) *apagado/a* ⓜ/ⓕ a·pa·*ga*·do/a
off (spoilt) *malo/a* ⓜ/ⓕ *ma*·lo/a
office *oficina* ⓕ o·fee·*see*·na
office worker *trabajador de oficina* ⓜ tra·ba·kha·*dor* de o·fee·*see*·na
often *a menudo* a me·*noo*·do
oil (cooking) *aceite* ⓜ a·*say*·te
oil (petrol) *petróleo* ⓜ pe·*tro*·le·o
old (age) *viejo/a* ⓜ/ⓕ *vye*·kho/a
olive *aceituna* ⓕ a·say·*too*·na
olive oil *aceite de oliva* ⓕ a·*say*·te de o·*lee*·va
Olympic Games *Juegos Olímpicos* ⓜ pl *khwe*·gos o·*leem*·pee·kos
omelette *omelet* ⓕ o·me·*let*
on *sobre* *so*·bre
on (power) *encendido/a* ⓜ/ⓕ en·sen·*dee*·do/a
once *una vez* *oo*·na ves
one *uno/a* ⓜ/ⓕ *oo*·no/a
one-way ticket *tiquete de ida* ⓕ tee·*ke*·te de *ee*·da
onion *cebolla* ⓕ se·*bo*·ya
only *sólo* *so*·lo
on time *a tiempo* a *tyem*·po
open *abrir* a·*breer*
open (business) *abierto/a* ⓜ/ⓕ a·*byer*·to/a
opening hours *horario* ⓜ o·*ra*·ryo
opera *ópera* ⓕ *o*·pe·ra
operation (medical) *operación* ⓕ o·pe·ra·*syon*
operator (telephone) *operador/operadora* ⓜ/ⓕ o·pe·ra·*dor*/o·pe·ra·*do*·ra
opinion *opinión* ⓕ o·pee·*nyon*
opposite *opuesto* o·*pwes*·to
optometrist *optometrista* ⓜ&ⓕ op·to·me·*trees*·ta
or *o* o
orange (colour) *anaranjado/a* ⓜ/ⓕ a·na·ran·*kha*·do/a
orange (fruit) *naranja* ⓕ na·*ran*·kha
orange juice *jugo de naranja* ⓜ *khoo*·go de na·*ran*·kha
orchestra *orquesta* ⓕ or·*kes*·ta
order (food) *pedido* ⓜ pe·*dee*·do
order *orden* ⓜ *or*·den
order v *ordenar* or·de·*nar*
ordinary *ordinario/a* ⓜ/ⓕ or·dee·*na*·ryo/a
orgasm *orgasmo* ⓜ or·*gas*·mo
original *original* ⓜ&ⓕ o·ree·khee·*nal*
other *otro/a* ⓜ/ⓕ *o*·tro/a
our *nuestro/a* ⓜ/ⓕ *nwes*·tro/a
out of order *fuera de servicio* *fwe*·ra de ser·*vee*·syo
outside *fuera de* *fwe*·ra de
ovarian cyst *quiste en los ovarios* ⓜ *kees*·te en los o·*va*·ryos
ovary *ovario* ⓜ o·*va*·ryo
oven *horno* ⓜ *or*·no
overcoat *abrigo* ⓜ a·*bree*·go
overdose *sobredosis* ⓕ so·bre·*do*·sees
overnight *por a noche* por a *no*·che
overseas *extranjero/a* ⓜ/ⓕ eks·tran·*khe*·ro/a
owe *deber* de·*ber*
owner *dueño/a* ⓜ/ⓕ *dwe*·nyo/a
oxygen *oxígeno* ⓜ ok·*see*·khe·no
oyster *ostra* ⓕ *os*·tra
ozone layer *capa de ozono* ⓕ *ka*·pa de o·*so*·no

P

pacemaker *marcapasos* ⓜ mar·ka·*pa*·sos
Pacific Ocean *Océano Pacífico* ⓜ o·*se*·a·no pa·*see*·fee·ko
pacifier (dummy) *chupeta* ⓕ choo·*pe*·ta
package *paquete* ⓜ pa·*ke*·te
packet *paquete* ⓜ pa·*ke*·te
padlock *candado* ⓜ kan·*da*·do
page *página* ⓕ *pa*·khee·na
pain *dolor* ⓜ do·*lor*
painful *doloroso/a* ⓜ/ⓕ do·lo·*ro*·so/a
painkiller *pastilla para el dolor* ⓕ pas·*tee*·ya *pa*·ra el do·*lor*
painter *pintor/pintora* ⓜ/ⓕ peen·*tor*/peen·*to*·ra
painting (artwork) *cuadro* ⓜ *kwa*·dro
painting (technique) *pintura* ⓕ peen·*too*·ra
pair (couple) *pareja* ⓕ pa·*re*·kha
palace *palacio* ⓜ pa·*la*·syo
pan *sartén* ⓜ sar·*ten*
Panama *Panamá* ⓕ pa·na·*ma*

english–costa rican spanish

pants (trousers) *pantalones* ⓜ pl pan·ta·*lo*·nes
pantyhose *pantys* ⓕ pl *pan*·tees
panty liners *protectores* ⓜ pl pro·tek·*to*·res
paper *papel* ⓜ pa·*pel*
paperwork *papeleo* ⓜ pa·pe·*le*·o
pap smear *papanicolau* ⓜ pa·pa·nee·ko·*low*
paraplegic *parapléjico/a* ⓜ/ⓕ pa·ra·*ple*·khee·ko/a
parcel *parcela* ⓕ par·*se*·la
parents *papás* ⓜ pl pa·*pas*
park *parque* ⓜ *par*·ke
park (vehicle) *parquear* par·ke·*ar*
parliament *parlamento* ⓜ par·la·*men*·to
parrot *loro/a* ⓜ/ⓕ *lo*·ro/a
part (component) *parte* ⓕ *par*·te
part-time *tiempo parcial* ⓜ *tyem*·po par·*syal*
party (night out) *fiesta* ⓕ *fyes*·ta
party (politics) *partido* ⓜ par·*tee*·do
pass *pasar* pa·*sar*
passenger *pasajero/a* ⓜ/ⓕ pa·sa·*khe*·ro/a
passionfruit *maracuyá* ⓕ ma·ra·koo·*ya*
passport *pasaporte* ⓜ pa·sa·*por*·te
passport number *número de pasaporte* ⓜ *noo*·me·ro de pa·sa·*por*·te
past *pasado* ⓜ pa·*sa*·do
pasta *pasta* ⓕ *pas*·ta
pastry *pastel* ⓜ pas·*tel*
path *camino* ⓜ ka·*mee*·no
pay *pagar* pa·*gar*
payment *pago* ⓜ *pa*·go
pea *petipoa* ⓕ pe·tee·*po*·a
peace *paz* ⓕ pas
peach *melocotón* ⓜ me·lo·ko·*ton*
peak (mountain) *cima* ⓕ *see*·ma
peanut *maní* ⓜ ma·*nee*
pear *pera* ⓕ *pe*·ra
pedal *pedal* ⓜ pe·*dal*
pedestrian *peatón* ⓜ pe·a·*ton*
pen (ballpoint) *lapicero* ⓜ la·pee·*se*·ro
pencil *lápiz* ⓜ *la*·pees
penis *pene* ⓜ *pe*·ne
penknife *navaja* ⓕ na·*va*·kha
pensioner *pensionado/a* ⓜ/ⓕ pen·syo·*na*·do/a
people *gente* ⓕ *khen*·te
pepper (bell) *pimentón* ⓜ pee·men·*ton*
pepper (spice) *pimienta* ⓕ pee·*myen*·ta
per (day) *por (día)* por (*dee*·a)
per cent *porcentaje* ⓜ por·sen·*ta*·khe

perfect *perfecto/a* ⓜ/ⓕ per·*fek*·to/a
performance *presentación* ⓕ pre·sen·ta·*syon*
perfume *perfume* ⓜ per·*foo*·me
period pain *dolores menstruales* ⓜ pl do·*lo*·res mens·*trwa*·les
permission *permiso* ⓜ per·*mee*·so
permit *permiso* ⓜ per·*mee*·so
person *persona* ⓕ per·*so*·na
petition *petición* ⓕ pe·tee·*syon*
petrol *gasolina* ⓕ ga·so·*lee*·na
petrol station *bomba* ⓕ *bom*·ba
pharmacist *farmacéutico/a* ⓜ/ⓕ far·ma·se·oo·tee·ko/a
pharmacy *farmacia* ⓕ far·*ma*·sya
phone book *guía telefónica* ⓕ *gee*·a te·le·*fo*·nee·ka
phone box *casetilla de teléfono* ⓕ ka·se·*tee*·ya de te·*le*·fo·no
phone card *tarjeta de teléfono* ⓕ tar·*khe*·ta de te·*le*·fo·no
photo *foto* ⓕ *fo*·to
photograph v *fotografiar* fo·to·gra·*fyar*
photographer *fotógrafo/a* ⓜ/ⓕ fo·*to*·gra·fo/a
photography *fotografía* ⓕ fo·to·gra·*fee*·a
phrasebook *libro de frases* ⓜ *lee*·bro de *fra*·ses
piano *piano* ⓜ pee·*a*·no
pickaxe *pico* ⓜ *pee*·ko
pickles *pepinillos* ⓜ pl pe·pee·*nee*·yos
picnic *picnic* ⓜ *peek*·neek
pie *pastel* ⓜ pas·*tel*
piece *pedazo* ⓜ pe·*da*·so
pig *cerdo* ⓜ • *chancho* ⓜ *ser*·do • *chan*·cho
pill *pastilla* ⓕ pas·*tee*·ya
the pill *pastilla anticonceptiva* ⓕ pas·*tee*·ya an·tee·kon·sep·*tee*·va
pillow *almohada* ⓕ al·mo·*a*·da
pillowcase *funda* ⓕ *foon*·da
pineapple *piña* ⓕ *pee*·nya
pink *rosado/a* ⓜ/ⓕ ro·*sa*·do/a
pistachio *pistacho* ⓜ pees·*ta*·cho
place *lugar* ⓜ loo·*gar*
place of birth *lugar de nacimiento* ⓜ loo·*gar* de na·see·*myen*·to
plane *avión* ⓜ a·*vyon*
planet *planeta* ⓜ pla·*ne*·ta
plant *mata* ⓕ *ma*·ta
plastic *plástico* ⓜ *plas*·tee·ko

plate *plato* ⓜ *pla*·to
plateau *meseta* ⓕ me·*se*·ta
platform *plataforma* ⓕ pla·ta·*for*·ma
play (cards, etc) *jugar* khoo·*gar*
play (instrument) *tocar* to·*kar*
play (theatre) *obra de teatro* ⓕ *o*·bra de te·*a*·tro
plug (bath) *tapón* ⓜ ta·*pon*
plug (electricity) *enchufe* ⓜ en·*choo*·fe
plum *ciruela* ⓕ see·*rwe*·la
plumber *plomero* ⓜ plo·*me*·ro
pocket *bolsillo* ⓜ bol·*see*·yo
pocketknife *cuchilla* ⓕ koo·*chee*·ya
poetry *poesía* ⓕ po·e·*see*·a
point *señalar* se·nya·*lar*
poisonous *venenoso/a* ⓜ/ⓕ ve·ne·*no*·so/a
police *policía* ⓕ po·lee·*see*·a
police officer (city) *policía* ⓜ&ⓕ po·lee·*see*·a
police officer (country) *guarda rural* ⓜ&ⓕ *gwar*·da roo·*ral*
police station *estación de policía* ⓕ es·ta·*syon* de po·lee·*see*·a
policy *política* ⓕ po·*lee*·tee·ka
politician *político* ⓜ po·*lee*·tee·ko
politics *política* ⓕ po·*lee*·tee·ka
pollen *polen* ⓜ *po*·len
pollution *contaminación* ⓕ kon·ta·mee·na·*syon*
pool (game) *pool* ⓜ pool
pool (swimming) *piscina* ⓕ pee·*see*·na
poor *pobre* ⓜ&ⓕ *po*·bre
popular *popular* ⓜ&ⓕ po·poo·*lar*
pork *cerdo* ⓜ • *chancho* ⓜ *ser*·do • *chan*·cho
port (harbour) *puerto* ⓜ *pwer*·to
positive *positivo/a* ⓜ/ⓕ po·see·*tee*·vo/a
possible *posible* ⓜ&ⓕ po·*see*·ble
post *mandar* man·*dar*
postage *franqueo* ⓜ fran·*ke*·o
postcard *postal* ⓕ pos·*tal*
poster *póster* ⓜ *pos*·ter
postcode *código postal* ⓜ *ko*·dee·go pos·*tal*
post office *correo* ⓜ ko·*re*·o
pot (ceramics) *vasija* ⓕ va·*see*·kha
pot (cooking) *olla* ⓕ *o*·ya
potato *papa* ⓕ *pa*·pa
pottery *alfarería* ⓕ al·fa·re·*ree*·a
pound (currency/weight) *libra* ⓕ *lee*·bra
poverty *pobreza* ⓕ po·*bre*·sa
powder *polvo* ⓜ *pol*·vo
power *poder* ⓜ po·*der*
prawn *gamba* ⓕ *gam*·ba
prayer *oración* ⓕ o·ra·*syon*
prayer book *libro de oraciones* ⓜ *lee*·bro de o·ra·*syo*·nes
prefer *preferir* pre·fe·*reer*
pregnancy test kit *prueba de embarazo* ⓕ *prwe*·ba de em·ba·*ra*·so
pregnant *embarazada* ⓕ em·ba·ra·*sa*·da
premenstrual tension *tensión premenstrual* ⓕ ten·*syon* pre·mens·*trwal*
prepare *preparar* pre·pa·*rar*
prescription (medical) *receta* ⓕ re·*se*·ta
present (gift) *regalo* ⓜ re·*ga*·lo
present (time) *presente* ⓜ pre·*sen*·te
president *presidente* ⓜ&ⓕ pre·see·*den*·te
pressure (tyre) *presión* ⓕ pre·*syon*
pretty *bonito/a* ⓜ/ⓕ bo·*nee*·to/a
price *precio* ⓜ *pre*·syo
priest *cura* ⓜ *koo*·ra
prime minister *primer ministro/primera ministra* ⓜ/ⓕ pree·*mer* mee·*nees*·tro/ pree·*me*·ra mee·*nees*·tra
printer (computer) *impresora* ⓕ eem·pre·*so*·ra
prison *cárcel* ⓕ *kar*·sel
prisoner *reo/a* ⓜ/ⓕ *re*·o/a
private *privado/a* ⓜ/ⓕ pree·*va*·do/a
produce *producir* pro·doo·*seer*
profit *lucrar* loo·*krar*
program *programa* ⓜ pro·*gra*·ma
projector *proyector* ⓜ pro·yek·*tor*
promise *prometer* pro·me·*ter*
prostitute *prostituto/a* ⓜ/ⓕ pros·tee·*too*·to/a
protect *proteger* pro·te·*kher*
protected *protegido/a* ⓜ/ⓕ pro·te·*khee*·do/a
protest *protesta* ⓕ pro·*tes*·ta
protest v *protestar* pro·tes·*tar*
provisions *provisiones* ⓕ pl pro·vee·*syo*·nes
public gardens *jardines públicos* ⓜ pl khar·*dee*·nes *poo*·blee·kos
public phone *teléfono público* ⓜ te·*le*·fo·no *poo*·blee·ko
public relations *relaciones públicas* ⓕ pl re·la·*syo*·nes *poo*·blee·kas
public toilet *baño público* ⓜ *ba*·nyo *poo*·blee·ko
pull *halar* a·*lar*

P

english–costa rican spanish

pump *bomba* ⓕ *bom*·ba
pumpkin *calabaza* ⓕ ka·la·*ba*·sa
puncture v *estallar* es·ta·*yar*
pure *puro/a* ⓜ/ⓕ *poo*·ro/a
purple *morado/a* ⓜ/ⓕ mo·*ra*·do/a
purse *cartera* ⓕ kar·*te*·ra
push *empujar* em·poo·*khar*
put *poner* po·*ner*

Q

quadriplegic *cuadrapléjico/a* ⓜ/ⓕ kwa·dra·*ple*·khee·ko/a
qualifications *cualidades* ⓕ pl kwa·lee·*da*·des
quality *calidad* ⓕ ka·lee·*dad*
quarantine *cuarentena* ⓕ kwa·ren·*te*·na
quarter *cuarto* ⓜ *kwar*·to
queen *reina* ⓕ *ray*·na
question *pregunta* ⓕ pre·*goon*·ta
queue *fila* ⓕ *fee*·la
quick *rápido/a* ⓜ/ⓕ *ra*·pee·do/a
quiet *callado/a* ⓜ/ⓕ ka·*ya*·do/a
quit *darse por vencido/a* ⓜ/ⓕ *dar*·se por ven·*see*·do/a

R

rabbit *conejo* ⓜ ko·*ne*·kho
rabies *rabia* ⓕ *ra*·bya
race (sport) *carrera* ⓕ ka·*re*·ra
racetrack *pista* ⓕ *pees*·ta
racing bike *bicicleta de carreras* ⓕ bee·see·*kle*·ta de ka·*re*·ras
racism *racismo* ⓜ ra·*sees*·mo
racquet *raqueta* ⓕ ra·*ke*·ta
radiator *radiador* ⓜ ra·dya·*dor*
radio *radio* ⓕ *ra*·dyo
radish *rábano* ⓜ *ra*·ba·no
railway station *estación de tren* ⓕ es·ta·*syon* de tren
rain *lluvia* ⓕ *yoo*·vya
raincoat *capa* ⓕ *ka*·pa
rainforest *bosque lluvioso* ⓜ *bos*·ke yoo·*vyo*·so
raisin *pasa* ⓕ *pa*·sa
rally (protest) *protesta* ⓕ pro·*tes*·ta
rape *violación* ⓕ vyo·la·*syon*
rape v *violar* vyo·*lar*
rare (steak) *poco cocido/a* *po*·ko ko·*see*·do/a
rare (uncommon) *raro/a* ⓜ/ⓕ *ra*·ro/a
rash *salpullido* ⓜ sal·poo·*yee*·do
raspberry *frambuesa* ⓕ fram·*bwe*·sa
rat *rata* ⓕ *ra*·ta
rave (party) *rave* ⓜ *ra*·ve
raw *crudo/a* ⓜ/ⓕ *kroo*·do/a
razor *rasuradora* ⓕ ra·soo·ra·*do*·ra
razor blade *navajilla* ⓕ na·va·*khee*·ya
read *leer* le·*er*
reading *lectura* ⓕ lek·*too*·ra
ready *listo/a* ⓜ/ⓕ *lees*·to/a
real estate agent *agente de bienes raíces* ⓜ a·*khen*·te de *bye*·nes ra·*ee*·ses
realistic *realista* ⓜ&ⓕ re·a·*lees*·ta
rear (location) *atrás* a·*tras*
reason *razón* ⓕ ra·*son*
receipt *recibo* ⓜ re·*see*·bo
recently *recientemente* re·syen·te·*men*·te
recommend *recomendar* re·ko·men·*dar*
record *grabar* gra·*bar*
recording *grabación* ⓕ gra·ba·*syon*
recyclable *reciclable* ⓜ&ⓕ re·see·*kla*·ble
recycle *reciclar* re·see·*klar*
red *rojo/a* ⓜ/ⓕ *ro*·kho/a
red wine *vino tinto* ⓜ *vee*·no *teen*·to
referee *árbitro* ⓜ *ar*·bee·tro
reference *referencia* ⓕ re·fe·*ren*·sya
reflexology *reflexología* ⓕ re·flek·so·lo·*khee*·a
refrigerator *refri* ⓜ *re*·free
refugee *refugiado/a* ⓜ/ⓕ re·foo·*khya*·do/a
refund *reintegro* ⓜ re·een·*te*·gro
refuse *negar* ne·*gar*
regional *regional* ⓜ&ⓕ re·khyo·*nal*
registered mail *correo certificado* ⓜ ko·*re*·o ser·tee·fee·*ka*·do
rehydration salts *sales para rehidratación* ⓕ pl *sa*·les *pa*·ra re·ee·dra·ta·*syon*
relationship *relación* ⓕ re·la·*syon*
relax *relajarse* re·la·*khar*·se
relic *reliquia* ⓕ re·*lee*·kya
religion *religión* ⓕ re·lee·*khyon*
religious *religioso/a* ⓜ/ⓕ re·lee·*khyo*·so/a
remote *remoto/a* ⓜ/ⓕ re·*mo*·to/a
remote control *control remoto* ⓜ kon·*trol* re·*mo*·to
rent *alquilar* al·kee·*lar*
repair *reparar* re·pa·*rar*
republic *república* ⓕ re·*poo*·blee·ka

reservation (booking) *reservación* ⓕ re·ser·va·*syon*
rest *descansar* des·kan·*sar*
restaurant *restaurante* ⓜ re·stow·*ran*·te
résumé (CV) *currículum* ⓜ koo·*ree*·koo·loom
retired *retirado/a* ⓜ/ⓕ re·tee·*ra*·do/a
return *volver* vol·*ver*
return ticket *tiquete de ida y vuelta* ⓜ tee·*ke*·te de *ee*·da ee *vwel*·ta
review *revisión* ⓕ re·vee·*syon*
rhythm *ritmo* ⓜ *reet*·mo
rib (body) *costilla* ⓕ kos·*tee*·ya
rice *arroz* ⓜ a·*ros*
rich *rico/a* ⓜ/ⓕ *ree*·ko/a
ride *aventón* ⓜ a·ven·*ton*
ride (bike, horse) *andar* an·*dar*
right (correct) *correcto/a* ⓜ/ⓕ ko·*rek*·to/a
right (direction) *derecha* ⓕ de·*re*·cha
right-wing *derechista* ⓜ&ⓕ de·re·*chees*·ta
ring (jewellry) *anillo* ⓜ a·*nee*·yo
ring (phone) *timbre* ⓜ *teem*·bre
rip-off *robo* ⓜ *ro*·bo
risk *riesgo* ⓜ *ryes*·go
river *río* ⓜ *ree*·o
road *calle* ⓕ *ka*·ye
road map *mapa de calles* ⓜ *ma*·pa de *ka*·yes
rob *robar* ro·*bar*
rock (music) *rock* ⓜ rok
rock (stone) *piedra* ⓕ *pye*·dra
rock climbing *escalada* ⓕ es·ka·*la*·da
rock group *grupo de rock* ⓜ *groo*·po de rok
roll (bread) *bollo (de pan)* ⓜ *bo*·yo (de pan)
rollerblading *patinaje sobre ruedas* ⓜ pa·tee·*na*·khe *so*·bre *rwe*·das
romantic n&a *romántico/a* ⓜ/ⓕ ro·*man*·tee·ko/a
room *habitación* ⓕ a·bee·ta·*syon*
room number *número de habitación* ⓜ *noo*·me·ro de a·bee·ta·*syon*
rope *cuerda* ⓕ *kwer*·da
round (drinks) *ronda* ⓕ *ron*·da
round (shape) *redondo/a* ⓜ/ⓕ re·*don*·do/a
roundabout *rotonda* ⓕ ro·*ton*·da
route *ruta* ⓕ *roo*·ta
rowing *remo* ⓜ *re*·mo
rubbish *basura* ⓕ ba·*soo*·ra
rubella *rubéola* ⓕ roo·*be*·o·la
rug *alfombra* ⓕ al·*fom*·bra
ruins *ruinas* ⓕ pl *rwee*·nas
rule *regla* ⓕ *re*·gla
rum *ron* ⓜ ron
run *correr* ko·*rer*
running *corriendo* ⓜ ko·*ryen*·do
runny nose *moquera* ⓕ mo·*ke*·ra

S

sad *triste* ⓜ&ⓕ *trees*·te
saddle *montura* ⓕ mon·*too*·ra
safe *seguro/a* ⓜ/ⓕ se·*goo*·ro/a
safe (for valuables) *caja fuerte* ⓕ *ka*·kha *fwer*·te
safe sex *sexo seguro* ⓜ *sek*·so se·*goo*·ro
sailboarding *windsurf* ⓜ *weend*·soorf
saint *santo/a* ⓜ/ⓕ *san*·to/a
salad *ensalada* ⓕ en·sa·*la*·da
salami *salami* ⓜ sa·*la*·mee
salary *salario* ⓜ sa·*la*·ryo
sale *promoción* ⓕ pro·mo·*syon*
sales assistant *asistente de ventas* ⓜ&ⓕ a·sees·*ten*·te de *ven*·tas
sales tax *impuesto de ventas* ⓜ eem·*pwes*·to de *ven*·tas
salmon *salmón* ⓜ sal·*mon*
salt *sal* ⓕ sal
same *mismo/a* ⓜ/ⓕ *mees*·mo/a
sand *arena* ⓕ a·*re*·na
sandals *chancletas* ⓕ pl chan·*kle*·tas
sanitary napkin *toalla sanitaria* ⓕ to·*a*·ya sa·nee·*ta*·rya
sardine *sardina* ⓕ sar·*dee*·na
Saturday *sábado* ⓜ *sa*·ba·do
sauce *salsa* ⓕ *sal*·sa
saucepan *olla* ⓕ *o*·ya
sauna *sauna* ⓜ *sow*·na
sausage *chorizo* ⓜ cho·*ree*·so
saxophone *saxofón* ⓜ sak·so·*fon*
say *decir* de·*seer*
scalp *cuero cabelludo* ⓜ *kwe*·ro ka·be·*yoo*·do
scarf *bufanda* ⓕ boo·*fan*·da
school *escuela* ⓕ es·*kwe*·la
science *ciencia* ⓕ *syen*·sya
scientist *científico/a* ⓜ/ⓕ syen·*tee*·fee·ko/a
scissors *tijeras* ⓕ pl tee·*khe*·ras
score *anotar* a·no·*tar*
scoreboard *marcador* ⓜ mar·ka·*dor*
Scotland *Escocia* ⓕ es·*ko*·sya

S

scrambled (eggs) *revuelto/a* ⓜ/ⓕ re·wel·to/a
sculpture *escultura* ⓕ es·kool·too·ra
sea *mar* ⓜ mar
seasick *mareado/a* ⓜ/ⓕ ma·re·a·do/a
seaside *costa* ⓕ kos·ta
season *temporada* ⓕ tem·po·ra·da
seat (place) *asiento* ⓜ a·syen·to
seatbelt *cinturón* ⓜ seen·too·ron
second (time unit) *segundo* ⓜ se·goon·do
second (number) *segundo/a* ⓜ/ⓕ se·goon·do/a
second class *segunda clase* ⓕ se·goon·da kla·se
secondhand *usado/a* ⓜ/ⓕ oo·sa·do/a
secondhand shop *tienda de artículos usados* ⓕ tyen·da de ar·tee·koo·los oo·sa·dos
secretary *secretario/a* ⓜ/ⓕ se·kre·ta·ryo/a
see *ver* ver
self-employed *tener su propio negocio* te·ner soo pro·pyo ne·go·syo
selfish *egoísta* ⓜ&ⓕ e·go·ees·ta
self-service ⓜ *auto servicio* ow·to ser·vee·syo
sell *vender* ven·der
send *enviar* en·vyar
sensible *sensible* ⓜ&ⓕ sen·see·ble
sensual *sensual* ⓜ&ⓕ sen·swal
separate *separado/a* ⓜ/ⓕ se·pa·ra·do/a
September *septiembre* ⓜ sep·tyem·bre
serious *serio/a* ⓜ/ⓕ se·ryo/a
service *servicio* ⓜ ser·vee·syo
service charge *servicio* ⓜ ser·vee·syo
service station *bomba* ⓕ bom·ba
serviette *servilleta* ⓕ ser·vee·ye·ta
several *varios/as* ⓜ/ⓕ pl va·ryos/as
sew *coser* ko·ser
sex *sexo* ⓜ sek·so
sexism *sexismo* ⓜ sek·sees·mo
shade *sombra* ⓕ som·bra
shadow *sombra* ⓕ som·bra
shampoo *champú* ⓜ cham·poo
shape *forma* ⓕ for·ma
share (with) *compartir (con)* kom·par·teer (kon)
shave *rasurar* ra·soo·rar
shaving cream *espuma de afeitar* ⓕ es·poo·ma de a·fay·tar
she *ella* e·ya
sheep *oveja* ⓕ o·ve·kha
sheet (bed) *sábana* ⓕ sa·ba·na
shelf *repisa* ⓕ re·pee·sa
shingles (illness) *herpes* ⓜ er·pes
ship *barco* ⓜ bar·ko
shirt *camisa* ⓕ ka·mee·sa
shoe *zapato* ⓜ sa·pa·to
shoelace *cordón de zapato* ⓜ kor·don de sa·pa·to
shoe shop *zapatería* ⓕ sa·pa·te·ree·a
shoot *disparar* dees·pa·rar
shop *tienda* ⓕ tyen·da
shop v *ir de compras* eer de kom·pras
shopping *compras* ⓕ pl kom·pras
shopping centre *centro comercial* ⓜ sen·tro ko·mer·syal
short (height) *bajo/a* ⓜ/ⓕ ba·kho/a
short (length) *corto/a* ⓜ/ⓕ kor·to/a
shortage *escasez* ⓕ es·ka·ses
shorts *chores* ⓜ pl cho·res
shoulder *hombro* ⓜ om·bro
shout *gritar* gree·tar
show *espectáculo* ⓜ es·pek·ta·koo·lo
show v *enseñar* en·se·nyar
shower (bath) *ducha* ⓕ doo·cha
shrine *santuario* ⓜ san·too·a·ryo
shut *cerrado/a* ⓜ/ⓕ se·ra·do/a
shy *tímido/a* ⓜ/ⓕ tee·mee·do/a
sick *enfermo/a* ⓜ/ⓕ en·fer·mo/a
side *lado* ⓜ la·do
sign *señal* ⓕ se·nyal
sign (one's name) v *firmar* feer·mar
signature *firma* ⓕ feer·ma
silk *seda* ⓕ se·da
silver *plata* ⓕ pla·ta
SIM card *tarjeta SIM* ⓕ tar·khe·ta seem
similar *similar* ⓜ&ⓕ see·mee·lar
simple *sencillo/a* ⓜ/ⓕ sen·see·yo/a
since (time) *desde* des·de
sing *cantar* kan·tar
singer *cantante* ⓜ&ⓕ kan·tan·te
single (person) *soltero/a* ⓜ/ⓕ sol·te·ro/a
single room *habitación sencilla* ⓕ a·bee·ta·syon sen·see·ya
sister *hermana* ⓕ er·ma·na
sit *sentarse* sen·tar·se
size (clothes) *talla* ⓕ ta·ya
size (general) *tamaño* ⓜ ta·ma·nyo
skate *patinar* pa·tee·nar
skateboarding *andar en patineta* ⓜ an·dar en pa·tee·ne·ta
ski *esquiar* es·kyar

DICTIONARY

skiing *esquí* ⓜ es·*kee*
skim milk *leche descremada* ⓕ *le*·che des·kre·*ma*·da
skin *piel* ⓕ pyel
skirt *enagua* ⓕ e·*na*·gwa
skull *cráneo* ⓜ *kra*·ne·o
sky *cielo* ⓜ *sye*·lo
sleep *sueño* ⓜ *swe*·nyo
sleep *dormir* dor·*meer*
sleeping bag *saco de dormir* ⓜ *sa*·ko de dor·*meer*
sleeping berth *litera* ⓕ lee·*te*·ra
sleeping pills *pastillas para dormir* ⓕ pl pas·*tee*·yas *pa*·ra dor·*meer*
slice *tajada* ⓕ ta·*kha*·da
slide (film) *diapositivas* ⓕ pl dya·po·see·*tee*·vas
slow *lento/a* ⓜ/ⓕ *len*·to/a
slowly *despacio* des·*pa*·syo
small *pequeño/a* ⓜ/ⓕ pe·*ke*·nyo/a
smaller *más pequeño/a* ⓜ/ⓕ mas pe·*ke*·nyo/a
(the) smallest *el/la más pequeño/a* ⓜ/ⓕ el/la mas pe·*ke*·nyo/a
smell *olor* ⓜ o·*lor*
smile *sonreír* son·re·*eer*
smoke (cigarettes) *fumar* foo·*mar*
snack *merienda* ⓕ me·*ryen*·da
snail *caracol* ⓜ ka·ra·*kol*
snake *culebra* ⓕ koo·*le*·bra
snorkelling *esnorclear* ⓜ es·nor·kle·*ar*
snow *nieve* ⓕ *nye*·ve
snowboarding *snowboarding* ⓜ es·*no*·bor·deen
snow pea *vainica china* ⓕ vai·*nee*·ka *chee*·na
soap *jabón* ⓜ kha·*bon*
soap opera *novela* ⓕ no·*ve*·la
soccer *fútbol* ⓜ *foot*·bol
socialist n&a *socialista* ⓜ&ⓕ so·sya·*lees*·ta
social welfare *bienestar social* ⓜ byen·*es*·tar so·*syal*
socks *medias* ⓕ pl *me*·dyas
soft-boiled (eggs) *tierno/a* ⓜ/ⓕ *tyer*·no/a
soft drink *refresco* ⓜ re·*fres*·ko
soldier *soldado* ⓜ sol·*da*·do
some *algún/alguna* ⓜ/ⓕ al·*goon*/al·*goo*·na
someone *alguien* *al*·gyen
something *algo* *al*·go
sometimes *a veces* a *ve*·ses
son *hijo* ⓜ *ee*·kho
song *canción* ⓕ kan·*syon*
soon *pronto* ⓜ *pron*·to
sore *adolorido/a* ⓜ/ⓕ a·do·lo·*ree*·do/a
soup *sopa* ⓕ *so*·pa
sour cream *natilla* ⓕ na·*tee*·ya
south *sur* ⓜ soor
souvenir *recuerdo* ⓜ re·*kwer*·do
souvenir shop *tienda de recuerdos* ⓕ *tyen*·da de re·*kwer*·dos
soy milk *leche de soya* ⓕ *le*·che de *so*·ya
soy sauce *salsa de soya* ⓕ *sal*·sa de *so*·ya
space (room) *campo* ⓜ *kam*·po
Spain *España* ⓕ es·*pa*·nya
Spanish (language) *castellano* • *español* ka·ste·*ya*·no • es·pa·*nyol*
sparkling wine *vino espumante* ⓜ *vee*·no es·poo·*man*·te
speak *hablar* a·*blar*
special *especial* ⓜ&ⓕ es·pe·*syal*
specialist *especialista* ⓜ&ⓕ es·pe·sya·*lees*·ta
speed (drug) *anfetamina* ⓕ an·fe·ta·*mee*·na
speed (travel) *velocidad* ⓕ ve·lo·see·*dad*
speed limit *límite de velocidad* ⓜ *lee*·mee·te de ve·lo·see·*dad*
speedometer *velocímetro* ⓜ ve·lo·*see*·me·tro
spider *araña* ⓕ a·*ra*·nya
spinach *espinaca* ⓕ es·pee·*na*·ka
spoilt (food) *podrido/a* ⓜ/ⓕ po·*dree*·do/a
spoilt (person) *chineado/a* ⓜ/ⓕ chee·ne·*a*·do/a
spoke (wheel) *radio* ⓜ *ra*·dyo
spoon *cuchara* ⓕ koo·*cha*·ra
sport *deporte* ⓜ de·*por*·te
sportsperson *deportista* ⓜ&ⓕ de·por·*tees*·ta
sports store *tienda deportiva* ⓕ *tyen*·da de·por·*tee*·va
sprain *esguince* ⓜ es·*geen*·se
spring (coil) *resorte* ⓜ re·*sor*·te
spring (season) *primavera* ⓕ pree·ma·*ve*·ra
square (town) *plaza* ⓕ *pla*·sa
stadium *estadio* ⓜ es·*ta*·dyo
stairway *escaleras* ⓕ pl es·ka·*le*·ras
stale *rancio/a* ⓜ/ⓕ *ran*·syo/a
stamp (postage) *estampilla* ⓕ es·tam·*pee*·ya
stand-by ticket *tiquete de stand-by* ⓜ tee·*ke*·te de stan·*bai*

star *estrella* ⓕ es·tre·ya
(four-)star *(cuatro) estrellas* (kwa·tro) es·tre·yas
start *inicio* ⓜ ee·nee·syo
start *empezar* em·pe·sar
station *estación* ⓕ es·ta·syon
stationer *librería* ⓕ lee·bre·ree·a
statue *estatua* ⓕ es·ta·twa
stay *quedarse* ke·dar·se
steak (beef) *bistec* ⓜ bee·stek
steal *robar* ro·bar
steep *empinado/a* ⓜ/ⓕ em·pee·na·do/a
step *grada* ⓕ gra·da
stereo *equipo de sonido* ⓜ e·kee·po de so·nee·do
still water *agua sin gas* ⓕ a·gwa seen gas
stockings *calcetines* ⓕ pl kal·se·tee·nes
stolen *robado/a* ⓜ/ⓕ ro·ba·do/a
stomach *estómago* ⓜ es·to·ma·go
stomachache *dolor de estómago* ⓜ do·lor de es·to·ma·go
stone *piedra* ⓕ pye·dra
stoned (drugged) *pijiado/a* ⓜ/ⓕ pee·khya·do/a
stop (bus, tram) *parada* ⓕ pa·ra·da
stop (cease) *parar* pa·rar
stop (prevent) *prevenir* pre·ve·neer
storm *tormenta* ⓕ tor·men·ta
story *cuento* ⓜ kwen·to
stove *cocina* ⓕ ko·see·na
straight *recto/a* ⓜ/ⓕ rek·to/a
strange *raro/a* ⓜ/ⓕ ra·ro/a
stranger *desconocido/a* ⓜ/ⓕ des·ko·no·see·do/a
strawberry *fresa* ⓕ fre·sa
stream *arrollo* ⓜ a·ro·yo
street *calle* ⓕ ka·ye
street market *mercado callejero* ⓜ mer·ka·do ka·ye·khe·ro
strike (hit) *golpe* ⓜ gol·pe
strike (stoppage) *huelga* ⓕ wel·ga
string *hilo* ⓜ ee·lo
stroke (health) *derrame* ⓜ de·ra·me
stroller *coche* ⓜ ko·che
strong *fuerte* ⓜ&ⓕ fwer·te
stubborn *terco/a* ⓜ/ⓕ ter·ko/a
student *estudiante* ⓜ&ⓕ es·too·dyan·te
studio *estudio* ⓜ es·too·dyo
stupid *estúpido/a* ⓜ/ⓕ es·too·pee·do/a
style *estilo* ⓜ es·tee·lo
subtitles *subtítulos* ⓜ pl soob·tee·too·los
suburb *suburbio* ⓜ soo·boor·byo
sugar *azúcar* ⓜ a·soo·kar
suitcase *maleta* ⓕ ma·le·ta
summer *verano* ⓜ ve·ra·no
sun *sol* ⓜ sol
sunblock *bloqueador* ⓜ blo·ke·a·dor
sunburn *quemadura de sol* ⓕ ke·ma·doo·ra de sol
Sunday *domingo* ⓜ do·meen·go
sunglasses *anteojos de sol* ⓜ pl an·te·o·khos de sol
sunny *soleado/a* ⓜ/ⓕ so·le·a·do/a
sunrise *amanecer* ⓜ a·ma·ne·ser
sunset *atardecer* ⓜ a·tar·de·ser
sunstroke *insolación* ⓕ een·so·la·syon
supermarket *supermercado* ⓜ soo·per·mer·ka·do
superstition *superstición* ⓕ soo·pers·tee·syon
supporter (politics) *partidario/a* ⓜ/ⓕ par·tee·da·ryo/a
supporter (sport) *aficionado/a* ⓜ/ⓕ a·fee·syo·na·do/a
surfing *surf* ⓜ soorf
surf v *surfear* soor·fe·ar
surface mail (land) *correo por tierra* ⓜ ko·re·o por tye·ra
surface mail (sea) *correo por mar* ⓜ ko·re·o por mar
surfboard *tabla de surf* ⓕ ta·bla de soorf
surfing *surf* ⓜ soorf
surname *apellido* ⓜ a·pe·yee·do
surprise *sorpresa* ⓕ sor·pre·sa
sweater *suéter* ⓜ swe·ter
Sweden *Suecia* ⓕ swe·sya
sweet *dulce* ⓜ&ⓕ dool·se
sweets *dulces* ⓜ pl dool·ses
swelling *hinchazón* ⓕ een·cha·son
swim *nadar* na·dar
swimming *nado* ⓜ na·do
swimming pool *piscina* ⓕ pee·see·na
swimsuit *vestido de baño* ⓜ ves·tee·do de ba·nyo
Switzerland *Suiza* ⓕ swee·sa
synagogue *sinagoga* ⓕ see·na·go·ga
synthetic *sintético/a* ⓜ/ⓕ seen·te·tee·ko/a
syringe *jeringa* ⓕ khe·reen·ga

T

table *mesa* ⓕ me·sa
tablecloth *mantel* ⓜ man·tel
table tennis *tenis de mesa* ⓜ te·nees de me·sa
tail *cola* ⓕ ko·la
tailor *sastre* ⓜ sas·tre
take *llevar* ye·var
take a photo *tomar una foto* to·mar oo·na fo·to
talk *hablar* a·blar
tall *alto/a* ⓜ/ⓕ al·to/a
tampon *tampón* ⓜ tam·pon
tanning lotion *bronceador* ⓜ bron·se·a·dor
tap (sink) *tubo* ⓜ too·bo
tap water *agua de tubo* ⓕ a·gwa de too·bo
tasty *rico/a* ⓜ/ⓕ ree·ko/a
tax *impuesto* ⓜ eem·pwes·to
taxi *taxi* ⓜ tak·see
taxi stand *parada de taxis* ⓕ pa·ra·da de tak·sees
tea *té* ⓜ te
teacher *maestro/a* ⓜ/ⓕ ma·es·tro/a
team *equipo* ⓜ e·kee·po
teaspoon *cucharita* ⓕ koo·cha·ree·ta
technique *técnica* ⓕ tek·nee·ka
teeth *dientes* ⓜ pl dyen·tes
telegram *telegrama* ⓜ te·le·gra·ma
telephone *teléfono* ⓜ te·le·fo·no
telephone *llamar* ya·mar
telephone centre *central telefónica* ⓕ sen·tral te·le·fo·nee·ka
telescope *telescopio* ⓜ te·les·ko·pyo
television *televisión* ⓕ te·le·vee·syon
tell *decir* de·seer
temperature (fever) *fiebre* ⓕ fye·bre
temperature (weather) *temperatura* ⓕ tem·pe·ra·too·ra
temple (building) *templo* ⓜ tem·plo
tennis *tenis* ⓜ te·nees
tennis court *cancha de tenis* ⓕ kan·cha de te·nees
tent *tienda de campaña* ⓕ tyen·da de kam·pa·nya
tent peg *clavija* ⓕ kla·vee·kha
terrible *terrible* ⓜ&ⓕ te·ree·ble
terrorism *terrorismo* ⓜ te·ro·rees·mo
test *prueba* ⓕ prwe·ba
thank *agradecer* a·gra·de·ser
that a *ese/a* ⓜ/ⓕ e·se/a
theatre *teatro* ⓜ te·a·tro
their *su* soo
there *ahí* a·ee
they *ellos/as* ⓜ/ⓕ pl e·yos/as
thick *grueso/a* ⓜ/ⓕ grwe·so/a
thief *ladrón/ladrona* ⓜ/ⓕ la·dron/la·dro·na
thin *delgado/a* ⓜ/ⓕ del·ga·do/a
think *pensar* pen·sar
third *tercero/a* ⓜ/ⓕ ter·se·ro/a
this a *este/a* ⓜ/ⓕ es·te/a
thread *hilo* ⓜ ee·lo
throat *garganta* ⓕ gar·gan·ta
thrush (health) *zorzal* ⓜ sor·sal
thunderstorm *tormenta eléctrica* ⓕ tor·men·ta e·lek·tree·ka
Thursday *jueves* ⓜ khwe·ves
ticket *tiquete* ⓜ tee·ke·te
ticket collector *colector de tiquetes* ⓜ ko·lek·tor de tee·ke·tes
ticket machine *máquina de tiquetes* ⓕ ma·kee·na de tee·ke·tes
ticket office *ventanilla* ⓕ ven·ta·nee·ya
tide *marea* ⓕ ma·re·a
tight *socado/a* ⓜ/ⓕ so·ka·do/a
time *tiempo* ⓜ tyem·po
time difference *diferencia de hora* ⓕ dee·fe·ren·sya de o·ra
timetable *itinerario* ⓜ ee·tee·ne·ra·ryo
tin (can) *lata* ⓕ la·ta
tin opener *abrelatas* ⓜ a·bre·la·tas
tiny *diminuto/a* ⓜ/ⓕ dee·mee·noo·to/a
tip (gratuity) *propina* ⓕ pro·pee·na
tire *llanta* ⓕ yan·ta
tired *cansado/a* ⓜ/ⓕ kan·sa·do/a
tissues *klíneks* ⓜ pl klee·neks
to *a* a
toast (food) *tostada* ⓕ tos·ta·da
toaster *tostador* ⓜ tos·ta·dor
tobacco *tabaco* ⓜ ta·ba·ko
tobacconist *tabaquería* ⓕ ta·ba·ke·ree·a
today *hoy* oi
toe *dedo del pie* ⓜ de·do del pye
together *juntos/as* ⓜ/ⓕ pl khoon·tos/as
toilet *baño* ⓜ ba·nyo
toilet paper *papel higiénico* ⓜ pa·pel ee·khye·nee·ko
tomato *tomate* ⓜ to·ma·te

tomato sauce *salsa de tomate* ⓕ sal·sa de to·ma·te
tomorrow *mañana* ma·nya·na
tonight *esta noche* es·ta no·che
too (much) *demasiado* de·ma·sya·do
too (also) *también* tam·byen
tooth *diente* ⓜ dyen·te
toothache *dolor de diente* ⓜ do·lor de dyen·te
toothbrush *cepillo de dientes* ⓜ se·pee·yo de dyen·tes
toothpaste *pasta de dientes* ⓕ pas·ta de dyen·tes
toothpick *palillo de dientes* ⓜ pa·lee·yo de dyen·tes
torch (flashlight) *foco* ⓜ fo·ko
touch *tocar* to·kar
tour *tour* ⓜ toor
tourist *turista* ⓜ&ⓕ too·rees·ta
tourist office *oficina de turismo* ⓕ o·fee·see·na de too·rees·mo
towards *hacia* a·see·a
towel *paño* ⓜ pa·nyo
tower *torre* ⓕ to·re
toxic waste *desecho tóxico* ⓜ de·se·cho tok·see·ko
toy shop *juguetería* ⓕ khoo·ge·te·ree·a
track (path) *camino* ⓜ ka·mee·no
track (sport) *pista* ⓕ pees·ta
trade *comercio* ⓜ ko·mer·syo
tradesperson *comerciante* ⓜ&ⓕ ko·mer·syan·te
traffic *tránsito* ⓜ tran·see·to
traffic light *semáforo* ⓜ se·ma·fo·ro
trail *camino* ⓜ ka·mee·no
train *tren* ⓜ tren
train station *estación de tren* ⓕ es·ta·syon de tren
tram *tranvía* ⓜ tran·vee·a
translate *traducir* tra·doo·seer
translator *traductor/traductora* ⓜ/ⓕ tra·dook·tor/tra·dook·to·ra
transport *transporte* ⓜ trans·por·te
travel *viajar* vya·khar
travel agency *agencia de viajes* ⓕ a·khen·sya de vya·khes
travellers cheque *cheque de viajero* ⓜ che·ke de vya·khe·ro
travel sickness *enfermedad del viajero* ⓕ en·fer·me·dad del vya·khe·ro
tree *árbol* ⓜ ar·bol
trip (journey) *viaje* ⓜ vya·khe
tropical plains *llanuras* ⓕ pl ya·noo·ras
trousers *pantalones* ⓜ pl pan·ta·lo·nes
truck *camión* ⓜ ka·myon
trumpet *trompeta* ⓕ trom·pe·ta
trust *confiar* kon·fyar
try (attempt) *tratar* tra·tar
T-shirt *camiseta* ⓕ ka·mee·se·ta
tube (tyre) *neumático* ⓜ ne·oo·ma·tee·ko
Tuesday *martes* ⓜ mar·tes
tumour *tumor* ⓜ too·mor
tuna *atún* ⓜ a·toon
tune *melodía* ⓕ me·lo·dee·a
turkey *pavo* ⓜ pa·vo
turn *dar vuelta* dar vwel·ta
TV *televisor* ⓜ te·le·vee·sor
tweezers *pinzas* ⓕ pl peen·sas
twice *dos veces* dos ve·ses
twin beds *camas sencillas* ⓕ pl ka·mas sen·see·yas
twins *gemelos/as* ⓜ/ⓕ pl khe·me·los/as
two *dos* dos
type *tipo* ⓜ tee·po
typhoid *tifoidea* ⓕ tee·foy·de·a
typical *típico/a* ⓜ/ⓕ tee·pee·ko/a
tyre *llanta* ⓕ yan·ta

U

ultrasound *ultrasonido* ⓜ ool·tra·so·nee·do
umbrella *sombrilla* ⓕ som·bree·ya
uncomfortable *incómodo/a* ⓜ/ⓕ een·ko·mo·do/a
understand *entender* en·ten·der
underwear *ropa interior* ⓕ ro·pa een·te·ryor
unemployed *desempleado/a* ⓜ/ⓕ de·sem·ple·a·do/a
unfair *injusto/a* ⓜ/ⓕ een·khoos·to/a
uniform *uniforme* ⓜ oo·nee·for·me
universe *universo* ⓜ oo·nee·ver·so
university *universidad* ⓕ oo·nee·ver·see·dad
unleaded (petrol) *sin plomo* seen plo·mo
unsafe *inseguro/a* ⓜ/ⓕ een·se·goo·ro/a
until *hasta* as·ta
unusual *raro/a* ⓜ/ⓕ ra·ro/a
up *arriba* a·ree·ba
uphill *cuesta arriba* kwes·ta a·ree·ba
urgent *urgente* ⓜ&ⓕ oor·khen·te

urinary infection *infección urinaria* ⓕ een·fek·syon oo·ree·na·rya
USA *Estados Unidos* ⓜ pl es·ta·dos oo·nee·dos
useful *útil* ⓜ&ⓕ oo·teel

V

vacancy *espacio disponible* ⓜ es·pa·syo dees·po·nee·ble
vacant *vacío/a* ⓜ/ⓕ va·see·o/a
vacation *vacación* ⓕ va·ka·syon
vaccination *vacunación* ⓕ va·koo·na·syon
vagina *vagina* ⓕ va·khee·na
validate *validar* va·lee·dar
valley *valle* ⓜ va·ye
valuable *valioso/a* ⓜ/ⓕ va·lyo·so/a
value (price) *valor* ⓜ va·lor
van *van* ⓕ van
veal *ternera* ⓕ ter·ne·ra
vegetable *vegetal* ⓜ ve·khe·tal
vegetarian n&a *vegetariano/a* ⓜ/ⓕ ve·khe·ta·rya·no/a
vein *vena* ⓕ ve·na
venereal disease *enfermedad venérea* ⓕ en·fer·me·dad ve·ne·re·a
venue *lugar* ⓜ loo·gar
very *muy* mooy
video camera *cámara de video* ⓕ ka·ma·ra de vee·de·o
video recorder *video* ⓜ vee·de·o
video tape *cinta de video* ⓕ seen·ta de vee·de·o
view *vista* ⓕ vees·ta
village *pueblo* ⓜ pwe·blo
vine *vid* ⓕ veed
vinegar *vinagre* ⓜ vee·na·gre
vineyard *viñedo* ⓜ vee·nye·do
violin *violín* ⓜ vee·o·leen
virus *virus* ⓜ vee·roos
visa *visa* ⓕ vee·sa
visit *visita* ⓕ vee·see·ta
vitamins *vitaminas* ⓕ pl vee·ta·mee·nas
visually impaired *discapacitado/a visual* ⓜ/ⓕ dees·ka·pa·see·ta·do/a vee·swal
voice *voz* ⓕ vos
volcano *volcán* ⓜ vol·kan
volleyball *volibol* ⓜ vo·lee·bol
volume *volumen* ⓜ vo·loo·men
vote *votar* vo·tar

W

wage *salario* ⓜ sa·la·ryo
wait *esperar* es·pe·rar
waiter *mesero/a* ⓜ/ⓕ me·se·ro/a
waiting room *sala de espera* ⓕ sa·la de es·pe·ra
wake (someone) up *despertar* des·per·tar
walk *caminar* ka·mee·nar
wall *pared* ⓕ pa·red
want *querer* ke·rer
war *guerra* ⓕ ge·ra
wardrobe *armario* ⓜ ar·ma·ryo
warm *caliente* ⓜ&ⓕ ka·lyen·te
warn *advertir* ad·ver·teer
wash (oneself) *lavarse* la·var·se
wash (something) *lavar* la·var
wash cloth (flannel) *toallita* ⓕ to·a·yee·ta
washing machine *lavadora* ⓕ la·va·do·ra
wasp *avispa* ⓕ a·vees·pa
watch (clock) *reloj* ⓜ re·lokh
watch *observar* ob·ser·var
water *agua* ⓕ a·gwa
water bottle *botella de agua* ⓕ bo·te·ya de a·gwa
water bottle (hot) *termo* ⓜ ter·mo
waterfall *catarata* ⓕ ka·ta·ra·ta
watermelon *sandía* ⓕ san·dee·a
waterproof *contra agua* kon·tra a·gwa
water-skiing *esquí acuático* ⓜ es·kee a·kwa·tee·ko
wave (beach) *ola* ⓕ o·la
way *camino* ⓜ ka·mee·no
we *nosotros/as* ⓜ/ⓕ pl no·so·tros/as
weak *débil* ⓜ&ⓕ de·beel
wealthy *rico/a* ⓜ/ⓕ ree·ko/a
wear *ponerse* po·ner·se
weather *tiempo* ⓜ tyem·po
wedding *boda* ⓕ bo·da
wedding cake *queque de bodas* ⓜ ke·ke de bo·das
wedding present *regalo de bodas* ⓜ re·ga·lo de bo·das
Wednesday *miércoles* ⓜ myer·ko·les
week *semana* ⓕ se·ma·na
weekend *fin de semana* ⓜ feen de se·ma·na
weigh *pesar* pe·sar
weight *peso* ⓜ pe·so
weights *pesas* ⓕ pl pe·sas

welcome *dar la bienvenida* dar la byen·ve·*nee*·da
welfare *bienestar* ⓜ byen·es·*tar*
well *bien* byen
west *oeste* ⓜ o·*es*·te
wet *mojado/a* ⓜ/ⓕ mo·*kha*·do/a
what *qué* ke
wheel *rueda* ⓕ *rwe*·da
wheelchair *silla de ruedas* ⓕ *see*·ya de *rwe*·das
when *cuándo* *kwan*·do
where *dónde* *don*·de
which *cuál* kwal
white *blanco/a* ⓜ/ⓕ *blan*·ko/a
white wine *vino blanco* ⓜ *vee*·no *blan*·ko
who *quién* kyen
wholemeal bread *pan integral* ⓜ pan een·te·*gral*
why *por qué* por ke
wide *ancho/a* ⓜ/ⓕ *an*·cho/a
wife *esposa* ⓕ es·*po*·sa
wildlife *flora y fauna silvestre* ⓕ *flo*·ra ee *fow*·na seel·*ves*·tre
win *ganar* ga·*nar*
wind *viento* ⓜ *vyen*·to
window *ventana* ⓕ ven·*ta*·na
windscreen *parabrisas* ⓜ pa·ra·*bree*·sas
wine *vino* ⓜ *vee*·no
wings *alas* ⓕ pl *a*·las
winner *ganador/ganadora* ⓜ/ⓕ ga·na·*dor*/ga·na·*do*·ra
winter *invierno* ⓜ een·*vyer*·no
wire *alambre* ⓜ a·*lam*·bre
wish *desear* de·se·*ar*
with *con* kon
within (time) *dentro de* *den*·tro de
without *sin* seen
woman *mujer* ⓕ moo·*kher*
wonderful *maravilloso/a* ⓜ/ⓕ ma·ra·vee·*yo*·so/a
wood (food) *madera* ⓕ ma·*de*·ra
wool *lana* ⓕ *la*·na
word *palabra* ⓕ pa·*la*·bra
work *trabajo* ⓜ tra·*ba*·kho
work (function) *funcionar* foon·syo·*nar*
work (job) *trabajar* tra·ba·*khar*
work experience *experiencia laboral* ⓕ eks·pe·*ryen*·sya la·bo·*ral*
workout *sesión de ejercicios* ⓕ se·*syon* de e·kher·*see*·syos
work permit *permiso de trabajo* ⓜ per·*mee*·so de tra·*ba*·kho
workshop *taller* ⓜ ta·*yer*
world *mundo* ⓜ *moon*·do
World Cup *Mundial* ⓜ moon·*dyal*
worms (intestinal) *lombrices* ⓕ pl lom·*bree*·ses
worried *preocupado/a* ⓜ/ⓕ pre·o·koo·*pa*·do/a
worship *adorar* a·do·*rar*
wrist *muñeca* ⓕ moo·*nye*·ka
write *escribir* es·kree·*beer*
writer *autor* ⓜ ow·*tor*
wrong *equivocado/a* ⓜ/ⓕ e·kee·vo·*ka*·do/a

Y

year *año* ⓜ *a*·nyo
yellow *amarillo/a* ⓜ/ⓕ a·ma·*ree*·yo/a
yes *sí* see
yesterday *ayer* a·*yer*
(not) yet *todavía (no)* to·da·*vee*·a (no)
you sg inf *tú* • *vos* too • vos
you sg pol *usted* oos·*ted*
you pl *ustedes* oos·*te*·des
young *joven* ⓜ&ⓕ *kho*·ven
your sg inf *tu* too
your sg pol&pl *su* so
youth hostel *albergue juvenil* ⓜ al·*ber*·ge khoo·ve·*neel*

Z

zip(per) *zipper* ⓜ *see*·per
zodiac *zodíaco* ⓜ so·*dee*·a·ko
zoo *zoológico* ⓜ so·o·*lo*·khee·ko
zoom lens *lente zoom* ⓜ *len*·te soom

costa rican spanish–english

The words in this dictionary are listed in Spanish alphabetical order (see the box **spanish alphabet**, page 13). Spanish nouns have their gender indicated with ⓜ (masculine) and ⓕ (feminine). If adjectives and nouns have just one form for both genders, it's marked as ⓜ&ⓕ. Where adjectives and nouns have separate masculine and feminine forms, the endings are divided by a slash (eg *bello/a* ⓜ/ⓕ). Where the letter *a* is added onto a masculine form to make a feminine form, the added ending is in brackets (eg *director(a)* ⓜ/ⓕ). See the **phrasebuilder** for more on gender. Words are also marked as n (noun), a (adjective), adv (adverb), v (verb), pl (plural), sg (singular), inf (informal) and pol (polite) where necessary. Verbs are given in the infinitive – for details on how to change verbs for use in a sentence, see the **phrasebuilder**, page 28.

A

a a *to*
  — **bordo** bor·do *aboard*
  — **menudo** me·noo·do *often*
  — **tiempo** tyem·po *on time*
  — **través** tra·ves *across*
  — **veces** ve·ses *sometimes*
abajo a·ba·kho *down*
abeja ⓕ a·be·kha *bee*
abierto/a ⓜ/ⓕ a·byer·to/a *open (business)*
abogado/a ⓜ/ⓕ a·bo·ga·do/a *lawyer*
abordar a·bor·dar *board (plane, ship)*
aborto ⓜ a·bor·to *abortion*
  — **natural** na·too·ral *miscarriage*
abrazar a·bra·sar *hug*
abrelatas ⓜ a·bre·la·tas *can opener*
abridor ⓜ a·bree·dor *bottle opener*
abrigo ⓜ a·bree·go *coat*
abril ⓜ a·breel *April*
abrir a·breer *open* v
abuela ⓕ a·bwe·la *grandmother*
abuelo ⓜ a·bwe·lo *grandfather*
aburrido/a ⓜ/ⓕ a·boo·ree·do/a *bored • boring*
acampar a·kam·par *camp* v
accidente ⓜ ak·see·den·te *accident*
aceite ⓜ a·say·te *oil (cooking)*
achaques ⓜ pl a·cha·kes *morning sickness*
ácido ⓜ a·see·do *acid*
acondicionador ⓜ a·kon·dee·syo·na·dor *hair conditioner*
acoso ⓜ a·ko·so *harassment*
acostarse a·kos·tar·se *lie (not stand)*
activista ⓜ&ⓕ ak·tee·vees·ta *activist*
actualidad ⓕ ak·twa·lee·dad *current affairs*
acupuntura ⓕ a·koo·poon·too·ra *acupuncture*
adaptador ⓜ a·dap·ta·dor *adaptor*
adelante a·de·lan·te *ahead*
adentro a·den·tro *indoor*
adicción ⓕ a·deek·syon *addiction*
adiós a·dyos *goodbye*
adivinar a·dee·vee·nar *guess*
adivino/a ⓜ/ⓕ a·dee·vee·no/a *fortune teller*
administración ⓕ ad·mee·nees·tra·syon *administration*
admisión ⓕ ad·mee·syon *admission (price)*
admitir ad·mee·teer *admit*
adolorido/a ⓜ/ⓕ a·do·lo·ree·do/a *sore*
adorar a·do·rar *worship* v
aduana ⓕ a·dwa·na *customs (immigration)*
adulto/a ⓜ/ⓕ a·dool·to/a *adult* n&a
advertir ad·ver·teer *warn*
aeróbicos ⓜ pl a·e·ro·bee·kos *aerobics*
aerolínea ⓕ a·e·ro·lee·ne·a *airline*
aeropuerto ⓜ a·e·ro·pwer·to *airport*
aficionado/a ⓜ/ⓕ a·fee·syo·na·do/a *fan (sport, etc)*
afortunado/a ⓜ/ⓕ a·for·too·na·do/a *lucky*
afuera a·fwe·ra *outside*
agencia ⓕ a·khen·sya *agency*
  — **de noticias** de no·tee·syas *newsagency*
  — **de viajes** de vya·khes *travel agency*
agenda ⓕ a·khen·da *diary*
agente de bienes raíces ⓜ a·khen·te de bye·nes ra·ee·ses *real estate agent*
agosto ⓜ a·gos·to *August*
agradecer a·gra·de·ser *thank*

agradecido/a ⓜ/ⓕ *a·gra·de·see·do/a* *grateful*
agricultura ⓕ *a·gree·kool·too·ra* *agriculture*
agua ⓕ *a·gwa* *water*
aguja ⓕ *a·goo·kha* *needle (sewing)*
ahí *a·ee* *there*
ahora *a·o·ra* *now*
aire ⓜ *ai·re* *air*
— acondicionado *a·kon·dee·syo·na·do* *air conditioning*
alas ⓕ pl *a·las* *wings*
albergue juvenil ⓜ *al·ber·ge khoo·ve·neel* *youth hostel*
alcalde(sa) ⓜ/ⓕ *al·kal·de/al·kal·de·sa* *mayor*
alcohol ⓜ *al·kol* *alcohol*
alemán *a·le·man* *German (language)*
alergia ⓕ *a·ler·khee·a* *allergy*
alfarería ⓕ *al·fa·re·ree·a* *pottery*
alfombra ⓕ *al·fom·bra* *rug*
algo *al·go* *something*
algodón ⓜ *al·go·don* *cotton*
alguien *al·gyen* *someone*
algún/alguna ⓜ/ⓕ *al·goon/al·goo·na* *some*
almohada ⓕ *al·mo·a·da* *pillow*
almuerzo ⓜ *al·mwer·so* *lunch*
alojamiento ⓜ *a·lo·kha·myen·to* *accommodation*
alquilar *al·kee·lar* *rent* v
alquiler de carros ⓜ *al·kee·ler de ka·ros* *car hire*
altar ⓜ *al·tar* *altar*
alto/a ⓜ/ⓕ *al·to/a* *high • tall*
altura ⓕ *al·too·ra* *altitude*
amable ⓜ&ⓕ *a·ma·ble* *kind • nice*
amanecer ⓜ *a·ma·ne·ser* *dawn • sunrise*
amante ⓜ&ⓕ *a·man·te* *lover*
amar *a·mar* *love* v
amargo/a ⓜ/ⓕ *a·mar·go/a* *bitter*
amarillo/a ⓜ/ⓕ *a·ma·ree·yo/a* *yellow*
ambos/as ⓜ/ⓕ pl *am·bos/am·bas* *both*
ambulancia ⓕ *am·boo·lan·sya* *ambulance*
amigo/a ⓜ/ⓕ *a·mee·go/a* *friend*
amor ⓜ *a·mor* *love*
ampolla ⓕ *am·po·ya* *blister*
anaranjado/a ⓜ/ⓕ *a·na·ran·kha·do/a* *orange (colour)*
anarquista ⓜ&ⓕ *a·nar·kees·ta* *anarchist* n&a
ancho/a ⓜ/ⓕ *an·cho/a* *wide*
andar *an·dar* *ride (bike, horse)*
— en bicicleta *en bee·see·kle·ta* *cycle* v
— en patineta *en pa·tee·ne·ta* *skateboard* v
anemia ⓕ *a·ne·mya* *anaemia*
anillo ⓜ *a·nee·yo* *ring (jewellery)*
animal ⓜ *a·nee·mal* *animal*
anotar *a·no·tar* *score* v
anteayer ⓜ *an·te·a·yer* *day before yesterday*
anteojos ⓜ pl *an·te·o·khos* *glasses*
— de sol *de sol* *sunglasses*
anterior ⓜ&ⓕ *an·te·ryor* *last (previous)*
antes *an·tes* *before*
antibióticos ⓜ pl *an·tee·byo·tee·kos* *antibiotics*
anticonceptivos ⓜ pl *an·tee·kon·sep·tee·vos* *contraceptives*
antigüedad ⓕ *an·tee·gwe·dad* *antique*
antiguo/a ⓜ/ⓕ *an·tee·gwo/a* *ancient*
antiséptico ⓜ *an·tee·sep·tee·ko* *antiseptic*
anuncio ⓜ *a·noon·syo* *advertisement*
año ⓜ *a·nyo* *year*
Año Nuevo ⓜ *a·nyo nwe·vo* *New Year*
apagado/a ⓜ/ⓕ *a·pa·ga·do/a* *off (power)*
apartamento ⓜ *a·par·ta·men·to* *apartment • flat*
apellido ⓜ *a·pe·yee·do* *surname*
apéndice ⓜ *a·pen·dee·se* *appendix (body)*
aplicadores ⓜ pl *a·plee·ka·do·res* *cotton buds (swabs)*
apodo ⓜ *a·po·do* *nickname*
apostar *a·pos·tar* *bet* v
aprender *a·pren·der* *learn*
apuesta ⓕ *a·pwes·ta* *bet*
apurado/a ⓜ/ⓕ *a·poo·ra·do/a* *in a hurry*
aquí *a·kee* *here*
araña ⓕ *a·ra·nya* *spider*
árbitro ⓜ *ar·bee·tro* *referee*
árbol ⓜ *ar·bol* *tree*
área de acampar ⓕ *a·re·a de a·kam·par* *camping ground*
arena ⓕ *a·re·na* *sand*
aretes ⓜ pl *a·re·tes* *earrings*
argumentar *ar·goo·men·tar* *argue*
armario ⓜ *ar·ma·ryo* *cupboard • wardrobe*
aromaterapia ⓕ *a·ro·ma·te·ra·pya* *aromatherapy*
arqueológico/a ⓜ/ⓕ *ar·ke·o·lo·khee·ko/a* *archaeological*
arquitecto/a ⓜ/ⓕ *ar·kee·tek·to/a* *architect*
arquitectura ⓕ *ar·kee·tek·too·ra* *architecture*
arrestar *a·res·tar* *arrest* v
arriba *a·ree·ba* *up*
arrollo ⓜ *a·ro·yo* *stream*
arte ⓜ *ar·te* *art*
artesanías ⓕ pl *ar·te·sa·nee·as* *handicraft*
artesano/a ⓜ/ⓕ *ar·te·sa·no/a* *craftsman/woman*
artes marciales ⓕ pl *ar·tes mar·sya·les* *martial arts*
artista ⓜ&ⓕ *ar·tees·ta* *artist*
— callejero *ka·ye·khe·ro* *busker*

asa ⓜ a·sa film speed
ascensor ⓜ a·sen·sor elevator (lift)
asesinar a·se·see·nar murder v
asesinato ⓜ a·se·see·na·to murder
asiento ⓜ a·syen·to seat (place)
asistente de ventas ⓜ&ⓕ a·sees·ten·te de ven·tas sales assistant
asma ⓕ as·ma asthma
aspirina ⓕ as·pee·ree·na aspirin
ataque al corazón ⓜ a·ta·ke al ko·ra·son heart attack
atardecer ⓜ a·tar·de·ser sunset
atletismo ⓜ at·le·tees·mo athletics
atmósfera ⓕ at·mos·fe·ra atmosphere
atrás a·tras back (position)
atraso ⓜ a·tra·so delay
audífono ⓜ ow·dee·fo·no hearing aid
autopista ⓕ ow·to·pees·ta highway
autor ⓜ ow·tor writer
auto servicio ⓜ ow·to ser·vee·syo self-service
avenida ⓕ a·ve·nee·da avenue
aventón ⓜ a·ven·ton ride
avergonzado/a ⓜ/ⓕ a·ver·gon·sa·do/a embarrassed
avión ⓜ a·vyon airplane
avispa ⓕ a·vees·pa wasp
ayer a·yer yesterday
ayuda ⓕ a·yoo·da help
ayudar a·yoo·dar help v
azúcar ⓜ a·soo·kar sugar
azul ⓜ&ⓕ a·sool blue

B

bailar bai·lar dance v
baile ⓜ bai·le dance
bajar ba·khar get off (bus, train)
bajo/a ⓜ/ⓕ ba·kho/a low • short (height)
balcón ⓜ bal·kon balcony
balde ⓜ bal·de bucket
balomano ⓜ ba·lo·ma·no handball
banco ⓜ ban·ko bank
bandera ⓕ ban·de·ra flag
baño ⓜ ba·nyo bath • bathroom • toilet
— público poo·blee·ko public toilet
bar ⓜ bar bar • pub
barato/a ⓜ/ⓕ ba·ra·to/a cheap
barbero ⓜ bar·be·ro barber
barco ⓜ bar·ko boat • ship
barra ⓕ ba·ra counter (at bar)
barro ⓜ ba·ro mud
básquetbol ⓜ bas·ket·bol basketball
basura ⓕ ba·soo·ra garbage
basurero ⓜ ba·soo·re·ro garbage can
batería ⓕ ba·te·ree·a battery • drums (kit)
bautismo ⓜ bow·tees·mo baptism
bebé ⓜ&ⓕ be·be baby
bebida ⓕ be·bee·da drink
béisbol ⓜ bays·bol baseball
bello/a ⓜ/ⓕ be·yo/a beautiful
besar be·sar kiss v
beso ⓜ be·so kiss
biblioteca ⓕ bee·blee·o·te·ka library
bibliotecario/a ⓜ/ⓕ bee·blee·o·te·ka·ryo/a librarian
bicho ⓜ bee·cho bug
bicicleta ⓕ bee·see·kle·ta bicycle
— de carreras de ka·re·ras racing bike
— montañera mon·ta·nye·ra mountain bike
bien byen fine • well
bienestar ⓜ byen·es·tar welfare
— social so·syal social welfare
billete de banco ⓜ bee·ye·te de ban·ko banknote
binoculares ⓜ pl bee·no·koo·la·res binoculars
blanco y negro blan·ko ee ne·gro B&W (film) a
blanco/a ⓜ/ⓕ blan·ko/a white
bloqueado/a ⓜ/ⓕ blo·ke·a·do/a blocked
bloqueador ⓜ blo·ke·a·dor sunblock
boca ⓕ bo·ka mouth
boda ⓕ bo·da wedding
bola ⓕ bo·la ball (sport)
bolitas de algodón ⓕ pl bo·lee·tas de al·go·don cotton balls
bollo de pan ⓜ bo·yo de pan bread roll
bolsa ⓕ bol·sa bag
bolsillo ⓜ bol·see·yo pocket
bolso ⓜ bol·so handbag
bomba ⓕ bom·ba gas station • petrol station
bombillo ⓜ bom·bee·yo light bulb
bonito/a ⓜ/ⓕ bo·nee·to/a pretty
borde ⓜ bor·de ledge
borracho/a ⓜ/ⓕ bo·ra·cho/a drunk
bosque ⓜ bos·ke forest
— lluvioso yoo·vyo·so rainforest
— nuboso noo·bo·so cloud forest
botas ⓕ pl bo·tas boots
— para caminata pa·ra ka·mee·na·ta hiking boots
botella ⓕ bo·te·ya bottle
— de agua de a·gwa water bottle
botón ⓜ bo·ton button
boxeo ⓜ bok·se·o boxing
bóxer ⓜ bok·ser boxer shorts
bracier ⓜ bra·syer bra
brazo ⓜ bra·so arm (body)

brillo ⓜ bree·yo lip balm
bronceador ⓜ bron·se·a·dor tanning lotion
bronquitis ⓕ bron·kee·tees bronchitis
brújula ⓕ broo·khoo·la compass
buceo ⓜ boo·se·o diving
budista ⓜ&ⓕ boo·dees·ta Buddhist n&a
bueno/a ⓜ/ⓕ bwe·no/a good • nice
bufanda ⓕ boo·fan·da scarf
bulto ⓜ bool·to lump
bus ⓜ boos bus • coach
buscar boos·kar look for
buzón ⓜ boo·son mailbox

C

caballo ⓜ ka·ba·yo horse
cabeza ⓕ ka·be·sa head
cabra ⓕ ka·bra goat
cacao ⓜ ka·kow cocoa
cada ⓜ&ⓕ ka·da each
cadena ⓕ ka·de·na chain • necklace
— de bicicleta de bee·see·kle·ta bike chain
caer ka·er fall v
café ⓜ ka·fe café • coffee • brown
— internet een·ter·net Internet café
caja ⓕ ka·kha box • cash register
— de cambios de kam·byos gearbox
— fuerte fwer·te safe (for valuables)
cajero/a ⓜ/ⓕ ka·khe·ro/a cashier
cajero automático ⓜ ka·khe·ro ow·to·ma·tee·ko ATM
calcetines ⓕ pl kal·se·tee·nes stockings
calculadora ⓕ kal·koo·la·do·ra calculator
calendario ⓜ ka·len·da·ryo calendar
calentado/a ⓜ/ⓕ ka·len·ta·do/a heated
calentador ⓜ ka·len·ta·dor heater
calentamiento ⓜ ka·len·ta·myen·to heating
calidad ⓕ ka·lee·dad quality
caliente ⓜ&ⓕ ka·lyen·te hot
callado/a ⓜ/ⓕ ka·ya·do/a quiet
calle ⓕ ka·ye road • street
— principal preen·se·pal main road
calor ⓜ ka·lor heat
cama ⓕ ka·ma bed
— matrimonial ma·tree·mo·nyal double bed
cámara ⓕ ka·ma·ra camera
— de video de vee·de·o video camera
camas sencillas ⓕ pl ka·mas sen·see·yas twin beds
cambiar kam·byar exchange (money)
— un cheque oon che·ke cash a cheque
cambio ⓜ kam·byo change • exchange
— de moneda de mo·ne·da currency exchange
caminar ka·mee·nar hike • walk
caminata ⓕ ka·mee·na·ta hiking
camino ⓜ ka·mee·no path • track • trail
— de montaña de mon·ta·nya mountain path
camión ⓜ ka·myon truck
— de todo-terreno de to·do·te·re·no all-terrain vehicle
camisa ⓕ ka·mee·sa shirt
camiseta ⓕ ka·mee·se·ta T-shirt
campeonatos ⓜ pl kam·pe·o·na·tos championships
campo ⓜ kam·po countryside • space (room)
— de golf de golf golf course
canasta ⓕ ka·nas·ta basket
cancelar kan·se·lar cancel
cáncer ⓜ kan·ser cancer
cancha de tenis ⓕ kan·cha de te·nees tennis court
canción ⓕ kan·syon song
candado ⓜ kan·da·do lock • padlock
— de bicicleta de bee·see·kle·ta bike lock
canoa ⓕ ka·no·a canoe
cansado/a ⓜ/ⓕ kan·sa·do/a tired
cantante ⓜ&ⓕ kan·tan·te singer
cantar kan·tar sing
capa ⓕ ka·pa raincoat
— de ozono de o·so·no ozone layer
cara ⓕ ka·ra face
caracol ⓜ ka·ra·kol snail
caravana ⓕ ka·ra·va·na caravan
cárcel ⓕ kar·sel jail
carne ⓕ kar·ne meat
carnicería ⓕ kar·nee·se·ree·a butcher's shop
carnicero ⓜ kar·nee·se·ro butcher
caro/a ⓜ/ⓕ ka·ro/a expensive
carpintero ⓜ kar·peen·te·ro carpenter
carrera ⓕ ka·re·ra race (sport)
carreras de caballo ⓕ pl ka·re·ras de ka·ba·yo horse racing
carro ⓜ ka·ro car
carta ⓕ kar·ta letter (mail)
cartera ⓕ kar·te·ra purse
cartón ⓜ kar·ton carton
casa ⓕ ka·sa house
casado/a ⓜ/ⓕ ka·sa·do/a married
casarse ka·sar·se marry
casco ⓜ kas·ko helmet
casetilla de teléfono ⓕ ka·se·tee·ya de te·le·fo·no phone box
casi ka·see almost
castellano kas·te·ya·no Spanish (language)
castillo ⓜ kas·tee·yo castle

catarata ⓕ ka·ta·*ra*·ta *waterfall*
catedral ⓕ ka·te·*dral* *cathedral*
católico/a ⓜ/ⓕ ka·*to*·lee·ko/a *Catholic* n&a
caza ⓕ *ka*·sa *hunting*
cédula de identificación ⓕ *se*·doo·la de ee·den·tee·fee·ka·*syon* *identification card*
celebración ⓕ se·le·bra·*syon* *celebration*
celoso/a ⓜ/ⓕ se·*lo*·so/a *jealous*
cementerio ⓜ se·men·*te*·ryo *cemetery*
cena ⓕ *se*·na *dinner*
cenicero ⓜ se·nee·*se*·ro *ashtray*
centavo ⓜ sen·*ta*·vo *cent*
centímetro ⓜ sen·*tee*·me·tro *centimetre*
central telefónica ⓕ sen·*tral* te·le·*fo*·nee·ka *telephone centre*
centro ⓜ *sen*·tro *centre*
— **comercial** ko·mer·*syal* *shopping centre*
— **de la ciudad** de la syoo·*dad* *city centre*
cepillo ⓜ se·*pee*·yo *brush* • *hairbrush*
— **de dientes** de *dyen*·tes *toothbrush*
cerámica ⓕ se·*ra*·mee·ka *ceramics*
cerca ⓕ *ser*·ka *fence*
cerca *ser*·ka *close* • *nearby*
cerdo ⓜ *ser*·do *pig* • *pork*
cerrado/a ⓜ/ⓕ se·*ra*·do/a *closed* • *shut*
— **con llave** kon *ya*·ve *locked*
cerrar se·*rar* *close* v
— **con llave** kon *ya*·ve *lock* v
certificado ⓜ ser·tee·fee·*ka*·do *certificate*
— **de nacimiento** de na·see·*myen*·to *birth certificate*
cerveza ⓕ ser·*ve*·sa *beer*
chaleco salvavidas ⓜ cha·*le*·ko sal·va·*vee*·das *life jacket*
champaña ⓕ cham·*pa*·nya *champagne*
champú ⓜ cham·*poo* *shampoo*
chancho ⓜ *chan*·cho *pig* • *pork*
chancletas ⓕ pl chan·*kle*·tas *sandals*
cheque ⓜ *che*·ke *check (banking)* • *cheque*
— **de viajero** de vya·*khe*·ro *travellers cheque*
chequeo ⓜ che·*ke*·o *check-in (desk)*
chicle ⓜ *chee*·kle *chewing gum*
chica ⓕ *chee*·ka *girl*
chico ⓜ *chee*·ko *boy*
chile ⓜ *chee*·le *chilli*
chineado/a ⓜ/ⓕ chee·ne·*a*·do/a *spoilt (person)*
chiquito/a ⓜ/ⓕ chee·*kee*·to/a *child*
chiste ⓜ *chees*·te *joke*
chivo ⓜ *chee*·vo *gig*
choque ⓜ *cho*·ke *crash*
chores ⓜ pl *cho*·res *shorts*
chupeta ⓕ choo·*pe*·ta *dummy* • *pacifier*
ciclismo ⓜ see·*klees*·mo *cycling*
ciclista ⓜ&ⓕ see·*klees*·ta *cyclist*
ciclo ⓜ *see*·klo *bike shop*
ciego/a ⓜ/ⓕ *sye*·go/a *blind*
cielo ⓜ *sye*·lo *sky*
cien ⓜ syen *hundred*
ciencia ⓕ *syen*·sya *science*
científico/a ⓜ/ⓕ syen·*tee*·fee·ko/a *scientist*
cigarrillo ⓜ see·ga·*ree*·yo *cigarette*
cigarro ⓜ see·*ga*·ro *cigar*
cilindro de gas ⓜ see·*leen*·dro de gas *gas cartridge*
cima ⓕ *see*·ma *mountain peak*
cine ⓜ *see*·ne *cinema*
cinta de video ⓕ *seen*·ta de vee·*de*·o *video tape*
cinturón ⓜ seen·too·*ron* *seatbelt*
circo ⓜ *seer*·ko *circus*
cistitis ⓕ sees·*tee*·tees *cystitis*
cita ⓕ *see*·ta *appointment*
ciudad ⓕ syoo·*dad* *city*
ciudadanía ⓕ syoo·da·da·*nee*·a *citizenship*
clarinete ⓜ kla·ree·*ne*·te *clarinet*
claro/a ⓜ/ⓕ *kla*·ro/a *light (colour)*
clase ⓕ *kla*·se *class (category)*
— **económica** e·ko·*no*·mee·ka *economy class*
— **ejecutiva** e·khe·koo·*tee*·va *business class*
clásico/a ⓜ/ⓕ *kla*·see·ko/a *classical*
clavija ⓕ kla·*vee*·kha *tent peg*
cliente ⓜ&ⓕ klee·*en*·te *client*
closh ⓜ klosh *clutch (car)*
club nocturno ⓜ kloob nok·*toor*·no *nightclub*
cobija ⓕ ko·*bee*·kha *blanket*
cocaína ⓕ ko·ka·*ee*·na *cocaine*
coche ⓜ *ko*·che *stroller*
cocina ⓕ ko·*see*·na *cooking* • *kitchen* • *stove*
cocinar ko·see·*nar* *cook* v
cocinero/a ⓜ/ⓕ ko·see·*ne*·ro/a *cook*
coco ⓜ *ko*·ko *coconut*
coctel ⓜ kok·*tel* *cocktail*
código postal ⓜ *ko*·dee·go pos·*tal* *postcode*
cola ⓕ *ko*·la *tail*
colchón ⓜ kol·*chon* *mattress*
colchoneta ⓕ kol·cho·*ne*·ta *mat*
colector de tiquetes ⓜ ko·lek·*tor* de tee·*ke*·tes *ticket collector*
colega ⓜ&ⓕ ko·*le*·ga *colleague*
colegio ⓜ ko·*le*·khyo *high school*
color ⓜ ko·*lor* *colour*
comedia ⓕ ko·*me*·dya *comedy*
comer ko·*mer* *eat*

comerciante ⓜ&ⓕ ko·mer·syan·te tradesperson
comercio ⓜ ko·mer·syo trade
comida ⓕ ko·mee·da food • meal
— de bebé de be·be baby food
cómo ko·mo how
cómodo/a ⓜ/ⓕ ko·mo·do/a comfortable
compañero/a ⓜ/ⓕ kom·pa·nye·ro/a companion
compañía ⓕ kom·pa·nyee·a company (firm)
compartir kom·par·teer share v
comprar kom·prar buy
compras ⓕ pl kom·pras shopping
comprometido/a ⓜ/ⓕ kom·pro·me·tee·do/a engaged (to marry)
compromiso ⓜ kom·pro·mee·so engagement (to marry)
computadora ⓕ kom·poo·ta·do·ra computer
comunicación ⓕ ko·moo·nee·ka·syon communications (profession)
comunión ⓕ ko·moo·nyon communion
comunista ⓜ&ⓕ ko·moo·nees·ta communist n&a
con kon with
— aire acondicionado ai·re a·kon·dee·syo·na·do air-conditioned
concierto ⓜ kon·syer·to concert
condición cardíaca ⓕ kon·dee·syon kar·dee·a·ka heart condition
conducir kon·doo·seer drive v
conejo ⓜ ko·ne·kho rabbit
conexión ⓕ ko·nek·syon connection
conferencia ⓕ kon·fe·ren·sya conference (small)
confesión ⓕ kon·fe·syon confession (religious)
confiar kon·fyar trust v
confirmar kon·feer·mar confirm (a booking)
confite ⓜ kon·fee·te candy
congelado/a ⓜ/ⓕ kon·khe·la·do/a frozen
congelar kon·khe·lar freeze
congreso ⓜ kon·gre·so conference (big)
conmoción ⓕ kon·mo·syon commission
conocer ko·no·ser know (someone)
conocerse ko·no·ser·se meet (first time)
consejo ⓜ kon·se·kho advice
conservador(a) ⓜ/ⓕ kon·ser·va·dor/kon·ser·va·do·ra conservative n&a
consigna ⓕ kon·seeg·na left-luggage office
constructor(a) ⓜ/ⓕ kons·trook·tor/kons·trook·to·ra builder
construir kons·troo·eer build
consulado ⓜ kon·soo·la·do consulate
contaminación ⓕ kon·ta·mee·na·syon pollution
contar kon·tar count v
contra agua kon·tra a·gwa waterproof
contratar kon·tra·tar hire • rent v
contrato ⓜ kon·tra·to contract
control remoto ⓜ kon·trol re·mo·to remote control
contusión ⓕ kon·too·syon concussion
convento ⓜ kon·ven·to convent
corazón ⓜ ko·ra·son heart
cordillera ⓕ kor·dee·ye·ra mountain range
cordón de zapato ⓜ kor·don de sa·pa·to shoelace
correcto/a ⓜ/ⓕ ko·rek·to/a right (correct)
correo ⓜ ko·re·o mail • post office
correr ko·rer run v
corriendo ⓜ ko·ryen·do running
corriente ⓕ ko·ryen·te current (electricity)
corrupción ⓕ ko·roop·syon corruption
corrupto/a ⓜ/ⓕ ko·roop·to/a corrupt
cortada ⓕ kor·ta·da cut
cortar kor·tar cut v
cortauñas ⓜ kor·ta·oo·nyas nail clippers
corte ⓕ kor·te court (legal)
corte de pelo ⓜ kor·te de pe·lo haircut
coser ko·ser sew
costa ⓕ kos·ta coast
costar kos·tar cost v
costilla ⓕ kos·tee·ya rib (body)
costumbre ⓕ kos·toom·bre custom
cráneo ⓜ kra·ne·o skull
crecer kre·ser grow
crédito ⓜ kre·dee·to credit
crema ⓕ kre·ma cream (food/lotion)
cricket ⓜ kree·ket cricket (sport)
cristiano/a ⓜ/ⓕ krees·tya·no/a Christian n&a
crudo/a ⓜ/ⓕ kroo·do/a raw
cruz ⓕ kroos cross (religious)
cuaderno ⓜ kwa·der·no notebook
cuadrapléjico/a ⓜ/ⓕ kwa·dra·ple·khee·ko/a quadriplegic
cuál kwal which
cualidades ⓕ pl kwa·lee·da·des qualifications
cualquier(a) ⓜ/ⓕ kwal·kyer/kwal·kye·ra any
cuándo kwan·do when
cuánto kwan·to how much
cuarentena ⓕ kwa·ren·te·na quarantine
cuarto ⓜ kwar·to bedroom • quarter
— doble do·ble double room
cubiertos ⓜ pl koo·byer·tos cutlery
cucaracha ⓕ koo·ka·ra·cha cockroach
cuchara ⓕ koo·cha·ra spoon

cucharita ⓕ koo·cha·ree·ta *teaspoon*
cuchilla ⓕ koo·chee·ya *pocketknife*
cuchillo ⓜ koo·chee·yo *knife*
cuello ⓜ kwe·yo *neck*
cuenta ⓕ kwen·ta *account • bill • cheque*
— **bancaria** ban·ka·rya *bank account*
cuento ⓜ kwen·to *story*
cuerda ⓕ kwer·da *rope*
cuero ⓜ kwe·ro *leather*
— **cabelludo** ka·be·yoo·do *scalp*
cuerpo ⓜ kwer·po *body*
cuesta abajo kwes·ta a·ba·kho *downhill*
cuesta arriba kwes·ta a·ree·ba *uphill*
cueva ⓕ kwe·va *cave*
cuidar de kwee·dar de *look after*
culebra ⓕ koo·le·bra *snake*
culpa ⓕ kool·pa *(someone's) fault*
culpable ⓜ&ⓕ kool·pa·ble *guilty*
cumpleaños ⓜ koom·ple·a·nyos *birthday*
cuna ⓕ koo·na *crèche • child-minding centre*
cupón ⓜ koo·pon *coupon*
cura ⓜ koo·ra *priest*
curita ⓕ koo·ree·ta *Band-Aid*
currículum ⓜ koo·ree·koo·loom *CV • résumé*

D

dar dar *give*
— **de comer** de ko·mer *feed* v
— **la bienvenida** la byen·ve·nee·da *welcome* v
— **vuelta** vwel·ta *turn* v
de de *from*
debajo de·ba·kho *below*
deber de·ber *owe*
débil ⓜ&ⓕ de·beel *weak*
decidir de·see·deer *decide*
decir de·seer *say • tell*
dedo ⓜ de·do *finger*
— **del pie** del pye *toe*
defectuoso/a ⓜ/ⓕ de·fek·two·so/a *faulty*
deforestación ⓕ de·fo·res·ta·syon *deforestation*
delgado/a ⓜ/ⓕ del·ga·do/a *thin*
demasiado de·ma·sya·do *too (much)*
democracia ⓕ de·mo·kra·sya *democracy*
demostración ⓕ de·mos·tra·syon *demonstration (display)*
dentista ⓜ&ⓕ den·tees·ta *dentist*
dentro den·tro *inside*
— **de** de *within (time)*
deporte ⓜ de·por·te *sport*
deportista ⓜ&ⓕ de·por·tees·ta *sportsperson*
depósito ⓜ de·po·see·to *deposit (bank)*
derecha ⓕ de·re·cha *right (direction)*
derechista ⓜ&ⓕ de·re·chees·ta *right-wing*
derecho ⓜ de·re·cho *law (profession)*
derechos civiles ⓜ pl de·re·chos see·vee·les *civil rights*
derechos humanos ⓜ pl de·re·chos oo·ma·nos *human rights*
derrame ⓜ de·ra·me *stroke (health)*
desayuno ⓜ de·sa·yoo·no *breakfast*
descansar des·kan·sar *rest* v
descendiente ⓜ de·sen·dyen·te *descendent*
descompuesto/a ⓜ/ⓕ des·kom·pwes·to/a *broken down (car, etc)*
desconocido/a ⓜ/ⓕ des·ko·no·see·do/a *stranger*
descuento ⓜ des·kwen·to *discount*
desde des·de *from • since*
desear de·se·ar *wish* v
desechos nucleares ⓜ pl de·se·chos noo·kle·a·res *nuclear waste*
desecho tóxico ⓜ de·se·cho tok·see·ko *toxic waste*
desempleado/a ⓜ/ⓕ de·sem·ple·a·do/a *unemployed*
desfase de horario ⓜ des·fa·se de o·ra·ryo *jet lag*
desierto ⓜ de·syer·to *desert*
desodorante ⓜ de·so·do·ran·te *deodorant*
despacio des·pa·syo *slowly*
despertar des·per·tar *wake (someone) up*
después des·pwes *after*
destino ⓜ des·tee·no *destination*
detallado/a ⓜ/ⓕ de·ta·ya·do/a *itemised*
detalles ⓜ pl de·ta·yes *details*
detrás de·tras *behind*
día ⓜ dee·a *day*
diabetes ⓕ dee·a·be·tes *diabetes*
diafragma ⓜ dya·frag·ma *diaphragm (contraceptive)*
diapositivas ⓕ pl dya·po·see·tee·vas *slide (film)*
diarrea ⓕ dee·a·re·a *diarrhoea*
diccionario ⓜ deek·syo·na·ryo *dictionary*
diciembre ⓜ dee·syem·bre *December*
diente ⓜ dyen·te *tooth*
dientes ⓜ pl dyen·tes *teeth*
dieta ⓕ dye·ta *diet*
diferencia de hora ⓕ dee·fe·ren·sya de o·ra *time difference*
diferente ⓜ&ⓕ dee·fe·ren·te *different*
difícil ⓜ&ⓕ dee·fee·seel *difficult*
digital ⓜ&ⓕ dee·khee·tal *digital*
diminuto/a ⓜ/ⓕ dee·mee·noo·to/a *tiny*
dinero ⓜ dee·ne·ro *money*
dios ⓜ dee·os *god*

dirección ⓕ dee·rek·*syon* *address • direction*
directo/a ⓜ/ⓕ dee·*rek*·to/a *direct • express*
director(a) ⓜ/ⓕ dee·rek·*tor*/dee·rek·*to*·ra *director • manager (sport)*
discapacitado/a ⓜ/ⓕ dees·ka·pa·see·*ta*·do/a *disabled*
— **visual** vee·*swal* *visually impaired*
discriminación ⓕ dees·kree·mee·na·*syon* *discrimination*
diseño ⓜ dee·*se*·nyo *design*
disfrutar dees·froo·*tar* *enjoy (oneself)*
disparar dees·pa·*rar* *shoot* v
disponible ⓜ&ⓕ dees·po·*nee*·ble *free (available)*
disquete ⓜ dees·*ke*·te *disk (floppy)*
DIU ⓜ de ee oo *IUD*
divertido/a ⓜ/ⓕ dee·ver·*tee*·do/a *fun*
divertirse dee·ver·*teer*·se *have fun*
divorciado/a ⓜ/ⓕ dee·vor·*sya*·do/a *divorced*
doble ⓜ&ⓕ *do*·ble *double*
docena ⓕ do·*se*·na *dozen*
doctor(a) ⓜ/ⓕ dok·*tor*/dok·*to*·ra *doctor*
documental ⓜ do·koo·men·*tal* *documentary*
dólar ⓜ *do*·lar *dollar*
doler do·*ler* *hurt (be painful)*
dolor ⓜ do·*lor* *pain*
— **de cabeza** de ka·*be*·sa *headache*
— **de diente** de *dyen*·te *toothache*
— **de estómago** de es·*to*·ma·go *stomachache*
dolores menstruales ⓜ pl do·*lo*·res mens·*trwa*·les *period pain*
doloroso/a ⓜ/ⓕ do·lo·*ro*·so/a *painful*
domingo ⓜ do·*meen*·go *Sunday*
dónde *don*·de *where*
dormir dor·*meer* *sleep* v
dos dos *two*
— **veces** *ve*·ses *twice*
drama ⓜ *dra*·ma *drama*
droga ⓕ *dro*·ga *drug (illicit)*
drogadicción ⓕ dro·ga·deek·*syon* *drug addiction*
drogadicto/a ⓜ/ⓕ dro·ga·*deek*·to/a *drug user*
ducha ⓕ *doo*·cha *shower (bath)*
dueño/a ⓜ/ⓕ *dwe*·nyo/a *landlord/lady • owner*
dulce ⓜ&ⓕ *dool*·se *sweet* a
dulces ⓜ pl *dool*·ses *sweets* n
duro/a ⓜ/ⓕ *doo*·ro/a *hard (not soft) • hard-boiled (egg) • loud*

E

eczema ⓕ ek·*se*·ma *eczema*
edad ⓕ e·*dad* *age*
edificio ⓜ e·dee·*fee*·syo *building*
educación ⓕ e·doo·ka·*syon* *education*
efectivo ⓜ e·fek·*tee*·vo *cash*
egoísta ⓜ&ⓕ e·go·*ees*·ta *selfish*
ejemplo ⓜ e·*khem*·plo *example*
ejército ⓜ e·*kher*·see·to *military*
él el *he • him*
elección ⓕ e·lek·*syon* *election*
electricidad ⓕ e·lek·tree·see·*dad* *electricity*
electricista ⓜ&ⓕ e·lek·tree·*sees*·ta *electrician*
ella *e*·ya *her • she*
ellos/as ⓜ/ⓕ pl *e*·yos/as *them • they*
embajada ⓕ em·ba·*kha*·da *embassy*
embajador(a) ⓜ/ⓕ em·ba·kha·*dor*/em·ba·kha·*do*·ra *ambassador*
embarazada ⓕ em·ba·ra·*sa*·da *pregnant*
emergencia ⓕ e·mer·*khen*·sya *emergency*
emocional ⓜ&ⓕ e·mo·syo·*nal* *emotional*
empezar em·pe·*sar* *start* v
empinado/a ⓜ/ⓕ em·pee·*na*·do/a *steep*
empleado/a ⓜ/ⓕ em·ple·*a*·do/a *employee*
empleador(a) ⓜ/ⓕ em·ple·a·*dor*/em·ple·a·*do*·ra *employer*
empujar em·poo·*khar* *push* v
en en *at • in*
— **frente de** *fren*·te de *in front of • opposite*
enagua ⓕ en·*a*·gwa *skirt*
encantador(a) ⓜ/ⓕ en·kan·ta·*dor*/en·kan·ta·*do*·ra *charming*
encendedor ⓜ en·sen·de·*dor* *cigarette lighter*
encendido/a ⓜ/ⓕ en·sen·*dee*·do/a *on (power)*
enchufe ⓜ en·*choo*·fe *plug (electricity)*
encías ⓕ pl en·*see*·as *gums (mouth)*
encontrar en·kon·*trar* *find*
encontrarse en·kon·*trar*·se *meet (get together)*
energía nuclear ⓕ e·ner·*khee*·a noo·kle·*ar* *nuclear energy*
enero ⓜ e·*ne*·ro *January*
enfadado/a ⓜ/ⓕ en·fa·*da*·do/a *angry*
enfermedad ⓕ en·fer·me·*dad* *disease*
— **del viajero** del vya·*khe*·ro *travel sickness*
— **venérea** ve·*ne*·re·a *venereal disease*
enfermero/a ⓜ/ⓕ en·fer·*me*·ro/a *nurse*
enfermo/a ⓜ/ⓕ en·*fer*·mo/a *ill*
enorme ⓜ&ⓕ e·*nor*·me *huge*

ensalada ⓕ en·sa·la·da *salad*
enseñar en·se·nyar *show* v • *teach*
entender en·ten·der *understand*
entrada ⓕ en·tra·da *cover charge* • *entry*
entrar en·trar *enter*
entre en·tre *between*
entrenador(a) ⓜ/ⓕ en·tre·na·dor/en·tre·na·do·ra *coach*
entrenar en·tre·nar *coach* v
entrevista ⓕ en·tre·vees·ta *interview*
enviar en·vyar *deliver* • *mail* • *send*
equipaje ⓜ e·kee·pa·khe *luggage*
equipo ⓜ e·kee·po *equipment* • *team*
— de buceo de boo·se·o *diving equipment*
— de sonido de so·nee·do *stereo*
equitación ⓕ e·kee·ta·syon *horse riding*
equivocado/a ⓜ/ⓕ e·kee·vo·ka·do/a *wrong*
error ⓜ e·ror *mistake*
escalada ⓕ es·ka·la·da *rock climbing*
escalar es·ka·lar *climb* v
escalas sociales ⓕ es·ka·las so·sya·les *class system*
escaleras ⓕ pl es·ka·le·ras *stairway*
escape ⓕ es·ka·pe *exhaust (car)*
escarcha ⓕ es·kar·cha *frost*
escasez ⓕ es·ka·ses *shortage*
escoger es·ko·kher *choose*
escribir es·kree·beer *write*
escuchar es·koo·char *listen*
escuela ⓕ es·kwe·la *school*
escultura ⓕ es·kool·too·ra *sculpture*
ese/a ⓜ/ⓕ e·se/a *that* a
esgrima ⓕ es·gree·ma *fencing (sport)*
esguince ⓜ es·geen·se *sprain*
esnorclear ⓜ es·nor·kle·ar *snorkelling*
espacio disponible ⓜ es·pa·syo dees·po·nee·ble *vacancy*
espalda ⓕ es·pal·da *back (body)*
España ⓕ es·pa·nya *Spain*
español es·pa·nyol *Spanish (language)*
especial ⓜ&ⓕ es·pe·syal *special*
especialista ⓜ&ⓕ es·pe·sya·lees·ta *specialist* n&a
espectáculo ⓜ es·pek·ta·koo·lo *show*
espejo ⓜ es·pe·kho *mirror*
esperar es·pe·rar *wait* v
espiral para mosquitos ⓕ es·pee·ral pa·ra mos·kee·tos *mosquito coil*
esposa ⓕ es·po·sa *wife*
esposo ⓜ es·po·so *husband*
espuma de afeitar ⓕ es·poo·ma de a·fay·tar *shaving cream*
esquí ⓜ es·kee *skiing*
— acuático a·kwa·tee·ko *water-skiing*
esquiar es·kyar *ski*
esquina ⓕ es·kee·na *corner*
esta noche e·sta no·che *tonight*
estación ⓕ es·ta·syon *station*
— de bus de boos *bus station*
— de policía de po·lee·see·a *police station*
— de tren de tren *railway station*
estadio ⓜ es·ta·dyo *stadium*
estado civil ⓜ es·ta·do see·veel *marital status*
Estados Unidos ⓜ pl es·ta·dos oo·nee·dos *USA*
estallar es·ta·yar *puncture*
estampilla ⓕ es·tam·pee·ya *stamp (postage)*
estar es·tar *be (temporary)*
— de acuerdo de a·kwer·do *agree*
— resfriado res·free·a·do *have a cold*
estatua ⓕ es·ta·twa *statue*
este/a ⓜ/ⓕ es·te/a *this* a
este ⓜ es·te *east*
estilista ⓜ&ⓕ es·tee·lees·ta *beautician*
estilo ⓜ es·tee·lo *style*
estómago ⓜ es·to·ma·go *stomach*
estrella ⓕ es·tre·ya *star*
estreñimiento ⓜ es·tre·nyee·myen·to *constipation*
estuario ⓜ es·twa·ryo *estuary*
estudiante ⓜ&ⓕ es·too·dyan·te *student*
estudio ⓜ es·too·dyo *studio*
estúpido/a ⓜ/ⓕ es·too·pee·do/a *stupid*
etiqueta del equipaje ⓕ e·tee·ke·ta del e·kee·pa·khe *luggage tag*
eutanasia ⓕ e·oo·ta·na·sya *euthanasia*
exactamente ek·sak·ta·men·te *exactly*
excelente ⓜ&ⓕ ek·se·len·te *excellent*
exceso de equipaje ⓜ ek·se·so de e·kee·pa·khe *excess baggage*
excluido/a ⓜ/ⓕ eks·kloo·ee·do/a *excluded*
exhibición ⓕ ek·see·bee·syon *exhibition*
experiencia ⓕ eks·pe·ryen·sya *experience*
— laboral la·bo·ral *work experience*
explotación eks·plo·ta·syon *exploitation*
éxtasis ⓜ eks·ta·sees *ecstacy (drug)*
extensión ⓕ eks·ten·syon *extension (visa)*
extranjero/a ⓜ/ⓕ eks·tran·khe·ro/a *foreign*
extrañar eks·tra·nyar *miss (feel absence of)*

F

fábrica ⓕ fa·bree·ka *factory*
fácil ⓜ&ⓕ fa·seel *easy*
faja del abanico ⓕ fa·kha del a·ba·nee·ko *fanbelt*
familia ⓕ fa·mee·lya *family*
famoso/a ⓜ/ⓕ fa·mo·so/a *famous*

fantástico fan·tas·tee·ko *great • fantastic*
farmacéutico/a ⓜ/ⓕ far·ma·se·oo·tee·ko/a *chemist • pharmacist*
farmacia ⓕ far·ma·sya *pharmacy*
faul ⓜ fa·ool *foul (soccer)*
fax ⓜ faks *fax machine*
febrero ⓜ fe·bre·ro *February*
fecha ⓕ fe·cha *date (day)*
— **de nacimiento** de na·see·myen·to *date of birth*
felicidades fe·lee·see·da·des *congratulations*
feliz ⓜ&ⓕ fe·lees *happy*
feriado ⓜ fe·ree·a·do *holiday*
ferretería ⓕ fe·re·te·ree·a *hardware store*
ficción ⓕ feek·syon *fiction*
fiebre ⓕ fye·bre *fever*
— **del heno** del e·no *hay fever*
fiesta ⓕ fyes·ta *festival • party (night out)*
fila ⓕ fee·la *queue*
filtrado/a ⓜ/ⓕ feel·tra·do/a *filtered*
fin ⓜ feen *end*
— **de semana** de se·ma·na *weekend*
finca ⓕ feen·ka *farm*
finquero/a ⓜ/ⓕ feen·ke·ro/a *farmer*
firma ⓕ feer·ma *signature*
firmar feer·mar *sign (one's name)*
flash ⓜ flash *flash (camera)*
flauta ⓕ flow·ta *flute*
flojo/a ⓜ/ⓕ flo·kho/a *loose*
flor ⓕ flor *flower*
flora y fauna ⓕ flo·ra ee fow·na *wildlife*
floristería ⓕ flo·rees·te·ree·a *florist (shop)*
foco ⓜ fo·ko *flashlight • torch*
focos ⓜ pl fo·kos *headlights*
fondo ⓜ fon·do *bottom (position)*
forma ⓕ for·ma *shape • manner*
fósforos ⓜ pl fos·fo·ros *matches (lighting)*
foto ⓕ fo·to *photo*
fotografía ⓕ fo·to·gra·fee·a *photography*
fotografiar fo·to·gra·fyar *photograph*
fotógrafo/a ⓜ/ⓕ fo·to·gra·fo/a *photographer*
frágil ⓜ&ⓕ fra·kheel *fragile*
francés fran·ses *French (language)*
franela ⓕ fra·ne·la *flannel (face cloth)*
franqueo ⓜ fran·ke·o *postage*
frasco ⓜ fras·ko *jar*
freír fre·eer *fry*
frenos ⓜ pl fre·nos *brakes*
fresco/a ⓜ/ⓕ fre·sko/a *cool • fresh*
frío/a ⓜ/ⓕ free·o/a *cold*
frito/a ⓜ/ⓕ free·to/a *fried*
frontera ⓕ fron·te·ra *border (geographic)*
fruta ⓕ froo·ta *fruit*
frutas secas ⓕ pl froo·tas se·kas *dried fruit*

fuego ⓜ fwe·go *fire*
fuera de servicio fwe·ra de ser·vee·syo *out of order*
fuerte ⓜ&ⓕ fwer·te *strong*
fumar foo·mar *smoke* v
funcionar foon·syo·nar *work (function)*
funda ⓕ foon·da *pillowcase*
funeral ⓜ foo·ne·ral *funeral*
fútbol ⓜ foot·bol *football • soccer*
futuro ⓜ foo·too·ro *future*

G

galería ⓕ ga·le·ree·a *gallery*
galleta ⓕ ga·ye·ta *biscuit (sweet) • cookie*
— **salada** sa·la·da *cracker*
ganador(a) ⓜ/ⓕ ga·na·dor/ga·na·do·ra *winner*
ganar ga·nar *earn • win*
garaje ⓜ ga·ra·khe *garage*
garantizado/a ⓜ/ⓕ ga·ran·tee·sa·do/a *guaranteed*
garganta ⓕ gar·gan·ta *throat*
gas ⓜ gas *gas (cooking)*
gasa ⓕ ga·sa *gauze*
gasolina ⓕ ga·so·lee·na *gas • petrol*
gastritis ⓕ gas·tree·tees *gastroenteritis*
gato/a ⓜ/ⓕ ga·to/a *cat*
gay ⓜ&ⓕ gay *gay* n&a
gemelos/as ⓜ/ⓕ pl khe·me·los/as *twins*
gente ⓕ khen·te *people*
gerente ⓜ&ⓕ khe·ren·te *manager (business)*
gimnasia ⓕ kheem·na·sya *gymnastics*
gimnasio ⓜ kheem·na·syo *gym (place)*
ginebra ⓕ khee·ne·bra *gin*
ginecólogo/a ⓜ/ⓕ khee·ne·ko·lo·go/a *gynaecologist*
gobierno ⓜ go·byer·no *government*
gol ⓜ gol *goal (sport)*
golpe ⓜ gol·pe *strike (hit)*
gordo/a ⓜ/ⓕ gor·do/a *fat*
gotas para los ojos ⓕ pl go·tas pa·ra los o·khos *eye drops*
grabación ⓕ gra·ba·syon *recording*
grabar gra·bar *record* v
grada ⓕ gra·da *step*
gradas ⓕ pl gra·das *escalator*
grados ⓜ pl gra·dos *degrees (temperature)*
gramo ⓜ gra·mo *gram*
grande ⓜ&ⓕ gran·de *big*
granola ⓕ gra·no·la *muesli*
gratis ⓜ&ⓕ gra·tees *complimentary (free)*
gripe ⓕ gree·pe *influenza*
gris ⓜ&ⓕ grees *grey*

gritar gree·*tar* *shout*
grueso/a ⓜ/ⓕ *grwe*·so/a *thick*
grupo ⓜ *groo*·po *group*
— **de rock** de rok *rock group*
— **musical** moo·see·*kal* *band (music)*
— **sanguíneo** san·*gee*·ne·o *blood group*
guantes ⓜ pl *gwan*·tes *gloves*
guapo/a ⓜ/ⓕ *gwa*·po/a *handsome*
guardaropa ⓜ gwar·da·*ro*·pa *cloakroom*
guarda rural ⓜ&ⓕ *gwar*·da roo·*ral* *police officer (country)*
guerra ⓕ *ge*·ra *war*
guía ⓕ *gee*·a *audio guide*
— **de entretenimiento** de en·tre·te·nee·*myen*·to *entertainment guide*
— **telefónica** te·le·*fo*·nee·ka *phone book*
— **turística** too·*rees*·tee·ka *guidebook*
guía ⓜ&ⓕ *gee*·a *guide (person)*
guitarra ⓕ gee·*ta*·ra *guitar*
gustar goos·*tar* *like* v

H

habitación ⓕ a·bee·ta·*syon* *room*
— **sencilla** sen·*see*·ya *single room*
hablar ab·*lar* *speak* • *talk*
hace (tres días) *a*·se (tres *dee*·as) *(three days) ago*
hacer a·*ser* *do* • *make*
hachís ⓜ a·*chees* *hashish*
hacia *a*·see·a *towards*
halal ⓜ&ⓕ a·*lal* *halal*
halar a·*lar* *pull*
hamaca ⓕ a·*ma*·ka *hammock*
hambriento/a ⓜ/ⓕ am·bree·*yen*·to/a *hungry*
hasta *as*·ta *until*
hecho/a a mano ⓜ/ⓕ *e*·cho/a a *ma*·no *handmade*
heladería ⓕ e·la·de·*ree*·a *ice-cream parlour*
helado ⓜ e·*la*·do *ice cream*
hembra ⓕ *em*·bra *female*
hepatitis ⓕ e·pa·*tee*·tees *hepatitis*
herida ⓕ e·*ree*·da *injury*
hermana ⓕ er·*ma*·na *sister*
hermano ⓜ er·*ma*·no *brother*
heroína ⓕ e·ro·*ee*·na *heroin*
herpes ⓜ *er*·pes *shingles (illness)*
hervido/a ⓜ/ⓕ er·*vee*·do/a *boiled*
hielo ⓜ *ye*·lo *ice*
hierba ⓕ *yer*·ba *dope (drugs)* • *herb*
hierbero/a ⓜ/ⓕ yer·*be*·ro/a *herbalist*
hija ⓕ *ee*·kha *daughter*
hijo ⓜ *ee*·kho *son*
hilo ⓜ *ee*·lo *string* • *thread*
— **dental** den·*tal* *dental floss*
hinchazón ⓕ een·cha·*son* *swelling*
hindú ⓜ&ⓕ een·*doo* *Hindu* n&a
historia ⓕ ees·*to*·rya *history*
histórico/a ⓜ/ⓕ ees·*to*·ree·ko/a *historical*
hogar ⓜ o·*gar* *home*
hoja ⓕ *o*·kha *leaf*
hombre ⓜ *om*·bre *man*
— **de negocios** de ne·*go*·syos *businessman*
hombro ⓜ *om*·bro *shoulder*
homeopatía ⓕ o·me·o·pa·*tee*·a *homeopathy*
homosexual ⓜ&ⓕ o·mo·*sek*·swal *homosexual* n&a
hondo/a ⓜ/ⓕ *on*·do/a *deep*
hora ⓕ *o*·ra *hour*
horario ⓜ o·*ra*·ryo *opening hours*
hormiga ⓕ or·*mee*·ga *ant*
horno ⓜ *or*·no *oven*
— **microondas** mee·kro·*on*·das *microwave oven*
horóscopo ⓜ o·*ros*·ko·po *horoscope*
horrible ⓜ&ⓕ o·*ree*·ble *awful*
hospital ⓜ os·pee·*tal* *hospital*
hospitalidad ⓕ os·pee·ta·lee·*dad* *hospitality*
hotel ⓜ o·*tel* *hotel*
hoy oy *today*
huelga ⓕ *wel*·ga *strike (stoppage)*
hueso ⓜ *we*·so *bone*
huevo ⓜ *we*·vo *egg*
humanidades ⓕ pl oo·ma·nee·*da*·des *humanities*
humectante ⓜ oo·mek·*tan*·te *moisturiser*

I

identificación ⓕ ee·den·tee·fee·ka·*syon* *identification*
idioma ⓜ ee·*dyo*·ma *language*
idiota ⓜ&ⓕ ee·*dyo*·ta *idiot*
iglesia ⓕ ee·*gle*·sya *church*
igualdad ⓕ ee·gwal·*dad* *equality*
— **de oportunidades** de o·por·too·nee·*da*·des *equal opportunity*
importante ⓜ&ⓕ eem·por·*tan*·te *important*
imposible ⓜ&ⓕ eem·po·*see*·ble *impossible*
impresora ⓕ eem·pre·*so*·ra *printer (computer)*
impuesto ⓜ eem·*pwes*·to *tax*
— **de salida** de sa·*lee*·da *airport tax*
— **de ventas** de *ven*·tas *sales tax*
incluido/a ⓜ/ⓕ een·kloo·*ee*·do/a *included*

incómodo/a ⓜ/ⓕ een·ko·mo·do/a *uncomfortable*
indicador ⓜ een·dee·ka·dor *indicator*
indigente ⓜ&ⓕ een·dee·khen·te *homeless* n&a
indigestión ⓕ een·dee·khes·tyon *indigestion*
industria ⓕ een·doos·tree·a *industry*
infección ⓕ een·fek·syon *infection*
— **urinaria** oo·ree·na·rya *urinary infection*
inflamación ⓕ een·fla·ma·syon *inflammation*
información ⓕ een·for·ma·syon *information*
informática ⓕ een·for·ma·tee·ka *IT*
ingeniería ⓕ een·khe·nye·ree·a *engineering*
ingeniero/a ⓜ/ⓕ een·khe·nye·ro/a *engineer*
Inglaterra ⓕ een·gla·te·ra *England*
inglés een·gles *English (language)*
ingrediente ⓜ een·gre·dyen·te *ingredient*
inicio ⓜ ee·nee·syo *start*
injusto/a ⓜ/ⓕ een·khoos·to/a *unfair*
inocente ⓜ&ⓕ e·no·sen·te *innocent*
insecto ⓜ een·sek·to *insect*
inseguro/a ⓜ/ⓕ een·se·goo·ro/a *unsafe*
insolación ⓕ een·so·la·syon *sunstroke*
instructor(a) ⓜ/ⓕ eens·trook·tor/eens·trook·to·ra *instructor*
interesante ⓜ&ⓕ een·te·re·san·te *interesting*
intermedio ⓜ een·ter·me·dyo *intermission*
internacional ⓜ&ⓕ een·ter·na·syo·nal *international*
intérprete ⓜ&ⓕ een·ter·pre·te *interpreter*
inundación ⓕ ee·noon·da·syon *flood*
invierno ⓜ een·vyer·no *winter*
invitar een·vee·tar *invite* v
inyección ⓕ een·yek·syon *injection*
inyectar een·yek·tar *inject*
ir eer *go*
— **de compras** de kom·pras *go shopping*
isla ⓕ ees·la *island*
itinerario ⓜ ee·tee·ne·ra·ryo *timetable*
izquierda ⓕ ees·kyer·da *left (direction)*
izquierdista ⓜ&ⓕ ees·kyer·dees·ta *left-wing*

J

jabón ⓜ kha·bon *soap*
jarabe para la tos ⓜ kha·ra·be pa·ra la tos *cough medicine*
jardín ⓜ khar·deen *garden*
— **botánico** bo·ta·nee·ko *botanic garden*
jardinería ⓕ khar·dee·ne·ree·a *gardening*
jardinero/a ⓜ/ⓕ khar·dee·ne·ro/a *gardener*
jardines públicos ⓜ pl khar·dee·nes poo·blee·kos *public gardens*
jeringa ⓕ khe·reen·ga *syringe*
joven ⓜ&ⓕ kho·ven *young*
joyas ⓕ pl kho·yas *jewellery*
judío/a ⓜ/ⓕ khoo·dee·o/a *Jewish*
juego de computadora ⓜ khwe·go de kom·poo·ta·do·ra *computer game*
Juegos Olímpicos ⓜ pl khwe·gos o·leem·pee·kos *Olympic Games*
jueves ⓜ khwe·ves *Thursday*
juez(a) ⓜ/ⓕ khwes/khwe·sa *judge*
jugar khoo·gar *play (cards, etc)*
jugo ⓜ khoo·go *juice*
juguetería ⓕ khoo·ge·te·ree·a *toy shop*
julio ⓜ khoo·lyo *July*
junio ⓜ khoo·nyo *June*
junto a khoon·to a *beside • next to*
juntos/as ⓜ/ⓕ pl khoon·tos/as *together*

K

kilogramo ⓜ kee·lo·gra·mo *kilogram*
kilómetro ⓜ kee·lo·me·tro *kilometre*
kínder ⓜ keen·der *kindergarten*
klínex ⓜ klee·neks *tissues*
kosher ⓜ&ⓕ ko·sher *kosher*

L

labios ⓜ pl la·byos *lips*
lado ⓜ la·do *side*
ladrón(a) ⓜ/ⓕ la·dron/la·dro·na *thief*
lagartija ⓕ la·gar·tee·kha *lizard*
lago ⓜ la·go *lake*
lana ⓕ la·na *wool*
lancha ⓕ lan·cha *motorboat*
lapicero ⓜ la·pee·se·ro *ballpoint pen*
lápiz ⓜ la·pees *pencil*
largo/a ⓜ/ⓕ lar·go/a *long*
lastimado/a ⓜ/ⓕ las·tee·ma·do/a *injured*
lastimar las·tee·mar *hurt (cause pain)*
lata ⓕ la·ta *can • tin*
lavadora ⓕ la·va·do·ra *washing machine*
lavandería ⓕ la·van·de·ree·a *launderette • laundry (place)*
lavar la·var *wash (something)*
lavarse la·var·se *wash (oneself)*
laxante ⓜ lak·san·te *laxative*
leche ⓕ le·che *milk*
lectura ⓕ lek·too·ra *reading*
leer le·er *read*
legal ⓜ&ⓕ le·gal *legal*
legislación ⓕ le·khees·la·syon *legislation*

DICTIONARY

lejos *le*·khos *far (away)*
lentes de contacto ⓜ pl *len*·tes de kon·*tak*·to *contact lenses*
lente zoom ⓜ *len*·te soom *zoom lens*
lento/a ⓜ/ⓕ *len*·to/a *slow*
leña ⓕ *le*·nya *firewood*
lesbiana ⓕ les·*bya*·na *lesbian* n&a
ley ⓕ lay *law (legislation)*
libra ⓕ *lee*·bra *pound (currency/weight)*
libre ⓜ&ⓕ *lee*·bre *free (not bound)*
librería ⓕ lee·bre·*ree*·a *book shop • stationer*
libro ⓜ *lee*·bro *book*
— **de frases** de *fra*·ses *phrasebook*
— **de oraciones** de o·ra·*syo*·nes *prayer book*
licencia ⓕ lee·*sen*·sya *licence*
— **de conductor** de kon·dook·*tor* *driving licence*
licorera ⓕ lee·ko·*re*·ra *bottle shop • liquor store*
líder ⓜ/ⓕ lee·*der* *leader*
ligar lee·*gar* *chat up (flirt)*
límite de equipaje ⓜ *lee*·mee·te de e·kee·*pa*·khe *baggage allowance*
límite de velocidad ⓜ *lee*·mee·te de ve·lo·see·*dad* *speed limit*
limonada ⓕ lee·mo·*na*·da *lemonade*
limpiar leem·*pyar* *clean* v
limpieza ⓕ leem·*pye*·sa *cleaning*
limpio/a ⓜ/ⓕ *leem*·pyo/a *clean*
lino ⓜ *lee*·no *linen (material)*
listo/a ⓜ/ⓕ *lees*·to/a *ready*
litera ⓕ lee·*te*·ra *sleeping berth*
liviano/a ⓜ/ⓕ lee·*vya*·no/a *light (weight)*
llamada a cobrar ⓕ ya·*ma*·da a ko·*brar* *collect call*
llamar ya·*mar* *call* v • *telephone* v
llanta ⓕ *yan*·ta *tire • tyre*
llanuras ⓕ pl ya·*noo*·ras *tropical plains*
llave ⓕ *ya*·ve *key (door etc)*
llegadas ⓕ pl ye·*ga*·das *arrivals (airport)*
llegar ye·*gar* *arrive*
llenar ye·*nar* *fill*
lleno/a ⓜ/ⓕ *ye*·no/a *full*
— **de gente** de *khen*·te *crowded*
llevar ye·*var* *carry • take*
lluvia ⓕ *yoo*·vya *rain*
local ⓜ&ⓕ lo·*kal* *local*
loco/a ⓜ/ⓕ *lo*·ko/a *crazy*
loma ⓕ *lo*·ma *hill*
lombrices ⓕ pl lom·*bree*·ses *intestinal worms*
loro/a ⓜ/ⓕ *lo*·ro/a *parrot*
lubricante ⓜ loo·bree·*kan*·te *lubricant*
lucrar loo·*krar* *profit* v
lugar ⓜ loo·*gar* *place • venue*
— **de nacimiento** de na·see·*myen*·to *place of birth*
lujoso/a ⓜ/ⓕ loo·*kho*·so/a *luxury*
luna ⓕ *loo*·na *moon*
— **de miel** de myel *honeymoon*
lunes ⓜ *loo*·nes *Monday*
luz ⓕ lus *light*

M

macrobiótica ⓕ ma·kro·*byo*·tee·ka *health-food store*
madera ⓕ ma·*de*·ra *wood*
madre ⓕ *ma*·dre *mother*
maestro/a ⓜ/ⓕ ma·*es*·tro/a *teacher*
malaria ⓕ ma·*la*·rya *malaria*
maleta ⓕ ma·*le*·ta *suitcase*
malo/a ⓜ/ⓕ *ma*·lo/a *bad • off (spoilt)*
mamografía ⓕ ma·mo·gra·*fee*·a *mammogram*
mandar man·*dar* *send*
mandíbula ⓕ man·*dee*·boo·la *jaw*
manglar ⓜ man·*glar* *mangrove*
manifestación ⓕ ma·nee·fes·ta·*syon* *demonstration (rally)*
manillar ⓜ ma·nee·*yar* *handlebars*
mano ⓕ *ma*·no *hand*
mantel ⓜ man·*tel* *tablecloth*
mañana ⓕ ma·*nya*·na *morning*
mañana ma·*nya*·na *tomorrow*
mapa ⓜ *ma*·pa *map*
— **de calles** de *ka*·yes *road map*
maquillaje ⓜ ma·kee·*ya*·khe *make-up*
máquina ⓕ *ma*·kee·na *machine*
— **de tiquetes** de tee·*ke*·tes *ticket machine*
mar ⓜ mar *sea*
maravilloso/a ⓜ/ⓕ ma·ra·vee·*yo*·so/a *wonderful*
marcación directa ⓕ mar·ka·*syon* dee·*rek*·ta *direct-dial*
marcador ⓜ mar·ka·*dor* *scoreboard*
marcapasos ⓜ mar·ka·*pa*·sos *pacemaker*
Mar Caribe ⓜ mar ka·*ree*·be *Caribbean Sea*
marea ⓕ ma·*re*·a *tide*
mareado/a ⓜ/ⓕ ma·re·*a*·do/a *dizzy • seasick*
margarina ⓕ mar·ga·*ree*·na *margarine*
marihuana ⓕ ma·ree·*wa*·na *marijuana*
mariposa ⓕ ma·ree·*po*·sa *butterfly*
martes ⓜ *mar*·tes *Tuesday*
martillo ⓜ mar·*tee*·yo *hammer*
marzo ⓜ *mar*·so *March*

más mas *more*
— **cerca** ser·ka *closer*
— **grande** ⓜ&ⓕ gran·de *bigger*
— **pequeño/a** ⓜ/ⓕ pe·ke·nyo/a *smaller*
— **tarde** tar·de *later*
masaje ⓜ ma·sa·khe *massage*
masajeador ⓜ ma·sa·khe·a·dor *masseur*
masajeadora ⓕ ma·sa·khe·a·do·ra *masseuse*
mascara ⓕ mas·ka·ra *goggles (diving)*
mascarilla ⓕ mas·ka·ree·ya *goggles (swimming)*
mata ⓕ ma·ta *plant*
matrimonio ⓜ ma·tree·mo·nyo *marriage*
mayo ⓜ ma·yo *May*
mecánico/a ⓜ/ⓕ me·ka·nee·ko/a *mechanic*
medianoche ⓕ me·dya·no·che *midnight*
medias ⓕ pl me·dyas *socks*
medicamento ⓜ me·dee·ka·men·to *medication*
medicina ⓕ me·de·see·na *medicine (profession)*
medidor de luz ⓜ me·dee·dor de lus *light meter*
medio ⓜ me·dyo *half*
— **ambiente** am·byen·te *environment*
mediodía ⓜ me·dyo·dee·a *midday • noon*
medios ⓜ pl me·dyos *media*
meditación ⓕ me·dee·ta·syon *meditation*
mejor me·khor *better*
melodía ⓕ me·lo·dee·a *tune*
mendigo/a ⓜ/ⓕ men·dee·go/a *beggar*
menos me·nos *less*
mensaje ⓜ men·sa·khe *message*
mentir men·teer *lie (not tell the truth)*
mentiroso/a ⓜ/ⓕ men·tee·ro·so/a *liar*
menú ⓜ me·noo *menu*
menudo ⓜ me·noo·do *loose change*
mercado ⓜ mer·ka·do *market*
— **callejero** ka·ye·khe·ro *street market*
— **de pulgas** de pool·gas *fleamarket*
— **negro** ne·gro *black market*
merienda ⓕ me·ryen·da *snack*
mes ⓜ mes *month*
mesa ⓕ me·sa *table*
mesero/a ⓜ/ⓕ me·se·ro/a *waiter*
meseta ⓕ me·se·ta *plateau*
meta ⓕ me·ta *finish*
metal ⓜ me·tal *metal*
metro ⓜ me·tro *metre*
mezclar mes·klar *mix*
mezquita ⓕ mes·kee·ta *mosque*
mi mee *my*
mí mee *me*
miembro/a ⓜ/ⓕ myem·bro/a *member*
miércoles ⓜ myer·ko·les *Wednesday*
migración ⓕ mee·gra·syon *immigration*
migraña ⓕ mee·gra·nya *migraine*
milímetro ⓜ mee·lee·me·tro *millimetre*
millón ⓜ mee·yon *million*
minuto ⓜ mee·noo·to *minute*
mirador ⓜ mee·ra·dor *lookout*
misa ⓕ mee·sa *mass (Catholic)*
mismo/a ⓜ/ⓕ mees·mo/a *same*
mitad ⓕ mee·tad *half*
mochila ⓕ mo·chee·la *backpack*
moda ⓕ mo·da *fashion*
módem ⓜ mo·dem *modem*
moderno/a ⓜ/ⓕ mo·der·no/a *modern*
mojado/a ⓜ/ⓕ mo·kha·do/a *wet*
monasterio ⓜ mo·nas·te·ryo *monastery*
monedas ⓕ pl mo·ne·das *coins*
monja ⓕ mon·kha *nun*
monje ⓜ mon·khe *monk*
mono ⓜ mo·no *monkey*
mononucleosis ⓕ mo·no·noo·kle·o·sees *glandular fever*
montaña ⓕ mon·ta·nya *mountain*
montañismo ⓜ mon·ta·nyees·mo *mountaineering*
montura ⓕ mon·too·ra *saddle*
monumento ⓜ mo·noo·men·to *monument*
moquera ⓕ mo·ke·ra *runny nose*
morado/a ⓜ/ⓕ mo·ra·do/a *purple*
mordida ⓕ mor·dee·da *bite (dog)*
moretón ⓜ mo·re·ton *bruise*
morir mo·reer *die*
mosca ⓕ mos·ka *fly*
mosquitero ⓜ mos·kee·te·ro *mosquito net*
mota ⓕ mo·ta *dope (drugs)*
motel ⓜ mo·tel *motel*
moto ⓕ mo·to *motorbike*
motor ⓜ mo·tor *engine*
mucho/a ⓜ/ⓕ moo·cho/a *(a) lot • much*
muchos/as ⓜ/ⓕ pl moo·chos/as *many*
mudo/a ⓜ/ⓕ moo·do/a *mute*
muebles ⓜ pl mwe·bles *furniture*
muerto/a ⓜ/ⓕ mwer·to/a *dead*
mujer ⓕ moo·kher *woman*
— **de negocios** de ne·go·syos *businesswoman*
multa ⓕ mool·ta *fine (payment)*
Mundial ⓜ moon·dyal *World Cup*
mundo ⓜ moon·do *world*
muñeca ⓕ moo·nye·ka *doll • wrist*
músculo ⓜ moos·koo·lo *muscle*
museo ⓜ moo·se·o *museum*
música ⓕ moo·see·ka *music*
músico/a ⓜ/ⓕ moo·see·ko/a *musician*

musulmán/musulmana ⓜ/ⓕ moo·sool·*man*/moo·sool·*ma*·na *Muslim* n&a
muy *mooy* *very*

N

nacionalidad ⓕ na·syo·na·lee·*dad* *nationality*
nada *na*·da *nothing*
nadar na·*dar* *swim*
nado ⓜ *na*·do *swimming*
naipes ⓜ pl *nai*·pes *cards (playing)*
narcotraficante ⓜ&ⓕ nar·ko·tra·fee·*kan*·te *drug dealer*
narcotráfico ⓜ nar·ko·*tra*·fee·ko *drug trafficking*
nariz ⓕ na·*rees* *nose*
naturaleza ⓕ na·too·ra·*le*·sa *nature*
náuseas ⓕ pl *now*·se·as *nausea*
navaja ⓕ na·*va*·kha *penknife*
navajilla ⓕ na·va·*khee*·ya *razor blade*
Navidad ⓕ na·vee·*dad* *Christmas*
necesario/a ⓜ/ⓕ ne·se·*sa*·ryo/a *necessary*
necesitar ne·se·see·*tar* *need* v
negar ne·*gar* *refuse* v
negativo/a ⓜ/ⓕ ne·ga·*tee*·vo/a *negative*
negativos ⓜ pl ne·ga·*tee*·vos *negatives (photos)*
negocio ⓜ ne·*go*·syo *business*
negro/a ⓜ/ⓕ *ne*·gro/a *black*
neumático ⓜ ne·oo·*ma*·tee·ko *tube (tyre)*
neuropatía ⓕ ne·oo·ro·pa·*tee*·a *naturopathy*
nieto/a ⓜ/ⓕ *nye*·to/a *grandchild*
nieve ⓕ *nye*·ve *snow*
ninguno/a ⓜ/ⓕ neen·*goo*·no/a *neither • none*
niñera ⓕ nee·*nye*·ra *babysitter*
niño/a ⓜ/ⓕ *nee*·nyo/a *child*
niños/as ⓜ/ⓕ pl *nee*·nyos/as *children*
no no *no • not*
— **fumado** foo·*ma*·do *nonsmoking*
noche ⓕ *no*·che *evening • night*
nombre ⓜ *nom*·bre *name*
— **cristiano** krees·*tya*·no *given name*
norte ⓜ *nor*·te *north*
nosotros/as ⓜ/ⓕ pl no·*so*·tros/as *we*
nostálgico/a ⓜ/ⓕ nos·*tal*·khee·ko/a *homesick*
noticias ⓕ pl no·*tee*·syas *news*
novela ⓕ no·*ve*·la *soap opera*
novia ⓕ *no*·vya *girlfriend*
noviembre ⓜ no·*vyem*·bre *November*
novio ⓜ *no*·vyo *boyfriend*
nube ⓕ *noo*·be *cloud*
nublado/a ⓜ/ⓕ noo·*bla*·do/a *cloudy*
nuestro/a ⓜ/ⓕ *nwes*·tro/a *our*
nuevo/a ⓜ/ⓕ *nwe*·vo/a *new*
número ⓜ *noo*·me·ro *number*
— **de habitación** de a·bee·ta·*syon* *room number*
— **de pasaporte** de pa·sa·*por*·te *passport number*
— **de placa** de *pla*·ka *license plate number*
nunca *noon*·ka *never*

O

o o *or*
objetivo ⓜ ob·khe·*tee*·vo *lens (camera)*
obra de teatro ⓕ *o*·bra de *te*·a·tro *play (theatre)*
observar ob·ser·*var* *watch* v
obtener ob·te·*ner* *get*
océano ⓜ o·*se*·a·no *ocean*
Océano Atlántico ⓜ o·se·*a*·no at·*lan*·tee·ko *Atlantic Ocean*
Océano Pacífico ⓜ o·se·*a*·no pa·*see*·fee·ko *Pacific Ocean*
octubre ⓜ ok·*too*·bre *October*
ocupado/a ⓜ/ⓕ o·koo·*pa*·do/a *busy • engaged (phone)*
oeste ⓜ o·*es*·te *west*
oficina ⓕ o·fee·*see*·na *office*
— **de objetos perdidos** de ob·*khe*·tos per·*dee*·dos *lost-property office*
— **de turismo** de too·*rees*·mo *tourist office*
oír o·*eer* *hear*
ojos ⓜ pl *o*·khos *eyes*
ola ⓕ *o*·la *wave (beach)*
olla ⓕ *o*·ya *pot • saucepan*
olor ⓜ o·*lor* *smell*
olvidar ol·vee·*dar* *forget*
operación ⓕ o·pe·ra·*syon* *operation (medical)*
operador(a) ⓜ/ⓕ o·pe·ra·*dor*/o·pe·ra·*do*·ra *telephone operator*
opinión ⓕ o·pee·*nyon* *opinion*
oportunidad ⓕ o·por·too·nee·*dad* *chance*
optometrista ⓜ&ⓕ op·to·me·*trees*·ta *optometrist*
opuesto o·*pwes*·to *opposite*
oración ⓕ o·ra·*syon* *prayer*
orden ⓜ *or*·den *command • order*
ordenar or·de·*nar* *order* v
ordinario/a ⓜ/ⓕ or·dee·*na*·ryo/a *ordinary*
oreja ⓕ o·*re*·kha *ear*
orgasmo ⓜ or·*gas*·mo *orgasm*
original ⓜ&ⓕ o·ree·khee·*nal* *original*
oro ⓜ *o*·ro *gold*

orquesta ⓕ or·kes·ta orchestra
oscuro/a ⓜ/ⓕ os·koo·ro/a dark (colour/night)
otoño ⓜ o·to·nyo autumn • fall
otra vez o·tra ves again
otro/a ⓜ/ⓕ o·tro/a another • other
ovario ⓜ o·va·ryo ovary
oveja ⓕ o·ve·kha sheep
oxígeno ⓜ ok·see·khe·no oxygen

P

padre ⓜ pa·dre father
pagar pa·gar pay
página ⓕ pa·khee·na page
pago ⓜ pa·go payment
país ⓜ pa·ees country
pájaro ⓜ pa·kha·ro bird
palabra ⓕ pa·la·bra word
palacio ⓜ pa·la·syo palace
palillo de dientes ⓜ pa·lee·yo de dyen·tes toothpick
palillos chinos ⓜ pl pa·lee·yos chee·nos chopsticks
pan ⓜ pan bread
panadería ⓕ pa·na·de·ree·a bakery
pancito ⓜ pan·see·to biscuit (savoury)
panfleto ⓜ pan·fle·to brochure
pantalones ⓜ pl pan·ta·lo·nes trousers
pañal ⓜ pa·nyal diaper • nappy
paño ⓜ pa·nyo towel
— para la cara pa·ra la ka·ra face cloth
pañuelo ⓜ pa·nywe·lo handkerchief
papá ⓜ pa·pa dad
papanicolau ⓜ pa·pa·nee·ko·low pap smear
papás ⓜ pl pa·pas parents
papel ⓜ pa·pel paper
— higiénico ee·khye·nee·ko toilet paper
papeleo ⓜ pa·pe·le·o paperwork
paperas ⓕ pl pa·pe·ras mumps
paquete ⓜ pa·ke·te package • packet
para pa·ra for
— siempre syem·pre forever
parabrisas ⓜ pa·ra·bree·sas windscreen
parada ⓕ pa·ra·da stop (bus, tram)
— de bus de boos bus stop
— de taxis de tak·sees taxi stand
parapléjico/a ⓜ/ⓕ pa·ra·ple·khee·ko/a paraplegic
parar pa·rar stop (cease)
parcela ⓕ par·se·la parcel
pared ⓕ pa·red wall
pareja ⓕ pa·re·kha couple • pair
parlamento ⓜ par·la·men·to parliament
parque ⓜ par·ke park
— nacional na·syo·nal national park
parquear par·ke·ar park (vehicle) v
parqueo ⓜ par·ke·o car park
parte ⓕ par·te part (component)
partidario/a ⓜ/ⓕ par·tee·da·ryo/a supporter (politics)
partido ⓜ par·tee·do game (sport) • match • party (politics)
partir par·teer depart
pasado ⓜ pa·sa·do past
— mañana ma·nya·na day after tomorrow
pasado/a ⓜ/ⓕ pa·sa·do/a last (previous)
pasajero/a ⓜ/ⓕ pa·sa·khe·ro/a passenger
pasaporte ⓜ pa·sa·por·te passport
pasar pa·sar pass v
Pascua ⓕ pas·kwa Easter
pasillo ⓜ pa·see·yo aisle (on plane)
pasta de dientes ⓕ pas·ta de dyen·tes toothpaste
pastel ⓜ pas·tel pastry • pie
pastelería ⓕ pas·te·le·ree·a cake shop
pastilla ⓕ pas·tee·ya pill
— anticonceptiva an·tee·kon·sep·tee·va the pill (contraceptive)
— para el dolor pa·ra el do·lor painkiller
pastillas para dormir ⓕ pl pas·tee·yas pa·ra dor·meer sleeping pills
patear pa·te·ar kick v
patinar pa·tee·nar skate v
paz ⓕ pas peace
peatón ⓜ pe·a·ton pedestrian
pecho ⓜ pe·cho breast • chest
pedal ⓜ pe·dal pedal
pedazo ⓜ pe·da·so piece
pedido ⓜ pe·dee·do order (food)
pedir pe·deer ask (for something)
— prestado pres·ta·do borrow
— un aventón oon a·ven·ton hitchhike
pegamento ⓜ pe·ga·men·to glue
peine ⓜ pay·ne comb
pelea ⓕ pe·le·a fight
película ⓕ pe·lee·koo·la film (cinema)
peligroso/a ⓜ/ⓕ pe·lee·gro·so/a dangerous
pelo ⓜ pe·lo hair
peluquero/a ⓜ/ⓕ pe·loo·ke·ro/a hairdresser
pene ⓜ pe·ne penis
pensar pen·sar think
pensión ⓕ pen·syon guesthouse
pensionado/a ⓜ/ⓕ pen·syo·na·do/a pensioner
pequeño/a ⓜ/ⓕ pe·ke·nyo/a small
perder per·der lose • miss
perdido/a ⓜ/ⓕ per·dee·do/a lost
perdonar per·do·nar forgive
perezoso/a ⓜ/ⓕ pe·re·so·so/a lazy
perfecto/a ⓜ/ⓕ per·fek·to/a perfect

perfume ⓜ per·foo·me *perfume*
periódico ⓜ pe·ryo·dee·ko *newspaper*
periodista ⓜ&ⓕ pe·ree·o·dees·ta *journalist*
permiso ⓜ per·mee·so *permission • permit*
— **de trabajo** de tra·ba·kho *work permit*
pero pe·ro *but*
perro/a ⓜ pe·ro/a *dog*
— **guía** gee·a *guide dog*
persona ⓕ per·so·na *person*
pesado/a ⓜ/ⓕ pe·sa·do/a *heavy*
pesar pe·sar *weigh*
pesas ⓕ pl pe·sas *weights*
pesca ⓕ pes·ka *fishing*
pescado ⓜ pes·ka·do *fish (meat)*
peso ⓜ pe·so *weight*
petición ⓕ pe·tee·syon *petition*
petróleo ⓜ pe·tro·le·o *oil (petrol)*
pez ⓜ pes *fish (animal)*
picada ⓕ pee·ka·da *bite (insect)*
picadillo ⓜ pee·ka·dee·yo *mince*
picazón ⓕ pee·ka·son *itch*
pico ⓜ pee·ko *pickaxe*
pie ⓜ pye *foot*
piedra ⓕ pye·dra *rock • stone*
piel ⓕ pyel *skin*
pierna ⓕ pyer·na *leg (body)*
pijiado/a ⓜ/ⓕ pee·khya·do/a *stoned (drugged)*
pimienta ⓕ pee·myen·ta *pepper (spice)*
pintor(a) ⓜ/ⓕ peen·tor/peen·to·ra *painter*
pintura ⓕ peen·too·ra *painting*
— **de labios** de la·byos *lipstick*
pinzas ⓕ pl peen·sas *tweezers*
piojos ⓜ pl pyo·khos *lice*
piscina ⓕ pee·see·na *swimming pool*
piso ⓜ pee·so *floor (storey)*
pista ⓕ pees·ta *racetrack*
pistola ⓕ pees·to·la *gun*
placa ⓕ pla·ka *numberplate*
plancha ⓕ plan·cha *iron (for clothes)*
planeta ⓜ pla·ne·ta *planet*
plano/a ⓜ/ⓕ pla·no/a *flat*
plástico ⓜ plas·tee·ko *plastic*
plata ⓕ pla·ta *silver*
plataforma ⓕ pla·ta·for·ma *platform*
plato ⓜ pla·to *dish (food) • plate*
— **hondo** on·do *bowl*
playa ⓕ pla·ya *beach*
plaza ⓕ pla·sa *square (town)*
plomero ⓜ plo·me·ro *plumber*
pobre ⓜ&ⓕ po·bre *poor*
pobreza ⓕ po·bre·sa *poverty*
poco/a ⓜ/ⓕ po·ko/a *few • little (quantity)*
poder ⓜ po·der *power*
poder po·der *can (be able/have permission)*

podrido/a ⓜ/ⓕ po·dree·do/a *spoilt (food)*
poesía ⓕ po·e·see·a *poetry*
polen ⓜ po·len *pollen*
policía ⓕ po·lee·see·a *police*
policía ⓜ&ⓕ po·lee·see·a *police officer (city)*
política ⓕ po·lee·tee·ka *policy • politics*
político ⓜ po·lee·tee·ko *politician*
político/a ⓜ/ⓕ po·lee·tee·ko/a *political*
polvo ⓜ pol·vo *powder*
poner po·ner *put*
ponerse po·ner·se *wear*
popular ⓜ&ⓕ po·poo·lar *popular*
por por *for*
— **a noche** a no·che *overnight*
— **qué** ke *why*
porcentaje ⓜ por·sen·ta·khe *per cent*
porque por·ke *because*
portero ⓜ por·te·ro *goalkeeper*
posible ⓜ&ⓕ po·see·ble *possible*
positivo/a ⓜ/ⓕ po·see·tee·vo/a *positive*
postal ⓕ pos·tal *postcard*
póster ⓜ pos·ter *poster*
postre ⓜ pos·tre *dessert*
precio ⓜ pre·syo *price*
precipicio ⓜ pre·see·pee·syo *cliff*
preferir pre·fe·reer *prefer*
pregunta ⓕ pre·goon·ta *question*
preguntar pre·goon·tar *ask (a question)*
preocupado/a ⓜ/ⓕ pre·o·koo·pa·do/a *worried*
preparar pre·pa·rar *prepare*
presentación ⓕ pre·sen·ta·syon *performance*
presente ⓜ pre·sen·te *present (time)*
preservativo ⓜ pre·ser·va·tee·vo *condom*
presidente ⓜ&ⓕ pre·see·den·te *president*
presión ⓕ pre·syon *pressure (tyre)*
— **sanguínea** san·gee·ne·a *blood pressure*
presupuesto ⓜ pre·soo·pwes·to *budget*
prevenir pre·ve·neer *stop (prevent)*
primavera ⓕ pree·ma·ve·ra *spring (season)*
primera clase ⓕ pree·me·ra kla·se *first class*
primer(a) ministro/a ⓜ/ⓕ pree·mer mee·nees·tro/pree·me·ra mee·nees·tra *prime minister*
primero/a ⓜ/ⓕ pree·me·ro/a *first*
primeros auxilios ⓜ pl pree·me·ros owk·see·lyos *first-aid kit*
principal ⓜ&ⓕ preen·see·pal *main*
privado/a ⓜ/ⓕ pree·va·do/a *private*
producir pro·doo·seer *produce* v
programa ⓜ pro·gra·ma *program* v
prometer pro·me·ter *promise*
prometido/a ⓜ/ⓕ pro·me·tee·do/a *fiancé/fiancée*

promoción ⓕ pro·mo·syon sale
pronto ⓜ pron·to soon
propina ⓕ pro·pee·na tip (gratuity)
prostituto/a ⓜ/ⓕ pros·tee·too·to/a prostitute
protectores ⓜ pl pro·tek·to·res panty liners
proteger pro·te·kher protect
protegido/a ⓜ/ⓕ pro·te·khee·do/a protected
protesta ⓕ pro·tes·ta protest
protestar pro·tes·tar protest v
provisiones ⓕ pl pro·vee·syo·nes provisions
próximo/a ⓜ/ⓕ prok·see·mo/a following • next
proyector ⓜ pro·yek·tor projector
prueba ⓕ prwe·ba test
— de embarazo de em·ba·ra·so pregnancy test kit
— de sangre de san·gre blood test
pruebas nucleares ⓕ pl prwe·bas noo·kle·a·res nuclear testing
pueblo ⓜ pwe·blo village
puente ⓜ pwen·te bridge (structure)
puerta ⓕ pwer·ta door • gate (airport, etc)
— de salida de sa·lee·da departure gate
puerto ⓜ pwer·to harbour • port
pulga ⓕ pool·ga flea
pulmón ⓜ pool·mon lung
punto de control ⓜ poon·to de kon·trol checkpoint (border)
puro/a ⓜ/ⓕ poo·ro/a pure

Q

qiropráctico ⓜ kee·ro·prak·tee·ko chiropractor
qué ke what
quebrado/a ⓜ/ⓕ ke·bra·do/a broken
quebrar ke·brar break (in general) v
quedarse ke·dar·se stay
— varado va·ra·do break down (car)
queja ⓕ ke·kha complaint
quejarse ke·khar·se complain
quemado/a ⓜ/ⓕ ke·ma·do/a burnt
quemadura ⓕ ke·ma·doo·ra burn
— de sol de sol sunburn
queque ⓜ ke·ke cake
querer ke·rer want
quién kyen who
quincena ⓕ keen·se·na fortnight
quiosco ⓜ kyos·ko kiosk
quiste en los ovarios ⓜ kees·te en los o·va·ryos ovarian cyst

R

rabia ⓕ ra·bya rabies
racismo ⓜ ra·sees·mo racism
radiador ⓜ ra·dya·dor radiator
radio ⓜ ra·dyo spoke (wheel)
radio ⓕ ra·dyo radio
rancio/a ⓜ/ⓕ ran·syo/a stale
rápido/a ⓜ/ⓕ ra·pee·do/a fast
raqueta ⓕ ra·ke·ta racquet
raro/a ⓜ/ⓕ ra·ro/a rare • strange • unusual
rasuradora ⓕ ra·soo·ra·do·ra razor
rasurar ra·soo·rar shave v
rata ⓕ ra·ta rat
ratón ⓜ ra·ton mouse (animal)
razón ⓕ ra·son reason
realista ⓜ&ⓕ re·a·lees·ta realistic
receta ⓕ re·se·ta prescription (medical)
recibo ⓜ re·see·bo receipt
reciclable ⓜ&ⓕ re·see·kla·ble recyclable
reciclar re·see·klar recycle
recientemente re·syen·te·men·te recently
reclamo de equipaje ⓜ re·kla·mo de e·kee·pa·khe baggage claim
recomendar re·ko·men·dar recommend
recto/a ⓜ/ⓕ rek·to/a straight
recuerdo ⓜ re·kwer·do souvenir
recursos humanos ⓜ pl re·koor·sos oo·ma·nos human resources
red ⓕ red net • network (phone/Internet)
redondo/a ⓜ/ⓕ re·don·do/a round
referencia ⓕ re·fe·ren·sya reference
reflexología ⓕ re·flek·so·lo·khee·a reflexology
refresco ⓜ re·fres·ko soft drink
refri ⓜ re·free refrigerator
refugiado/a ⓜ/ⓕ re·foo·khya·do/a refugee
regalo ⓜ re·ga·lo gift
— de bodas de bo·das wedding present
regional ⓜ&ⓕ re·khyo·nal regional
registro del carro ⓜ re·khees·tro del ka·ro car registration
regla ⓕ re·gla menstruation • rule
reina ⓕ ray·na queen
reintegro ⓜ re·een·te·gro refund
reír re·eer laugh v
relación ⓕ re·la·syon relationship
relaciones públicas ⓕ pl re·la·syo·nes poo·blee·kas public relations
relajarse re·la·khar·se relax
religión ⓕ re·lee·khyon religion
religioso/a ⓜ/ⓕ re·lee·khyo·so/a religious
reliquia ⓕ re·lee·kya relic
reloj ⓜ re·lokh clock • watch
— despertador des·per·ta·dor alarm clock

remo ⓜ *re·mo rowing*
remoto/a ⓜ/ⓕ *re·mo·to/a remote*
reo/a ⓜ/ⓕ *re·o/a prisoner*
reparar *re·pa·rar repair*
repelente ⓜ *re·pe·len·te insect repellent*
repisa ⓕ *re·pee·sa shelf*
república ⓕ *re·poo·blee·ka republic*
reservación ⓕ *re·ser·va·syon reservation (booking)*
reservar *re·ser·var book (make a booking)*
resorte ⓜ *re·sor·te spring (coil)*
responder *res·pon·der answer* v
respuesta ⓕ *res·pwes·ta answer*
restaurante ⓜ *res·tow·ran·te restaurant*
retirado/a ⓜ/ⓕ *re·tee·ra·do/a retired*
revisar *re·vee·sar check* v
revisión ⓕ *re·vee·syon review*
revista ⓕ *re·vees·ta magazine*
revuelto/a ⓜ/ⓕ *re·vwel·to/a scrambled (eggs)*
rey ⓜ *ray king*
rico/a ⓜ/ⓕ *ree·ko/a rich • tasty • wealthy*
riesgo ⓜ *ryes·go risk*
riñón ⓜ *ree·nyon kidney*
río ⓜ *ree·o river*
ritmo ⓜ *reet·mo rhythm*
robado/a ⓜ/ⓕ *ro·ba·do/a stolen*
robar *ro·bar steal*
robo ⓜ *ro·bo rip-off*
rodilla ⓕ *ro·dee·ya knee*
rojo/a ⓜ/ⓕ *ro·kho/a red*
rollo ⓜ *ro·yo film (for camera)*
romántico/a ⓜ/ⓕ *ro·man·tee·ko/a romantic* n&a
romper *rom·per break (smash)*
ron ⓜ *ron rum*
ronda ⓕ *ron·da round (drinks)*
ropa ⓕ *ro·pa clothing • laundry*
— **de cama** *de ka·ma bedding*
— **interior** *een·te·ryor underwear*
rosado/a ⓜ/ⓕ *ro·sa·do/a pink*
rotonda ⓕ *ro·ton·da roundabout*
rubéola ⓕ *roo·be·o·la rubella*
rueda ⓕ *rwe·da wheel*
ruidoso/a ⓜ/ⓕ *rwee·do·so/a noisy*
ruinas ⓕ pl *rwee·nas ruins*
ruta ⓕ *roo·ta route*

S

sábado ⓜ *sa·ba·do Saturday*
sábana ⓕ *sa·ba·na sheet (bed)*
sábanas ⓕ pl *sa·ba·nas linen (sheets)*
saber *sa·ber know (something)*
sacacorchos ⓜ *sa·ka·kor·chos corkscrew*
saco de dormir ⓜ *sa·ko de dor·meer sleeping bag*
sal ⓕ *sal salt*
sala de espera ⓕ *sa·la de es·pe·ra waiting room*
salario ⓜ *sa·la·ryo salary*
saldo ⓜ *sal·do balance (account)*
salida ⓕ *sa·lee·da departure • exit*
— **de noche** *de no·che night out*
salir *sa·leer go out*
— **con** *kon go out with (date)*
salón de belleza ⓜ *sa·lon de be·ye·sa beauty salon*
salpullido ⓜ *sal·poo·yee·do nappy rash*
salsa ⓕ *sal·sa sauce*
saltar *sal·tar jump* v
salud ⓕ *sa·lood health*
sangre ⓕ *san·gre blood*
santo/a ⓜ/ⓕ *san·to/a saint*
santuario ⓜ *san·too·a·ryo shrine*
sarampión ⓜ *sa·ram·pyon measles*
sartén ⓜ *sar·ten frying pan*
sastre ⓜ *sas·tre tailor*
secar *se·kar dry (clothes, etc)* v
secarse *se·kar·se dry (oneself)* v
seco/a ⓜ/ⓕ *se·ko/a dried • dry*
secretario/a ⓜ/ⓕ *se·kre·ta·ryo/a secretary*
seda ⓕ *se·da silk*
seguir *se·geer follow*
segunda clase ⓕ *se·goon·da kla·se second class*
segundo ⓜ *se·goon·do second (time unit)*
segundo/a ⓜ/ⓕ *se·goon·do/a second (number)*
seguro ⓜ *se·goo·ro insurance*
seguro/a ⓜ/ⓕ *se·goo·ro/a safe*
semáforo ⓜ *se·ma·fo·ro traffic light*
semana ⓕ *se·ma·na week*
sencillo/a ⓜ/ⓕ *sen·see·yo/a simple*
sendero ⓜ *sen·de·ro footpath • hiking route*
— **de bicicleta** *de bee·see·kle·ta bike trail*
senos ⓜ pl *se·nos breasts (body)*
sensible ⓜ&ⓕ *sen·see·ble sensible*
sensual ⓜ&ⓕ *sen·swal sensual*
sentarse *sen·tar·se sit*
sentimientos ⓜ pl *seen·tee·myen·tos feelings*
sentir *sen·teer feel (emotions)*
señal ⓕ *se·nyal sign*
señalar *se·nya·lar point* v
separado/a ⓜ/ⓕ *se·pa·ra·do/a separate*
septiembre ⓜ *sep·tyem·bre September*
ser *ser be (permanent)*
serio/a ⓜ/ⓕ *se·ryo/a serious*
servicio ⓜ *ser·vee·syo service • service charge*
— **militar** *mee·lee·tar military service*

servilleta ⓕ ser·vee·ye·ta *serviette*
sesión de ejercicios ⓕ se·syon de e·kher·see·syos *workout*
sexismo ⓜ sek·sees·mo *sexism*
sexo ⓜ sek·so *sex*
— **seguro** se·goo·ro *safe sex*
si see *if*
sí see *yes*
SIDA ⓜ see·da *AIDS*
siempre syem·pre *always*
silla ⓕ see·ya *chair*
— **de comer para niños** de ko·mer pa·ra nee·nyos *highchair*
— **de ruedas** de rwe·das *wheelchair*
— **para niños** pa·ra nee·nyos *child seat*
similar ⓜ&ⓕ see·mee·lar *similar*
sin seen *without*
— **espacio** es·pa·syo *booked out*
— **plomo** plo·mo *unleaded (petrol)*
sinagoga ⓕ see·na·go·ga *synagogue*
sintético/a ⓜ/ⓕ seen·te·tee·ko/a *synthetic*
sobornar so·bor·nar *bribe* v
soborno ⓜ so·bor·no *bribe*
sobre so·bre *about • above • on*
sobre ⓜ so·bre *envelope*
sobredosis ⓕ so·bre·do·sees *overdose*
socado/a ⓜ/ⓕ so·ka·do/a *tight*
socialista ⓜ&ⓕ so·sya·lees·ta *socialist* n&a
sol ⓜ sol *sun*
solamente so·la·men·te *only*
soldado ⓜ sol·da·do *soldier*
soleado/a ⓜ/ⓕ so·le·a·do/a *sunny*
sólo so·lo *only*
solo/a ⓜ/ⓕ so·lo/a *alone*
soltero/a ⓜ/ⓕ sol·te·ro/a *single (person)*
sombra ⓕ som·bra *shade • shadow*
sombrero ⓜ som·bre·ro *hat*
sombrilla ⓕ som·bree·ya *umbrella*
sonreír son·re·eer *smile* v
sopa ⓕ so·pa *soup*
sordo/a ⓜ/ⓕ sor·do/a *deaf*
sorpresa ⓕ sor·pre·sa *surprise*
su soo *her • his • their • your* sg pol&pl
subtítulos ⓜ pl soob·tee·too·los *subtitles*
suburbio ⓜ soo·boor·byo *suburb*
sucio/a ⓜ/ⓕ soo·syo/a *dirty*
suegra ⓕ swe·gra *mother-in-law*
suegro ⓜ swe·gro *father-in-law*
suelo ⓜ swe·lo *floor (ground)*
sueño ⓜ swe·nyo *dream • sleep*
suerte ⓕ swer·te *luck*
suéter ⓜ swe·ter *jumper • sweater*
suficiente soo·fee·syen·te *enough*
súper ⓜ soo·per *convenience store*
supermercado ⓜ soo·per·mer·ka·do *supermarket*
superstición ⓕ soo·per·stee·syon *superstition*
sur ⓜ soor *south*
surf ⓜ soorf *surfing*
surfear soor·fe·ar *surf* v

T

tabaco ⓜ ta·ba·ko *tobacco*
tabaquería ⓕ ta·ba·ke·ree·a *tobacconist*
tabla de surf ⓕ ta·bla de soorf *surfboard*
tabla para picar ⓕ ta·bla pa·ra pee·kar *chopping board*
tajada ⓕ ta·kha·da *slice*
talcos ⓜ pl tal·kos *baby powder*
taller ⓜ ta·yer *workshop*
tal vez tal ves *maybe*
tamaño ⓜ ta·ma·nyo *size (general)*
también tam·byen *also • too*
tambor ⓜ tam·bor *drum (instrument)*
tampón ⓜ tam·pon *tampon*
tapón ⓜ ta·pon *plug (bath)*
tapones para los oídos ⓜ pl ta·po·nes pa·ra los o·ee·dos *earplugs*
tarde ⓕ tar·de *afternoon*
tarde tar·de *late* adv
tarifa ⓕ ta·ree·fa *fare*
tarjeta ⓕ tar·khe·ta *card*
— **de crédito** de kre·dee·to *credit card*
— **de memoria** de me·mo·rya *memory card*
— **de teléfono** de te·le·fo·no *phone card*
— **SIM** seem *SIM card*
taxi ⓜ tak·see *taxi*
taza ⓕ ta·sa *cup*
té ⓜ te *tea*
teatro ⓜ te·a·tro *theatre*
teclado ⓜ te·kla·do *keyboard*
técnica ⓕ tek·nee·ka *technique*
tela ⓕ te·la *fabric*
teleférico ⓜ te·le·fe·ree·ko *cable car*
teléfono ⓜ te·le·fo·no *telephone*
— **celular** se·loo·lar *cell/mobile phone*
— **público** poo·blee·ko *public phone*
telegrama ⓜ te·le·gra·ma *telegram*
telescopio ⓜ te·les·ko·pyo *telescope*
televisión ⓕ te·le·vee·syon *television*
televisor ⓜ te·le·vee·sor *TV*
temperatura ⓕ tem·pe·ra·too·ra *temperature (weather)*
templo ⓜ tem·plo *temple (building)*
temporada ⓕ tem·po·ra·da *season*
temprano tem·pra·no *early* adv
tendedero ⓜ ten·de·de·ro *clothesline*
tenedor ⓜ te·ne·dor *fork*
tener te·ner *have*
— **sed** sed *be thirsty*
— **sueño** swe·nyo *be sleepy*

tenis ⓜ te·nees tennis
— de mesa de me·sa table tennis
tensión premenstrual ⓕ ten·syon pre·mens·trwal premenstrual tension
tercero/a ⓜ/ⓕ ter·se·ro/a third
terco/a ⓜ/ⓕ ter·ko/a stubborn
terminar ter·mee·nar finish v
termo ⓜ ter·mo hot water bottle
ternera ⓕ ter·ne·ra veal
terremoto ⓜ te·re·mo·to earthquake
terrible ⓜ&ⓕ te·ree·ble terrible
terrorismo ⓜ te·ro·rees·mo terrorism
ti tee you sg inf
tía ⓕ tee·a aunt
tibio/a ⓜ/ⓕ tee·byo/a warm
tiempo ⓜ tyem·po time • weather
— completo kom·ple·to full-time
— parcial par·syal part-time
tienda ⓕ tyen·da shop
— de artículos usados de ar·tee·koo·los oo·sa·dos secondhand shop
— de cámaras de ka·ma·ras camera shop
— de campaña de kam·pa·nya tent
— de electrónicos de e·lek·tro·nee·kos electrical store
— de música de moo·see·ka music shop
— de recuerdos de re·kwer·dos souvenir shop
— de ropa de ro·pa clothing store
— deportiva de·por·tee·va sports store
— por departamentos por de·par·ta·men·tos department store
tierno/a ⓜ/ⓕ tyer·no/a soft-boiled (eggs)
tierra ⓕ tye·ra Earth • land
tifoidea ⓕ tee·foy·de·a typhoid
tijeras ⓕ pl tee·khe·ras scissors
timbre ⓜ teem·bre ring (phone)
tímido/a ⓜ/ⓕ tee·mee·do/a shy
tío ⓜ tee·o uncle
típico/a ⓜ/ⓕ tee·pee·ko/a typical
tipo ⓜ tee·po type
— de cambio de kam·byo exchange rate
tiquete ⓜ tee·ke·te ticket
— de abordaje de a·bor·da·khe boarding pass
— de ida de ee·da one-way ticket
— de ida y vuelta de ee·da ee vwel·ta return ticket
— de stand-by de stan·bai stand-by ticket
título de propiedad ⓜ tee·too·lo de pro·pye·dad car owner's title
toalla sanitaria ⓕ to·a·ya sa·nee·ta·rya sanitary napkin
toallita ⓕ to·a·yee·ta wash cloth (flannel)
tobillo ⓜ to·bee·yo ankle
tocar to·kar touch • play (instrument)
todavía (no) to·da·vee·a (no) (not) yet
todo to·do everything
todo/a ⓜ/ⓕ to·do/a all • every
todos/as ⓜ/ⓕ pl to·dos/as everyone
todos los días to·dos los dee·as every day
tomar to·mar take • drink
— una foto oo·na fo·to take a photo
tono ⓜ to·no dial tone
tormenta ⓕ tor·men·ta storm
— eléctrica e·lek·tree·ka thunderstorm
torre ⓕ to·re tower
tos ⓕ tos cough
toser to·ser cough v
tostada ⓕ tos·ta·da toast (food)
tostador ⓜ tos·ta·dor toaster
tour ⓜ toor tour
— con guía kon gee·a guided tour
trabajador(a) ⓜ/ⓕ tra·ba·kha·dor/ tra·ba·kha·do·ra labourer • worker
trabajar tra·ba·khar work v
trabajo ⓜ tra·ba·kho work
— temporal tem·po·ral casual work
traducir tra·doo·seer translate
traductor(a) ⓜ/ⓕ tra·dook·tor/tra·dook·to·ra translator
traer tra·er bring
trago ⓜ tra·go alcoholic drink
tramposo/a ⓜ/ⓕ tram·po·so/a cheat
tránsito ⓜ tran·see·to traffic
transporte ⓜ trans·por·te transport
tranvía ⓜ tran·vee·a tram
trasero ⓜ tra·se·ro bottom (body)
tratar tra·tar try (attempt)
tren ⓜ tren train
triste ⓜ&ⓕ trees·te sad
trompeta ⓕ trom·pe·ta trumpet
trotar ⓜ tro·tar jogging
tu too your sg inf
tú too you sg inf
tubo ⓜ too·bo faucet • tap
— interno een·ter·no inner tube (tyre)
tumba ⓕ toom·ba grave
tumor ⓜ too·mor tumour
turista ⓜ&ⓕ too·rees·ta tourist

último/a ⓜ/ⓕ ool·tee·mo/a last (final)
ultrasonido ⓜ ool·tra·so·nee·do ultrasound
una vez oo·na ves once
uniforme ⓜ oo·nee·for·me uniform
universidad ⓕ oo·nee·ver·see·dad university
universo ⓜ oo·nee·ver·so universe
uno/a ⓜ/ⓕ oo·no/a one n&a
urgente ⓜ&ⓕ oor·khen·te urgent

usado/a ⓜ/ⓕ oo·sa·do/a *secondhand*
usted oos·ted *you* sg pol
ustedes oos·te·des *you* pl
útil ⓜ&ⓕ oo·teel *useful*

V

vaca ⓕ va·ka *cow*
vacación ⓕ va·ka·syon *holidays • vacation*
vacilón/vacilona ⓜ/ⓕ va·see·lon/va·see·lo·na *funny*
vacío/a ⓜ/ⓕ va·see·o/a *empty*
vacunación ⓕ va·koo·na·syon *vaccination*
vagina ⓕ va·khee·na *vagina*
validar va·lee·dar *validate*
valiente ⓜ&ⓕ va·lyen·te *brave*
valija ⓕ va·lee·kha *briefcase*
valioso/a ⓜ/ⓕ va·lyo·so/a *valuable*
valle ⓜ va·ye *valley*
valor ⓜ va·lor *value (price)*
van ⓕ van *van*
varicela ⓕ va·ree·se·la *chicken pox*
varios/as ⓜ/ⓕ pl va·ryos/as *several*
vasija ⓕ va·see·kha *pot (ceramics)*
vaso ⓜ va·so *glass (drinking)*
vegetal ⓜ ve·khe·tal *vegetable*
vegetariano/a ⓜ/ⓕ ve·khe·ta·rya·no/a *vegetarian* n&a
vejiga ⓕ ve·khee·ga *bladder*
vela ⓕ ve·la *candle*
velocidad ⓕ ve·lo·see·dad *speed (travel)*
velocímetro ⓜ ve·lo·see·me·tro *speedometer*
vena ⓕ ve·na *vein*
vendaje ⓜ ven·da·khe *bandage*
vendedor de pescado ⓜ ven·de·dor de pes·ka·do *fishmonger*
vender ven·der *sell*
venenoso/a ⓜ/ⓕ ve·ne·no·so/a *poisonous*
venir ve·neer *come*
venta de periódicos ⓕ ven·ta de pe·ryo·dee·kos *newsstand*
ventana ⓕ ven·ta·na *window*
ventanilla ⓕ ven·ta·nee·ya *ticket office*
ventilador ⓜ ven·tee·la·dor *fan (machine)*
ver ver *look • see*
verano ⓜ ve·ra·no *summer*
verde ⓜ&ⓕ ver·de *green*
verdurería ⓕ ver·doo·re·ree·a *greengrocer*
vestíbulo ⓜ ves·tee·boo·lo *foyer*
vestido ⓜ ves·tee·do *dress*
— **de baño** de ba·nyo *bathing suit*
vestidores ⓜ pl ves·tee·do·res *changing room*
viajar vya·khar *travel*
viaje ⓜ vya·khe *journey*
vid ⓕ veed *vine*
vida ⓕ vee·da *life*
viejo/a ⓜ/ⓕ vye·kho/a *old (age)*
viento ⓜ vyen·to *wind*
viernes ⓜ vyer·nes *Friday*
VIH ⓜ ve ee a·che *HIV*
vinagre ⓜ vee·na·gre *vinegar*
vino ⓜ vee·no *wine*
viñedo ⓜ vee·nye·do *vineyard*
violación ⓕ vyo·la·syon *rape*
violar vyo·lar *rape* v
violín ⓜ vee·o·leen *violin*
virus ⓜ vee·roos *virus*
visa ⓕ vee·sa *visa*
visita ⓕ vee·see·ta *visit*
vista ⓕ vees·ta *view*
vitaminas ⓕ pl vee·ta·mee·nas *vitamins*
vivir vee·veer *live*
volar vo·lar *fly* v
volcán ⓜ vol·kan *volcano*
volibol ⓜ vo·lee·bol *volleyball*
— **de playa** de pla·ya *beach volleyball*
volumen ⓜ vo·loo·men *volume*
volver vol·ver *return*
vos vos *you* sg inf
votar vo·tar *vote* v
voz ⓕ vos *voice*
vuelo ⓜ vwe·lo *flight*
vuelto ⓜ vwel·to *change (coins)*

Y

y ee *and*
ya ya *already*
yo yo *I*

zacate ⓜ sa·ka·te *grass (lawn)*
zancudo ⓜ san·koo·do *mosquito*
zapatería ⓕ sa·pa·te·ree·a *shoe shop*
zapato ⓜ sa·pa·to *shoe*
zodíaco ⓜ so·dee·a·ko *zodiac*
zoológico ⓜ so·o·lo·khee·ko *zoo*
zorzal ⓜ sor·sal *thrush (health)*

A

B

C

D

E

INDEX

F

G

H

I

J

K

L

M

N

O

P

Q

R

S

T

U

V

W

The topics covered in this book are listed below in Spanish. Show this page to your Costa Rican friends if you're having trouble understanding them.

NOTES

KEY PATTERNS

When's (the next bus)?	¿A qué hora sale (el próximo bus)?	a ke *o*·ra *sa*·le (el *prok*·see·mo boos)
Where's (the bank)?	¿Dónde está (el banco)?	*don*·de es·*ta* (el *ban*·ko)
Where can I (buy a ticket)?	¿Dónde puedo (comprar un tiquete)?	*don*·de *pwe*·do (kom·*prar* oon tee·*ke*·te)
How much is (a room)?	¿Cuánto cuesta (una habitación)?	*kwan*·to *kwes*·ta (*oo*·na a·bee·ta·*syon*)
I'm looking for (a cabin).	Estoy buscando (una cabina).	es·*toy* boos·*kan*·do (*oo*·na ka·*bee*·na)
Do you have (a map)?	¿Tiene (un mapa)?	*tye*·ne (oon *ma*·pa)
Is there (a toilet)?	¿Hay (un baño)?	ai (oon *ba*·nyo)
I'd like (a coffee).	Quisiera (un café).	kee·*sye*·ra (oon ka·*fe*)
I'd like (to hire a car).	Quisiera (alquilar un carro).	kee·*sye*·ra (al·kee·*lar* oon *ka*·ro)
Can I (park here)?	¿Puedo (parquear aquí)?	*pwe*·do (par·ke·*ar* a·*kee*)
Could you please (help me)?	¿Podría (ayudarme), por favor?	po·*dree*·a (a·yoo·*dar*·me) por fa·*vor*
Do I have to (get a visa)?	¿Necesito (obtener una visa)?	ne·se·*see*·to (ob·te·*ner* *oo*·na *vee*·sa